ULTIMATE WOODWORKING COURSE

NICK GIBBS

COLLINS & BROWN

First published in Great Britain in
2005 by
Collins & Brown
The Chrysalis Building
Bramley Road
London W10 6SP

An imprint of **Chrysalis** Books Group plc

1 3 5 7 9 8 6 4 2

British Library Cataloguing-in-
Publication Data:
A catalogue record for this book is
available from the British Library.

ISBN 1 84340 126 6

Designers: Caroline Hill and
Bet Ayer
Project editor: Miranda Sessions
Photographer: Michael Wicks
Copy editor: Phil Hunt
Additional illustrations: Kang Chen
Reproduction by Anorax Imaging
Ltd, England
Printed in Singapore by Imago

Contents

ULTIMATE
WOODWORKING
COURSE

CONTENTS

Introduction

Some furniture makers are fortunate enough to find their vocation early in life, and receive a full-time training that prepares them for any task. The rest of us may have learnt some basic skills at school or from our fathers, but spend the next 20 years forgetting everything we were taught.

Wood is the most remarkable material, which anyone with an interest in making things will want to use, not just because it is beautiful, strong and sustainable, but for the challenge of taming its qualities and flaws. To do so successfully you need skills and tools, but you'd be surprised what can be achieved with only a limited range of both.

So, unlike most woodworking books, we will start at the beginning with only a few tools, wood from hardware stores, a portable workbench and the ambition to make some simple projects. I still use the same set of chisels I chose when I first became a carpenter in the 1980s, and the same tenon saw and the same mallet, which is looking a bit worse for wear but is an old friend now.

Gradually we will introduce you to tools and techniques that will enable the learning woodworker to take on ever more complicated projects. The aim is to become self-sufficient, able to choose the right joint, the right lumber and the right glues, abrasives, and finishes. You will find useful advice to help you buy the most suitable machines and power tools, and tips on maintaining and using your equipment.

At every stage there are projects to test your skills and techniques. During Part One these are essentially simple, using ready-planed materials and basic joints. Part Two introduces the backbone of woodworking joints that you will be using again and again, as well as showing you how to make or buy a workbench and the best machines to pick first. With Part Three come the confidence and advanced skills to take on any project. By the time you reach the end you will have the abilities and equipment to achieve whatever you want and, hopefully, the journey will have been both challenging and enjoyable!

Nick Gibbs

Learning
the Basics

What you will find in this section

What to expect

Tools

Fortunately, novice woodworkers need only a few key tools to get going, and it is those we will study in this first section. Working with prepared timber, little more than a good saw and combination square are needed to make a basic birdbox, but soon you'll need a plane, some chisels, a mallet and basic marking tools. We will be showing you what to buy, and how to judge what is good and bad, with tips on sharpening and using tools effectively and safely.

Materials

All timberyards have a supply of prepared softwood boards ready to be converted into projects. There is no better place to start for a novice woodworker, because the wood is generally dry and easy to use. As your skills improve, we will be introducing some common hardwoods, explaining what to look out for and how to overcome the challenges of using less forgiving timber. There will be sections on sheet materials and on the glues, finishes and abrasives you will need to enhance projects.

You will be using the measuring gauge for all of the projects in this section (see page 44).

You will learn how to treat wood with a stain to create impressive results (see page 49).

Find out how to sharpen and hone the blade of a plane (see page 27).

Find out how to stop knots weeping (see page 49).

Discover how to use a chisel to pare a joint and to scribe an accurate shoulder (see page 46).

Learn about the standard sizes of softwood available in the DIY store or timberyard (see page 69).

Techniques

More often than not, the key to successful woodworking is preparing pieces of timber before jointing them together. From the initial cutting of boards to length, accuracy is essential, and subsequent operations will never be easy if the first cuts are poor. In this section we will be learning the most basic techniques for holding tools, starting and completing cuts, and good preparation.

Cutting to length with a simple saw is an essential skill you will learn (see page 13).

You'll be drilling holes in cabinet doors (see page 35).

Planing wood is a highly satisfying technique (see page 64).

Projects

These are the eight projects in this first section, Learning the Basics. As you will see, the projects increase in complexity, and they all incorporate key techniques for you to learn along the way.

Birdbox **p18**

Bookends **p60**

Toy lorry **p30**

Knife block **p70**

Shoe rack **p38**

Noticeboard **p80**

Towel rail **p50**

Wall cabinet **p90**

Lesson 1
Cutting to length

Getting started

With so much pre-prepared timber sold in DIY stores, you can make many projects with very few tools, cutting boards to length by hand and joining them with screws or nails. You only need a saw and the ability to cut cleanly and accurately, though the most important lesson to learn is that successful woodworking relies entirely upon a flat, solid surface on which to work. Fortunately, this can be a folding workbench, of which there are many versions. I worked for many years on site with no more than the simplest portable workbench, which I still own and still use occasionally.

Accurate cutting also relies on good marking out and careful cuts, so we will be studying how to prepare well and I will be explaining how to start and finish a cut without damaging the board. We will be introducing the simplest of joints, the butt joint, which depends only on glue and screws or nails to hold it together. It requires little by way of preparation, but if cut inaccurately, it will be very weak.

I am assuming that most people aiming to start woodworking will already own a few tools for doing tasks around the home, and these will be useful for many projects. There's no need, for instance, to buy a new drill until you choose to expand your toolkit with specialist woodworking equipment. However, you will soon learn that the heavy claw hammer that works so well around the house and garden isn't easy to use for tapping in fine moulding pins for a woodworking project.

Marking out

First you must check that the board you are using has straight and square edges, even if it is a pre-cut board from a DIY store or timberyard. Use the combination square or a try square, with the stock against an edge and blade across the face, to check that the edges and faces are square to one another. Look for any thin shafts of light between the blade and the face. If the piece isn't square, you'll need to plane it (see page 64).

Lesson planner

Key techniques	Key tools and materials
• Marking out • Holding a saw • Starting a cut • Surveying the cut • Butt joints	• Hand saw • Tenon saw • Combination square • Portable workbench • Small G-clamp • Pencil, pen or knife • Small hammer • Combination screwdriver • Countersink bit • Nail set • Nails and screws • Wood glue and filler

Start by marking across the face of the board, creating a clear line you can see easily.

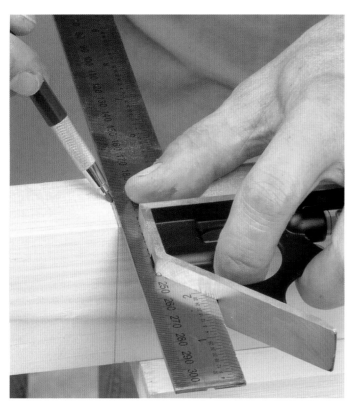

Once you are satisfied that the board is square, use the square to mark a line across a face, with the stock against the edge. Then mark a line across that edge, holding the stock against the face you've just marked. Work your way around the board from those lines, and if all's well, the lines will meet in the far corner. Always hold the stock against either the edge or the face where you started.

Holding a saw

By making a straight cut, woodworkers can save themselves considerable time, since the wood will not need to be cleaned up with a block plane or abrasives. To do this well, you need control of the saw blade, which is achieved by holding the saw properly. When you grip the saw, extend your index finger along the handle to help guide the cut by using the rigidity within the tendon that runs from the knuckle along the forearm. Many people hold planes and power tools in the same way.

Always hold the stock of the combination square against the first face and mark up the edges.

By extending your index finger along the handle of the saw, you gain more control through the tendons in your arm.

Starting a cut

A board can easily be damaged when you cut it, with the result that you may have to repair an edge or face, wasting both time and wood. To start a cut, rub the saw blade against the thumb or index finger of your other hand, keeping the teeth away from your flesh, and with the saw resting on the far corner of the board. Mark the line of cut. Make sure the teeth are to the waste side of the drawn line, rather than on the centre of the mark. Holding the saw at a low angle, gently draw the blade towards you until you've made a shallow groove and can increase the stroke, potentially cutting on both the push and pull. Notice how smaller teeth damage the fibres less, but cut more slowly.

Surveying the cut

When cutting a board to length, you need to follow marked lines across the top face and the nearest edge, even though to start with, you will often mark lines around all four sides of a workpiece. Once you have started cutting along the line across the top, you'll need to cut down the edge nearest you to ensure the cut is square. With time you will do this automatically, from muscle memory, but to start, you need to follow both lines carefully. Once you've made the cut down the nearest edge, you can use the groove as a guide and extend the cut down the back edge. Some woodworkers actually start their cut at the near corner, which is more awkward, but it makes it easier to follow the two lines.

Use the tip of your index finger or your thumb joint to guide the saw.

Trade secret

Don't push the saw

The traditional maxim is to let the weight of the saw do the cutting, and it is certainly best not to force the teeth into the wood. It's better to use the full length of the blade in long, gentle strokes than to make hurried, short efforts. When you get near the end of the cut, more damage can be done by the waste falling away and tearing the board. The safest way to resolve this is to clamp the board to a sawhorse or bench and then use your spare hand to hold the waste as you cut it off.

Don't remove your guiding finger until the cut is well under way.

Butt joints

When boards have been cut to length, you may need to join them, depending on the project. Butt joints can be used to fix two boards together, edge to edge, to produce a wider board or panel. This joint is glued and sometimes reinforced with biscuits or dowels (see Using the dowel joint, page 54, and Using a biscuit jointer, page 138).

Boards may also be fixed at 90° to one another, usually using glue and nails or screws for security. This joint isn't very strong and tends to be employed for basic projects or utility jobs in the workshop. It is often used when joining sheet materials and can be reinforced with biscuits or dowels (see Assembling a panel, page 85).

Pros
• Simple and quick to cut and assemble
• Efficient, since it requires no interlocking pieces
Cons
• Weak without reinforcement
• Can be difficult to tighten
• Any inaccuracy in cutting will be conspicuous

Use a combination drill bit and countersink to drill holes to fix the battens.

How to cut a butt joint

The simple rule is that the meeting edges or face and edge must be smooth, straight and square. If there is any inaccuracy, the joint will wobble and assembly will be difficult. The easiest way to join pieces at 90° is to hold one piece with the edge flush with the top of a worksurface. Then smear glue along the edge and screw or nail the second piece to the edge.

With the batten held in the portable workbench, screw the 'table' of the bench hook to the batten.

Trade secret

The weakest of joints

The strength of the butt joint relies largely upon the accuracy of cutting. It is very important that the mating surfaces are flat and true, otherwise there is a high risk of movement, however well reinforced the joint is. It is a real test of hand skills to cut a board squarely across the end, but this is essential for a good butt joint. A tenon saw, with its reinforced back, will cut more accurately than a hand saw. Professionals will use a table saw (Machine Cutting, page 218) or disc sander (page 224) to get a superb finish to end grain.

Tools

It doesn't matter if you only have a small collection of tools, as long as they are all useful and of good quality. Though there are more sophisticated alternatives to most of the tools listed here, the ones I've chosen to get you started will always be handy and don't require too much initial outlay. The idea is to gradually build up a toolkit, adding new items as your horizons (or budget) widen.

Hand saws

There are various types of hand saw, some with a reinforced spine or back. Most woodworkers start off with a tenon saw for cutting small items or for cutting accurate joints and a hand saw for cutting wider boards. Backsaws, of which the tenon saw is the most common example, have a restricted depth of cut, so they can't be used for cutting wide boards and certainly not thick boards. They are also short, so cut less per stroke, and they have small teeth for fine but slow cutting. However, the reinforced back keeps the blade square and improves accuracy.

Most people start with a medium tenon saw, about 254 mm (10 in) long and with about 13 teeth per inch (tpi). It's worth buying a saw with hardened teeth, which can cut any material and is thrown away once blunt. As your confidence and skills develop, you can buy traditional saws that you can sharpen yourself. I tend to favour Japanese saws, which cut on both the push and pull strokes. Fortunately, even the most basic tenon saws and hand saws are available with what are known as triple tooth-form teeth, which can also cut both ways.

For a hand saw I also recommend hardened teeth, with 8 tpi and a blade about 508 mm (20 in) long. Check the blade. If it's too flimsy, it will bend as you cut. Both these and the tenon saws are designed for cutting across the grain rather than with it. Few woodworkers cut boards along the grain by hand, since you ideally need a special rip saw and plenty of energy (see Japanese Tools, page 212 and see Band Saw, page 109).

Combination square

Though you can, of course, buy a dedicated try square, a good compromise is the combination square.
This provides you with a straight edge, which can be removed from the stock, usually a spirit level, and 90° and 45° angles for marking up. Some even have variable angles in between. Check the accuracy of the combination square by holding the stock against the edge and drawing a line

along the blade. Then flip the square over so the stock is pointing the other way and draw another line beside the first. The two lines should be parallel.

Portable workbench

A surface on which to work is essential for successful woodworking, and you can get going well enough with a portable workbench. Various manufacturers make these, but my recommendation is to go for something simple. I have owned a few of them over the years but always tend to return to the very simplest Workmate I bought when I started woodworking. Characterized by its crossed legs at each end, it has a small worksurface and not much flexibility in the vice, but I like it for being easy to erect and having no pieces that can fall off. Choose something solid, and it will last for years.

Small G-clamp

They say you can never have enough clamps, and for assembling projects just with glue, you will need a number of them. Initially, a couple will do, mainly for holding a board on the worksurface while you cut joints or clean up edges. Choose 102-mm (4-in) G-clamps, but always go for quality items, as they should last a lifetime and cheap clamps are a nightmare to use. A quality lightweight clamp is far better than a cheap heavyweight version.

Pencil, ballpoint pen or knife

Find a marking tool that you're happy with as soon as possible. Some favour a ballpoint pen, saying that it has a finer line for greater accuracy, though pencil-lovers tend to believe that the ink can leach into the fibres. Few woodworkers use a carpenter's pencil for fine work because the lead is too wide, so a good HB or H pencil is more suitable. The mark of a pencil with hard lead can be difficult to see, while softer pencils will smudge. Other people use a craft knife or box cutter for marking, but the consequences of a slip are more serious.

Small hammer

I love small hammers and I have a few of them in my workshop, ranging from about 99 g (3.5 oz) to 170 g (6 oz). I'm not fussy about them having a ball pein or wedge-shaped cross pein, but I like the hammer to be nicely balanced for tapping home nails.

Combination screwdriver

You probably own a variety of screwdrivers for working around the home, but I've discovered that I prefer having one good-quality combination driver that always returns to the same place in the workshop. I find it useful to have dedicated screwdrivers for the car, the kitchen and the workshop. The trick is to match the screws you use to your screwdrivers. Mine has two bits for slot-headed screws and two bits for cross-headed screws.

Countersink bit

Assuming you already have a power drill, cordless or otherwise, you will need a countersink for tidy screwed joints. Some screws have sharpened heads that will self-countersink beautifully, but the best solution is to buy a couple of combination countersink/counterbore units, with a fluted collar to attach to a drill bit with a set screw. Don't go for cheap units as the screws tend to fail.

Nail set

To sink nail heads below the surface you will need a nail set. You can always make do with a nail with a flattened tip if you don't have, or don't want to buy, a dedicated hole punch. I thoroughly encourage you to start creating your own tools and solutions, as it can save you money.

Materials

Screws or nails

I rarely use nails for woodworking, preferring the certainty of screws. The disadvantage of a screw is that it is more expensive, needs more preparation in the drilling of a clearance hole and a pilot hole, and takes up more room with its head, which may need to be hidden with filler or a bung. On the plus side, it is more secure than a nail, and you don't necessarily need any glue. Nails are quick to install, and are ideal for small components as long as the wood doesn't split.

Which screws?

Though I tend to use flat-headed brass slot screws for hinges and other fittings, I favour cross-headed screws for all other purposes. I buy them by the box and always have a good range of sizes and lengths. I tend not to keep old steel screws unless they are exceptionally large or long, since the slots are usually damaged and will cause as many problems being inserted as a new one would cost. I generally have 50 mm

(2 in), 38 mm (1½ in), 32 mm (1¼ in), and 25 mm (1 in) (no. 8); 25 mm (1 in) and 19 mm (¾ in) (no. 6); and 12 mm (½ in) and 9 mm (⅜ in) (no. 4). Purchasing sets of screws can be good value, and I particularly like those that have a serrated tip for catching the grain faster.

Which nails?

I keep a very limited range of nails, with 50 mm (2 in), 38 mm (1½ in), and 25 mm (1 in) in both oval heads and flat heads, plus a few boxes of moulding pins, panel pins, and escutcheon pins which I've bought for specific projects. You don't need many to get going.

Wood filler

You can buy all sorts of wood filler, but a general rule is to use filler that's a bit darker than the wood you're working on. Though filler will take a stain, darker filler tends not to show up as much, but the best thing to do is experiment first and make up your own mind which works best.

Buying softwood

Softwood in the UK is sold in metric measurements, in increments of 25 mm. It will usually be referred to by its rough-sawn size; that is, after it has left the saw and before it is planed. The most common thicknesses are 25 mm, 50 mm and 75 mm. Widths usually start at 25 mm, going up through 50 mm, 75 mm, 100 mm, 125 mm, 150 mm, 175 mm, 225 mm and even 300 mm, though you may also be able to find both rough-sawn and prepared 200-mm wide boards.

Standard sizes of softwood

Prepared sizes are roughly 5 mm narrower than sawn boards, but this is not consistent and cannot be relied upon from one timberyard to another.

Rough-sawn (width x thickness)	
25 x 25/50/75 mm (1 x 1/2/3 in)	150 x 25/50/75 mm (6 x 1/2/3 in)
50 x 25/50/75 mm (2 x 1/2/3 in)	175 x 25/50/75 mm (7 x 1/2/3 in)
75 x 25/50/75 mm (3 x 1/2/3 in)	200 x 25/50/75 mm (8 x 1/2/3 in)
100 x 25/50/75 mm (4 x 1/2/3 in)	225 x 25/50/75 mm (9 x 1/2/3 in)
125 x 25/50/75 mm (5 x 1/2/3 in)	300 x 25/50/75 mm (12 x 1/2/3 in)

Project **Birdbox**

For the birds

This birdbox is designed for small birds and should
be fitted high up on a wall, in a tree, or on a post.
Make sure it is safe from cats and other predators.
It is designed to be waterproof, so use waterproof
adhesive and galvanized nails.

178 mm (7 in)

197 mm (7¾ in)

406 mm (16 in)

203 mm (8 in)

B

A

E

B

C

Drainage hole

Metal entrance hole protector

114 mm (4½ in)

133 mm (5¼ in)

Cutting list

Part	Material	Quantity	Dimensions length, width, thickness
A Back	softwood	1	400 x 184 x 19 mm (16 x 7¼ x ¾ in)
B Sides	softwood	2	254 x 133 x 19 mm (10 x 5½ x ¾ in)
C Front	softwood	1	203 x 140 x 19 mm (8 x 5½ x ¾ in)
D Base	softwood	1	121 x 102 x 19 mm (4¾ x 4 x ¾ in)
E Top	plywood	1	197 x 152 x 13 mm (7¾ x 6 x ½ in)

Shopping list

Tools and materials

Hinge: tough leather or webbing, roughly 197 x 51 mm (7¾ x 2 in)
Entrance hole protection: thin metal sheet 63 x 63 mm (2½ x 2⅛ in)
Nails to assemble box: 30 x 38 mm (1½ in)
Galvanized tacks for hinge: 8 x 13 mm (½ in)
Screws for fixing back: 10 x 32 mm (1¼ in) no. 8 flat-headed screws
Wood filler: for holes made by nail heads
Exterior varnish
Drill and bits: for making the drainage holes in the base of the box. Drill press, see page 185
Flat bit for the entrance hole: 25 mm (1 in) in diameter
Sliding bevel to mark up angles of any degree
Protractor for marking up angles for this project

1 Cut the back (**A**) to length and then mark out the board for the sides. Use a protractor or combination square to mark up a 60° angle on the sides (**B**) and cut all components to length. When it comes to cutting the front (**C**), remember to angle your saw to 60° to match the angle of the roof. This will save you time cleaning up later.

2 Drill the front for the entrance hole, centred and about 38 mm (1½in) from the top edge. When using a flat bit, make sure you drill into a piece of waste wood underneath to reduce tearing. You may need to get the hole in the metal protection sheet drilled by an engineer, since metal can be difficult to drill with a flat bit. Pin it to the front of the birdbox front (**C**).

3 Drill ventilation/drainage holes in the base. Position the box sides (**B**) on a flat worksurface, with the front edge facing upwards. Spread glue along those edges, and place the birdbox front on top. Use your fingers to align the front with the sides, and then nail the front to the sides. Before the glue dries, apply some glue to the front and side edges of the base and insert it inside the front and sides. Nail in place.

4 Once the glue has set, mark up where the fixing screws should go. Drill these holes in the back, and holes for screws to fit the birdbox to its home. Then screw the back to the house. Tap all the nail heads below the surface with a hammer and nail set. Cut out the top from a piece of scrap plywood, and use the galvanized nails to fix the hinge. Fill the nail-head holes with filler and sand the whole project. Finish with an exterior varnish.

Lessons learned

- Notice how joining the front to the sides is made much easier because the edges are straight and square. In this project, you didn't need to join the cut edges because they were already planed, but imagine how the quality of your cut would have implicated the quality of a joint.

- How did your cuts start and finish? Did you need to sand back any tears on the corners? Practice will improve that.

- When you drilled, did the wood tear? This is a common problem and is only solved at the back by drilling into waste wood and at the front by using quality drill bits and a good drill or drill press (see Drill press, page 185).

- You can save a little timber by carefully cutting the sides from a board. Because the top edges are angled, you can overlap them a little on the board, and you'll want to use this technique frequently in the future to save wood.

Lesson 2
Sheet materials

Getting started

When I was editing a woodworking magazine some years ago, I was asked to comment about medium-density fibreboard (MDF) on a television programme, as I'd just written a column stating how much I disliked the stuff. My dislike of this heavy, dusty, lifeless material remains, and I will not allow it in my workshop. That's not true, however, of all sheet materials.

Birch plywood is one of my favourite materials. It cuts well, the edges can be planed really smooth, and the surfaces are fine. Its smell is particularly distinctive. This sort of high-quality plywood is easy to use because it cuts so well and is ideal for projects of all sizes and shapes. Plywood generally is a very good place for novices to start because the thickness is consistent and all you need to do is cut out the shape to suit your needs. It isn't as heavy as MDF – you almost feel as if you're using real wood. You can even buy certified ply these days (though it can be hard to find), which is guaranteed to have been harvested from a sustainable source.

Sheet materials of all types are extremely useful to have around the workshop. Even odd little pieces can prove to be invaluable, so don't throw the offcuts away. Each type of sheet has its own special uses, and even exterior shuttering ply can be useful for more functional jobs.

Lesson planner

Key techniques	Key tools and materials
• Cutting plywood • Planing plywood and end grain • Cutting shapes	• Block plane • Large drill bits • Scroll saw • Files, rasps and Microplanes • Jigsaw • Sawhorses • Plywood and fibreboard • Clear finishes

Cutting plywood

Plywood is a superb material for newcomers to woodworking, but it isn't always easy to work with, especially if you buy it in large 1220 X 2440 mm (4 X 8 ft) sheets. Fortunately, DIY stores sell it in smaller sizes and timberyards are usually willing to make a couple of cuts for free. All other cutting can be done with a hand saw.

The challenge, when working with plywood, is cutting it without tearing the grain. Here are five tips for cutting plywood effectively.

1 Thin plywood will often chatter as you cut. Clamp it to the workbench with the line of cut very close to the edge, to reduce the amount of flexing and give you more control.

2 Mark the line of cut with a pencil and score it with a craft knife to break the fibres along the cut. This should reduce tearing, especially when cutting across the grain.

3 If tearing is a real problem when cutting across the grain, you can try laying masking tape along the line. This reduces tearing and also means that you don't have a pencil line to clean up afterwards.

4 Use a fine-toothed hand saw (up to 12 tpi) for cutting plywood if tearing is an issue. If you are using a jigsaw, turn off the pendulum action and fit fine-toothed blades.

TIP: Buy a band saw. Though a band saw's throat limits the width of cut, you can achieve superb results (see Using a table saw, page 218).

Planing plywood and end grain

Obviously, you don't need to plane the surface of plywood, though if you do, it can reveal superb shapes and colours. The best tool for smoothing the edges is a block plane because the low angle of the cutter is designed to deal with end grain. The block plane is also easy to use one-handed in case you need to support a wobbling piece of ply with your other hand. A further option is the modern Microplane (see page 28), which is a bit like a cheese-grater but designed for wood.

Even when you are following the grain of the face layers of the ply, you will be planing end grain of some core layers. There is a risk that at the end of the cut, the end grain will break out because the fibres are easily split there. The same is true for solid wood. There are a couple of ways that you can avoid this.

1 Plane first from one end, then reverse the workpiece and work from the other end.

As a slight adaptation, plane a very angled section at the beginning of the board, down to the finish line, then plane down to it from the other end.

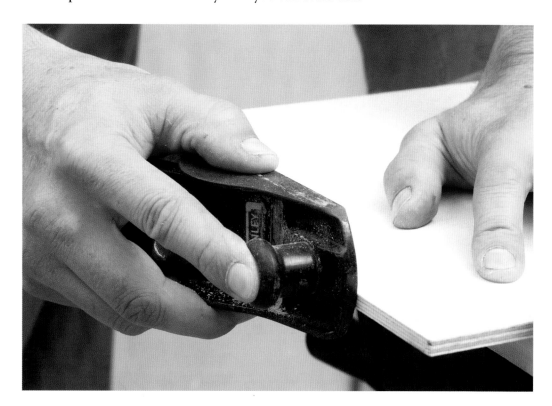

2 Clamp a sacrificial piece of scrap wood to the end of the board to reduce the tendency of the fibres to split. This is difficult to do on thin ply, though one tip is to tape the scrap in place and then hold it firmly in the vice.

Ultimately, a fixed disc sander (see photo on page 224) or belt sander (see Belt-sanding a board, page 118) is ideal for cleaning up the edges of plywood.

A coping saw is a superb first tool for a child learning woodwork; it is also useful for cutting shapes in plywood. Twist the blade in the frame as you work your way around a curve.

Cutting shapes

One of the most significant advantages of plywood is that it can be used very effectively for cutting shaped components because the alternating grain direction provides strength where solid wood might snap. That's why it is so good for toymaking. If you get into making jigsaw puzzles or lots of toys, you will probably eventually want to buy a powered scroll saw (see Buying a scroll saw, page 58). For now, a coping saw will do. Obviously, you need to drill an access hole through which to feed the blade if you are making internal cuts. Clean up the cuts afterwards with a rasp, metal file, or a Microplane.

Tools

How does a plane work?

A plane is no more than a chisel (known as the cutter or iron) held within a wooden or metal body. The adjustments help you fine-tune the cut, and differences in the shape and style of the body are designed for specific woodworking jobs. In most planes the cutter is actually inverted, with the bevel facing downwards so that there is metal behind the edge to support it as it cuts.

On some planes the opening (mouth) through which the cutter protrudes is adjustable. This is because the sole in front of the edge stops the shaving tearing from the board. For fine cuts, the mouth needs to be smaller because the shaving is thinner. The cutter sits on the frog of the plane, at an angle to the sole. A cap iron above the cutter curls the shaving out of the plane, so that it doesn't get jammed in the mechanism. The cap iron must be adjusted nearer the edge for finer shavings, with the distance varying between 0.4 mm (1/64 in) and 1.6 mm (1/16 in). The block plane is almost identical except that the bevel faces upwards because the angle is lower and there's less stress on the edge. The bevel does the curling of the shaving.

Block planes

Over the years, I've advocated the use of the short block plane – usually about 152 mm (6 in) long – as being essential for woodworking. It is certainly a delightful tool, especially if you work as a jobbing carpenter and need to tidy up bits here and there. As a woodworker with an established workshop, I find myself needing it less and less as a short plane, but it is useful for cleaning up end grain. I would spend a little more than normal and buy a low-angle block plane designed for working with end grain, which is harder to cut than long grain and less likely to tear. There are other features you should consider:

• Lateral adjustment enables you to line up the cutter edge with the sole.

• Depth control offers fine adjustment and is much easier to work than the cheaper block planes that you have to tap to control the depth of cut.

• An adjustable mouth helps you control the shaving, closing it up tightly for fine cuts and opening it to give more space for a thicker shaving.

Sharpening a block plane

To sharpen a block plane, you will need an oilstone and a honing guide, which helps you keep the bevel of the cutter level on the oilstone as you sharpen. The same tool is used

1 The block plane is very simple, with the cap iron holding the cutter in place.

2 To sharpen a block plane, use a straightedge to line up the bevel in the honing guide.

for sharpening chisels (see Sharpening a chisel, page 48). Use a straightedge to line up the bevel in the honing guide, then run it back and forth over the oilstone (which has to be primed with honing oil). Once the single bevel is smooth, adjust the cutter in the honing guide so that the bevel is at a slightly higher angle. This produces the honing bevel, which can be sharpened more quickly and more easily. Work the back a little on the oilstone.

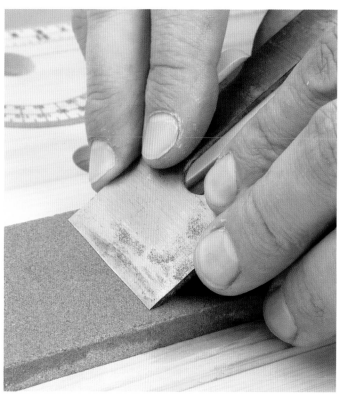

3 Lubricate the oilstone with oil.

4 Holding the honing guide firmly with your fingers around the front of the blade, place it on the oilstone and run it back and forth.

5 Once the bevel has been sharpened, tidy up the back on the oilstone.

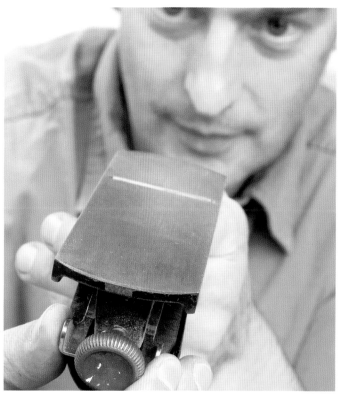

6 When reassembling the plane, look down it to make sure that the cutter doesn't project, even by a fraction.

Large drill bits

Anyone who owns an electric drill will already have a collection of drill bits, which are probably in a condition ranging from moderate to atrocious. When you start buying them for woodwork, try keeping them only for that purpose or they'll soon get ruined. For removing the waste from mortises, you will need some larger bits than you find in the average set, which are usually limited to a maximum diameter of 10 mm (⅜ in). The best solution is to buy flat bits when you need them. Use a file to sharpen their edges and to make sure the point is centred. Later we will discuss more advanced types of drill bit, but most of these are only worth considering once you have a drill press (see Drill press, page 185).

A flat bit needs to be sharp, or it will tear the grain.

Make sure the point of the flat bit is ground centrally.

The scroll saw

The scroll saw is one of the first tools young woodworkers try because it is safe and fun to use. Twisting the handle tightens the blade, which can be positioned to cut on the pull or the push stroke and can be fed through an access hole for internal cuts. A slight refinement of the scroll saw is the adjustable piercing saw, with a system for shortening the amount of exposed saw blade for more controlled cutting of thin material (see Cutting out shapes, page 58).

Files, rasps and Microplanes

There have always been rasps and files for cleaning up edges, especially curves, and for many years the Surform range of planes and files were considered to be the best. I was given a Surform block plane as a child and I loved it. But for serious woodworking, you will find them quite frustrating. There is, however, a new kid on the block, the Microplane range of tools, which is American. This tool is superb and cuts brilliantly; it is great for cleaning up.

Trade secret

Buying a jigsaw

After a drill, the jigsaw is often one of the first power tools a woodworker buys. They are quite useful around the home and can be used for all sorts of cutting, especially curves. There is no harm in owning one, but it is not an essential tool in the workshop. In the long term, you will find a band saw a much more useful piece of equipment, and it can often make the jigsaw redundant (see page xx).

When I was working as a site carpenter, I bought a very expensive jigsaw, with lots of power and weight. It has survived well and has been used extensively. However, now that my woodworking is limited to a workshop, I hardly ever use it, and I could happily cope with a much cheaper model for the one or two occasions a year it's needed. If you only plan to use a jigsaw from time to time, like I do, I recommend that you choose something solid but inexpensive, and without too many features. Always pay for good blades, though, ideally tungsten carbide, as they last longer.

Sawhorses

For cutting sheets of plywood and long lengths of wood, you need a pair of sawhorses. Many woodworkers are encouraged to make these as their first project. Personally, (and especially for those with limited space), I favour buying a pair of foldable plastic sawhorses that can be tucked away most of the time.

Materials

SHEET MATERIALS

Using sheet materials is an ideal way for woodworkers to get going, as they are stable, a consistent thickness, and don't have the challenges associated with movement (see Designing cabinet-making projects, page 166). After a while they become frustratingly uniform, but they are a valuable resource, especially as small sizes. Usually sold in 610-mm (2-ft) intervals, and available from DIY stores.

In the projects in this book, some caution has to be paid to the thickness of plywood, as the conversions from metric to imperial will not always be consistent from one source to another. You may need to use plywood as close as possible to the measurements that we have given and adjust the plans accordingly.

Plywood

In my opinion, plywood is the king of sheet materials, and whenever possible, I pay a little extra for birch ply. It tends to be more dense than ply made with tropical hardwoods, and I have a little more faith that the birch comes from a sustainable source. If you want a guarantee of this, you will need to buy certified plywood, but I'm not sure any exists yet! (See All About Wood – Sustainability, pages 168–9.)

I always try to have some sheets or offcuts of 6-mm (¼-in), 10-mm (⅜-in) and 13-mm (½-in) birch ply around the workshop. I also like the 1.6-mm (1⁄16-in) microply, which is really useful for making templates and writing lists but is not so easy to find! Model-making shops sometimes stock it.

Fibreboards

Some people love medium-density fibreboard (MDF). I hate the stuff because it's heavy, dusty, and blunts your tools. It has very little strength and given the opportunity, it will bend. The health scares that it is carcinogenic are the least of my concerns, though you must wear a respirator or dust mask when using MDF, and indeed for any dust-producing operations with

wood and other sheet materials. I try not to have any in my workshop, though it does have its uses for very specific purposes, particularly when you want to rout a profile on the edge. Similar to MDF, chipboard has larger chips of wood and isn't as dense, but it is even weaker than MDF and can't be routed along the edge easily. I have used it for worksurfaces, but I'd prefer to use plywood any day (see Lesson 5, page 136).

CLEAR FINISHES

Clear finishes are used to protect the surface and enhance the colour and pattern of wood. There is a wide range of options, but here are some you might consider. I favour oils for furniture and shellac/wax for smaller, more decorative pieces. Varnish is good for utility jobs and for outside surfaces.

Varnish and wax

The most common type of finish in DIY stores is generically termed 'varnish', but it applies to various mixes of resin and oil or water. You're likely to find polyurethane, in water- and oil-based versions, and in matt, gloss and satin finishes. The water-based varnish dries faster and is easier to use. After a couple of coats I usually rub the surface with wax, using a flexible abrasive pad, then buff with a soft cloth. However, I don't use this approach very often, as polyurethane tends to dry very hard and is very difficult to repair if it deteriorates.

Oils

I often use oil finishes because they are so easy to apply and produce a more natural effect. Some are pure, like linseed and tung oils, while others, such as Danish and teak oils, are mixed with resins to produce better protection. You can wipe oils on a surface, and when they start to lose their lustre, you simply add another layer, but this does mean that they need long-term maintenance.

Sanding sealer and wax

The quickest finish I know is to use a sanding sealer and then polish with wax. Sanding sealer is similar to varnish and can be brushed or wiped on. It is either shellac- or cellulose-based, and you can dilute it with thinners to suit your needs. I prefer the cellulose product because it is slightly less messy. Both types dry very quickly, and you can then apply wax as for varnish. However, they do not offer much protection, and the wax finish will need additional coats in the future.

Project **Toy lorry**

For playtime

Toys are superb projects for home woodworkers –
my children still play with the plywood garage my
father made me when he took up the hobby. The joy
of this lorry is that it is made almost entirely from
birch plywood, and there is also plenty of room to
customize the design.

Shopping list

Materials

Axles: 3 x 5 mm (⅕₆ in)
Plastic wheels: 6
Spring hubcaps: 6
Glue
Moulding pins: box each of
18 mm (¾ in) and 25 mm (1 in)

Cutting list

Part	Material	Quantity	Dimensions length, width, thickness	Part	Material	Quantity	Dimensions length, width, thickness
A Chassis	Birch ply	1	295 x 45 x 6 mm (11⅝ x 1¾ x ¼ in)	**J** Tailgate	Birch ply	1	152 x 41 x 6 mm (6 x 1⅝ x ¼ in)
B Chassis side	Birch ply	2	121 x 64 x 12 mm (4¾ x 2½ x ½ in)	**K** Flatbed Sorter box	Birch ply	1	225 x 152 x 6 mm (8⅞ x 6 x ¼ in)
C Cab front	Birch ply	1	114 x 89 x 6 mm (4½ x 3½ x ¼ in)	**L** Base	Birch ply	1	219 x 120 x 12 mm (8⅝ x 4¾ x ½ in)
D Cab side	Birch ply	2	121 x 59 x 12 mm (4¾ x 2⅜ x ½ in)	**M** Side	Birch ply	2	219 x 98 x 12 mm (8⅝ x 3⅞ x ½ in)
E Cab back	Birch ply	1	121 x 76 x 10 mm (4¾ x 3 x ⅜ in)	**N** Back	Birch ply	1	120 x 45 x 12 mm (4¾ x 1¾ x ½ in)
F Cab roof	Birch ply	1	89 x 51 x 4 or 3 mm (3½ x 2 x ⅛ in)	**O** Front	Birch ply	1	120 x 85 x 12 mm (4¾ x 3⅜ x ½ in.)
G Wheel arch	Birch ply	1	140 x 21 x 6 mm (5½ x ⅞ x ¼ in)	**P** Top	Birch ply	1	219 x 146 x 6 mm (8⅝ x 5¾ x ¼ in)
H Bumper	Birch ply	1	140 x 21 x 6 mm (5½ x ⅞ x ¼ in)	**Q** Sorter fixing	Dowel	4	12 x 10 x 10 mm (½ x ⅜ x ⅜ in)
I Lights/rad	Birch ply	1	140 x 19 x 6 mm (5½ x ¾ x ¼ in)	**R** Shapes			Each shape is 50 mm (2 in) long and cut to suit the holes you make in the roof. Cut these from whatever offcuts you have.

1 Cut out all the parts for the chassis. Drill the holes in the sides (**B**) for the axles, then glue and nail the sides (**B**) to the chassis (**A**).

TIP: When it comes to cutting shaped parts, you may find it easier to cut the shaped windows and other parts before cutting the piece from the plywood sheet.

2 Cut out the cab sides (**D**) and cut the window and wheel arch shapes using a coping saw (see Cutting out shapes, page 58).

3 Cut the wheel arches to suit the wheels you have bought. Nail and glue the cab sides to the chassis sides, making sure the front edge of the cab side is flush with the front edge of the chassis side.

4 Cut out the cab front (**C**), back (**E**) and roof (**F**) to fit within the cab sides. This should be a snug fit, but must not push the side outwards. Use a block plane or rasp to angle the leading edge of the roof to match the angle on the front edge of the cab sides.

5 Use a nail set to tap all the nail heads below the surface for filling later. Nail and glue the cab front, back and roof in place, and while the glue sets, cut out the bumper (**H**) and lights and radiator piece (**I**). Once again, you may find it easier to drill the light holes and cut out the grille before cutting the piece from the sheet of ply. Cut out all the sorter box parts, making sure the front (**O**) and back (**N**) are exactly as long as the base (**L**) is wide. Cut out the shapes in the top. Also cut out the flatbed (**K**). Position the sorter box base on the flatbed, and temporarily attach with sticky tape so that you can drill the locating holes for the sorter nails (**Q**).

6 Nail and glue the sides (**M**) to the base, then fix the front and back in place, and finally the top (**P**). Leave the glue to set between steps.

Make the blocks to fit the holes you've cut in the sorter box top, then sand and clean up all the parts and apply the finish of your choice, which must be child-friendly. Finally, add the wheels and perhaps some stickers to personalize the truck.

Lessons learned

- **TIP:** If you don't have the right length of moulding pin, or think a pin will protrude through the wood, snip off the excess from a 25-mm (1-in) pin before insertion.

- This is the ideal opportunity to discover how many components can be nailed and glued in one operation. Too many, and it will go awfully wrong. You may also have found that clothespegs or bulldog clips are useful temporary clamps to hold pieces in position while you pin them in place.

- Gradually, a project becomes increasingly sturdy as you add more parts.

- The dimensions of one component may have a significant impact on the fit of another one. Look out for components that have identical measurements or those that are critical to the construction. In this project, for instance, the relationship between the width of the chassis sides (**B**), the length of the cab sides (**D**), the width of the cab back (**E**), and the thickness of the cab roof (**F**) is absolutely critical to the success of that part of the project.

Lesson 3
Drilling basic joints

Getting started

The round hole is about as simple as it gets in woodworking terms, and yet it remains one of the most effective tools for joining pieces of wood together. Where you use the hole for screws or for a dowel rod, it is easy to position accurately and is quick to cut.

1 Use an awl to mark the position of the hole.

In fact, the introduction of the cordless drill has been one of the most dramatic revolutions for woodworking over the last 20-odd years. The router and its multitude of cutters and jigs have led to a greater leap in terms of opening up new techniques and methods to all woodworkers, but battery technology has made life so much more convenient. I can't remember the last time I used a brace and bit – certainly not since the development of the more powerful cordless drills.

Though drilled joints have been superseded by biscuits and other modern approaches, this is still an important technique to learn, since the drilled joint is extremely versatile and often strong. In this lesson we will also be looking at the use of softwoods and how you have to watch out for movement in wood and be able to adjust your work accordingly.

Drilling holes

Drilling a hole is certainly one of the easiest woodworking tasks, but take my word for it, things can go wrong, and there are some key tips for successful drilling.

2 Drill slowly to start, while the bit settles. Keep backing out every 6 mm (¼ in) or so to remove the waste and stop the bit from burning the wood.

Lesson planner

Key techniques	Key tools and materials
• Drilling holes • Drilling for screws • Cutting with the grain • Making a bench hook • How to solve cupping	• Cordless drill • Types of drill bit • Bradawl • Tenon saw • Dowel rod • Strip wood

3 You can buy collars to fit drill bits to set the depth, or you can create a depth stop for the drill bit. This can be done with a piece of tape, but the drill or the hole (or both) can end up getting clogged. A better solution is to drill through a short piece of narrow dowel that you can push up or down the drill bit as a depth guide or stop, but watch that it doesn't mark the wood. Take care using flat bits, as the point is long, and you can easily drill through the workpiece accidentally. You won't be able to use one for the Shoe Rack project in this lesson, for instance, because the bit will break through the sides.

Drilling for screws

When joining two pieces of wood with screws, you need to drill two different holes. In the guest piece – the one being held by the screw – you need a clearance hole through which the screw slips. In the host piece you need a pilot or thread hole into which the screw bites. It makes screwing easier and reduces the risk of splitting. Sometimes, for softwoods that aren't likely to split, you can get away without a pilot hole or perhaps just a very thin one. In fact, modern screws are designed to be self-tapping, without a pilot hole, and many have serrated tips to cut their way into the wood. Cordless drills also make it simpler, but there is still a risk of splitting.

Cutting with the grain

To create the Shoe Rack on page 38, you have to make an angled cut along the grain, known as ripping. You will soon discover this is harder than cutting across the grain. This is because the fibres tend to tear more when cutting with the grain, and these larger particles get clogged up in the saw's teeth. The hand saw you bought for Lesson 1 may be tough to use for this job, as it is designed for

Choosing a drill bit for screws

You may want to reduce the diameter of the pilot hole for softer species.

Screw size	Clearance hole	Pilot hole
No. 2	2.5 mm (0.095 in or ⁵⁄₆₄ in)	1.6 mm (0.058 in or ¹⁄₁₆ in)
No. 4	3 mm (0.110 in or ⁷⁄₆₄ in)	1.65 mm (0.065 in or ³⁄₃₂ in)
No. 6	3.5 mm (0.140 in or ⁹⁄₆₄ in)	2 mm (0.085 in or ⁵⁄₆₄ in)
No. 8	4.5 mm (0.175 in or ¹¹⁄₆₄ in)	2.5 mm (0.095 in or ⁵⁄₆₄ in)
No. 10	5 mm (0.200 in or ¹³⁄₆₄ in)	3 mm (0.110 in or ⁷⁄₆₄ in)

When cutting with the grain, use a wedge to stop the blade binding in the cut.

cutting across the grain, and is further proof that buying a table saw is a good idea (see Using a table saw, page 218).

To rip a long board in half, it's best to place it on a pair of sawhorses and then move it when you are likely to cut one of them. For shorter pieces, as in the Shoe Rack, clamp the board to the workbench, overhanging to one side. You will need to plane the sawn edge afterwards, with the block plane doing this perfectly.

Making a bench hook

A useful addition to any workbench is a home-made bench hook to hold a board as you cut. It is very simple to make, and can be adapted to suit your needs. A batten underneath at the front holds the bench hook securely against the front edge of the working surface, while another batten along the top at the back is used as a fence against which to hold the timber.

Most people use bench hooks for cutting thin pieces of wood, where the waste is not heavy enough to tear the corner as the cut finishes. But notice how the table extends beyond the end of the back fence, both to support the waste and to reduce tearing as the saw cuts through the bottom of the board. A simple bench hook can be customized to include pre-cut grooves for cutting at 90° or 45°, or other regularly used angles.

Clamp each batten to the plywood base to dry.

Run a glue bead along both battens.

Spread the glue with a brush or finger.

A batten glued to the centre of the underside of the bench hook allows it to be held in a workbench or vice.

Tools

Cordless drill

We've assumed, up to this point, that you can make do with the electric drill you use around the house for drilling operations as a woodworker. That may continue to be the case, but I'd also recommend you look at buying a cordless drill. There is no need for a hand drill or a brace and bit (unless you want to try chair-making, or like the crunch of the bit and the waste wood peacefully emerging from the hole).

The big decisions, if you are in the market for a cordless drill, concern its power and whether you buy one with hammer action. A really powerful, 18-volt hammer-action cordless drill is superb for drilling into masonry. But in the workshop you can probably make do with something smaller, say 9 volt or 12 volt. Make sure it has a chuck you can tighten and loosen by hand, forward and backward. You don't need many speeds, but torque control can help if you are inserting delicate screws (though I have to admit I've never used it).

Drill bits

There are two main types of drill bit for home woodworkers, though there are many other specialized bits we will come to later. Both main drill bits can be fitted with a countersinking collar so that you can drill and countersink a hole in one operation (see Countersink bit, page 17).

Twist bit

This is the most common drill bit and is used for drilling into both wood and metal. It works perfectly well for woodworking, but the point isn't always that easy to position. You can buy twist bits up to almost any size, but few sets go beyond 10 mm (⅜ in), and you will have to buy larger bits separately.

Lip and spur bit

A better bit for drilling wood is the lip and spur, sometimes referred to as the dowel bit. This has a central point, and is much easier to position on a mark. It is also less likely to wander than a twist bit. These are a bit more expensive than twist bits, but worth buying and keeping to one side for woodworking. If you regularly use dowels of a particular diameter, as for the Shoe Rack project in this lesson, it is worth buying a special dowel bit to suit. You can buy sets up to 13 mm (½ in) in diameter.

Bradawl

You will use an awl time and time again. A cheap one will do, or you can even make one yourself by knocking a nail into a piece of dowel and sharpening the point if you have a grinder. Considering they cost so little, I'd buy one.

Tenon saw

Most woodworkers start off with a tenon saw for cutting small items or for cutting accurate joints and a crosscut saw for cutting wider boards. Backsaws, of which the tenon saw is the most common example, have a restricted depth of cut, so they can't be used for cutting wide boards and certainly not thick boards. They are also short, so cut less per stroke, and they have small teeth for fine but slow cutting. However, the reinforced back keeps the blade square and improves accuracy.

Most people start with a medium tenon saw, about 254 mm (10 in) long and with about 13 teeth per inch (tpi). It's worth buying a saw with hardened teeth, which can cut any material and is thrown away once blunt. As your confidence and skills develop, you can buy traditional saws that you can sharpen yourself. I tend to favour Japanese saws, which cut on both the push and pull strokes. Fortunately, even the most basic tenon saws and hand saws are available with triple tooth-form teeth, which can also cut both ways (see Japanese tools, page 212).

Materials

Dowel rod

Pre-rounded lengths of wood are known as dowel or dowelling. This is commonly available in a few standard sizes, in steps from about 3 mm (⅛ in) to 38 mm (1½ in). Dowel is, however, notoriously inaccurate, and one length can be fractionally bigger or smaller than others supposedly of the same diameter. This can lead to sloppy joints and great frustration. So once you find a supply that suits your drill bits, buy plenty and stick to it.

Dowel is supplied in softwood or hardwood, with the former being far cheaper. More often than not, softwood dowel will do the job, and you are more likely to find FSC-certified supplies of this than of hardwood dowelling, which can be of uncertain origin (see All about wood – sustainability, page 168).

Problems with wood

Any project incorporating wood has to be designed with the material's inherent instability in mind, acknowledging that the material expands and contracts depending on the ambient humidity of its surroundings. We will look at how this affects designs later in the book (see Designing cabinet-making projects, page 166).

When you buy wood, you will notice that it is not always flat and straight. A board that is curved or bowed along its length shouldn't present too many problems for the woodworker, as you are likely to be cutting it up into shorter lengths. Boards that are twisted along their length should, however, be avoided because you will lose much of the material in trying to flatten them.

Cupping across the width is the most common problem, but it isn't difficult to resolve, and projects should be designed with the risks of further cupping in mind. If you look at the end of a board, you'll notice the growth rings of the tree. By cutting through those rings to produce a flat board, the level of tension on the two sides will be different, and the growth rings will try to flatten themselves. This actually forces the board to cup, rising at the edges.

How to solve cupping

Cupped boards can easily be planed flat and used to make a project, just like the Shoe Rack in this lesson. But if you move the rack from the workshop into a warm bedroom, the moisture content and tensions in the wood will change. The sides of the rack may not be able to bow or twist, because they are held by the front and back rails and by the dowel. They could, however, cup.

The effects of cupping are more likely to be noticed on wide boards than thin boards, because the tensions are amplified since the difference between the two sides is greater. One way to avoid this is to use quarter-sawn boards, but you won't find much softwood timber milled this way. The solution is to glue up wide boards from a number of thin strips, alternating the direction of the growth rings to minimize the consequences of cupping (see Quarter-sawing a log or a board, page 212).

Strip wood

To help you when making projects, you can buy ready-prepared wide boards of thin strips (before you own the machines or have the skills to glue panels from narrow boards). Strip wood reduces the risk of cupping but is more expensive than plain-sawn boards, even those planed on all four sides (PAR).

Project **Shoe rack**

For your bedroom

Using strip wood reduces the risk of the sides of the
shoe rack cupping. This project relies on accurate
drilling of the holes for the dowel racking and
straight cutting of the notches at the back.

230 mm (9in)

4 in. (100 mm)

50 mm (2 in)

230 mm (9 in)

70 mm (2¾ in)

60 mm (2⅜ in)   100 mm (4 in)

50 mm (2 in)

575 mm (22⅝ in)   230 mm (9 in)

100 mm (4 in)

D

648 mm (25½ in)

C

A

B

Cutting list

Part	Material	Quantity	Dimensions length, width, thickness
A Side	strip wood	2	549 x 229 x 19 mm (21⅝ x 9 x ¾ in)
B Front rail	softwood	1	648 x 63 x 19 mm (25½ x 2½ x ¾ in)
C Back rail	softwood	2	648 x 38 x 19 mm (25½ x 1½ x ¾ in)
D Shoe rail	dowel	4	622 x 19 x 19 mm (24½ x ¾ x ¾ in)

Shopping list

Tools and materials

Screws: 8 x 32 mm (1¼ in), no. 8

Flat bit: 19 mm (¾ in), to drill the dowel holes, or

Suitable twist bit (since you'll get a better finish and can drill the holes deeper for more stability)

1 Cut the sides (**A**) to length and mark up the tapers with a straightedge and pencil. Cut the tapers and clean up with a block plane.

2 Mark out the positions for the dowel holes, making sure the sides are paired and you don't end up drilling the inside face of one and the outside face of the other.

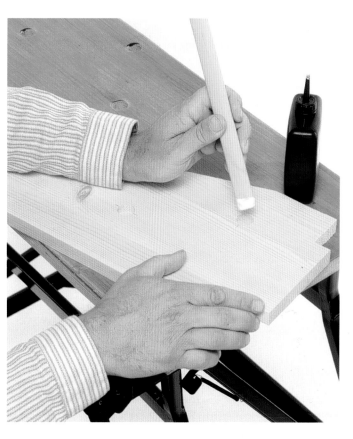

3 With a twist bit or flat bit, drill the dowel holes, making sure you use a depth stop or mark on the bit so as not to pierce the sides. Check the fit of the dowel after you've cut one hole, then do the rest.

Cut the notches at the back of the sides with a tenon saw, using the back rails (**C**) themselves to mark out the notches.

Use the sliding bevel I introduced in Lesson 1, and set it to the angle of the taper. Then mark the ends of the front rail (**B**) to that angle and plane the top edge with a block plane.

4 Drill and countersink the ends of the rails for inserting screws. Offer the rails up to the sides and use screws to mark where you need to drill pilot or thread holes in the sides. If you don't drill pilot holes in the sides you are likely to split the wood.

Do a dry run, and when you are satisfied, apply glue, using the screwed rails to hold it all together. If you are worried about the amount of gluing you are doing in one go, glue the dowels in place initially, but use screws for the rails. Once the glue for the dowels has set, you can carefully undo the rails one by one and glue them in place.

Clean up and apply a finish; varnish is an ideal choice.

Lessons learned

- Screws inserted into thin softwood are likely to split the wood.

- Flat bits tear wood fibres, and twist bits are far better if you can afford them.

- Wood will cup over wide boards unless you take precautions.

Lesson 4
Interlocking joints

Getting started

Though there are plenty of ways to join pieces of wood with metal fasteners and other connectors, the most satisfying method is to create interlocking joints from the timber itself. These rely upon the fit and glue to varying degrees, with truly mechanical joints like the drawer-bored mortise and tenon requiring no adhesive at all.

The first type of joint to try is the lap joint, which is used for simple constructions. The shoulders on the joint provide good lateral support, to stop twist, but the joint relies largely upon glue, though a good fit will improve its longevity. The good thing is that in learning how to cut the lap joint, you have to develop skills with tools that will help with all future woodworking. In particular, you will have to master the marking gauge for marking up joints, the tenon saw for cutting shoulders, and the chisel for paring back the cheeks of joints.

This lesson's project, the Towel Rail, employs various types of lap joint, between pieces of softwood and plywood. What you will discover is that this technique may be simple, but everything about the joint is on show, so any mistakes are on display. Other joints, later on, hide the link more cleverly but are more complicated to cut.

Lesson planner

Key techniques	Key tools and materials
• When to use the lap joint • Types of lap joint • Marking up a lap joint • Cutting a lap joint • Using a marking gauge • Colouring wood • Dealing with knots	• Chisels Selecting a chisel isn't the hardest choice you'll have to make as a woodworker, but these are tools you will use for years, and they'll also need regular sharpening • Mallet • Marking gauge

Trade secret

Gluing end grain
Glue does not take well to end grain because it is unable to grip the fibres. Any joint that relies on the end grain being glued is vulnerable. Instead, we try to make sure that any glued joint has a section of long grain meeting long grain. This is known as the gluing area. The larger the gluing area in a joint, the better the chances of its survival.

How to choose a joint

One of the most important skills to develop is learning which joint to use and when. While it is tempting to rely upon glues and metal fasteners to join two or more pieces of wood – as are employed in knock-down furniture – the strongest long-term solution is to produce a mechanical joint with interlocking wooden components. The joint you select depends on the dimensions of the stock you are using, the tools and equipment you own, and the stresses and tension exerted on the finished project.

Since a chair has to cope with severe pressure in many directions, it needs a particularly strong joint – so the value of the mortise and tenon is that the male part slots deeply into its partner for strength. A box, on the other hand, suffers only from the risk of the sides bowing and breaking the corner joints, so for that purpose we use dovetails that lock the boards in an embrace that cannot easily be broken. A picture frame needs very little strength, but must look good, for which the mitre is ideal. And then there are simple projects, especially around the workshop itself, that don't need much strength and for which speed is the key. Here, the lap joint is functional and quick.

When to use the lap joint
Up to now we have largely used butt joints and drilled joints to assemble our projects. The time comes, though, when you need to join square- or rectangular-section

components with some strength. Though it's not particularly strong itself, a very simple introduction to joint-cutting is the lap or halving joint.

The principle of this joint is that components overlap one another, often by reducing the thickness of each by half – hence the two names often associated with this joint. It is ideal for joining two pieces of identical section at right angles. The shoulders of the joint help to align the pieces, and there is plenty of long grain to long grain to glue.

Types of lap joint

There are numerous variations on the lap joint. Though it is usually the case, the components don't have to be cut at 90° to one another, and angled versions of all these joints can be used.

- **The end lap.** Very quick to cut, the end lap is used in frame corners but has very little sideways strength. Often it will be screwed or pegged to reduce the risk of breaking.
- **The centre lap.** Otherwise known as the cross-halving joint, the centre lap is surprisingly strong and can be cut very tightly. The shoulders stop any twist, but there is very little margin for error in cutting, as a loose joint looks sloppy and is weak.
- **The T-lap.** Very similar to the centre lap, but one component ends in the 'housing', making it an end lap for one part and centre lap for the other.
- **The full lap.** The components are of unequal thickness, with the full depth of one part fitting into a housing or lap on the other.
- **Dovetailed lap joint.** A version of the T-lap, with the male and female parts cut to a dovetail shape. This is particularly useful if you have no way of holding a frame together while it is being assembled and the glue is setting.

Marking up a lap joint

The quickest way to mark up a lap joint is to offer one component up to the other and use it to mark the shoulder lines. Remember, though, that this marks the outside of the joint, so the shoulders have to be cut to the inside of the lines or the joint will be sloppy.

Once the position is finalized, you can set the depth for the joint to be cut. You do this with a marking gauge. The idea is to scribe a thin groove along the sides (and across the end grain on an end or T-lap). This groove should mark the midpoint of the thickness, assuming both components are the same. You will cut down the shoulders to this mark and then use it to guide the chisel.

Cut the pieces roughly to length: it doesn't matter if they are a little long.

Use one piece to mark up the shoulder line on the other board.

Mark around the board using a knife and combination square.

Using a marking gauge

To use a marking gauge, at least to start, it's best to hold the workpiece in a vice or the jaws of a portable workbench, though with practice you can hold it by hand, resting one end of the board against your leg or the bench. Grasp the marking gauge with your fingers around the stock and hold the stock against the board,

resting on the shaft. Twist the marking gauge till the point breaks the surface and move from around the joint. If you push, you get a better view of the pin and line, but I find pulling gives you better control even if the visibility is worse. Try it for yourself. A few gentle passes are better than one heavy one, which might slip and damage the surface.

Set the marking gauge by marking with the stock held against each face.

Marking across the end grain can be more awkward.

Cup the marking gauge in your hand and run it down the grain.

Trade secret

Setting the marking gauge

The marking gauge must be set accurately if you are going to be able to use it repetitively for all your joints. Take the board and set the stock roughly half the board's thickness from the pin. Hold the stock against the board and make a light puncture. Do the same from the other side. Now adjust the stock to position the pin exactly between the first two holes. For fine adjustment, release the locking nut on the stock a fraction, then knock the gauge shaft on the bench.

Cutting a lap joint

The way you cut the joint depends a little on the type of lap you are forming, though the initial steps are the same for all. The guiding principle is that you cut the shoulders with a saw, and remove the waste and clean up the joint cheek with a chisel.

1 Cut the shoulders down to the depth mark, with the wood held in the jaws of the vice. This could also easily be done with a bench hook to speed up the process. Make sure you cut to the waste side of the drawn lines, and follow the lines you've squared around the sides as well as across the top. Ideally, cut exactly to the line you want, or you'll have to do some boring chisel work.

2 For an end lap you can remove the waste by using the chisel from the end, with the grain. Don't try to remove all the waste in one go, as you don't know how the grain is running and you may find a split chases down below the depth mark. For cleaning up the joint, discard the mallet and use gentle pressure.

3 Once you have cleaned up the joint cheek, use the corner of the chisel to cut through the shavings and to clean up the bottom corner of the shoulder. The face of the shoulder should be clean from the saw cut.

4 For a centre lap or T-lap, you have to chop away the waste across the grain. The end-lap process of working your way down applies, but you have to work from both sides, making sure the final cuts along the edge are tidy, since that is where any mistakes will be seen.

Tools

Your first mechanical joints can be cut with a few tools, but the lessons learned in using and maintaining chisels, in particular, will reinforce most woodworking you will do in the future.

Choosing a chisel

Chisels are produced in various forms, but initially you'll only need a few bevel-edged types, either bought as a set or individually. You can buy plenty of specialized chisels from secondhand stores.

• **Bevel-edged chisels.** As you might expect, these chisels are angled towards the edges to make them easier to get in and out of mortises, but they offer little lateral control and can easily wander.

• **Firmer chisels.** These chisels offer more control than a bevel-edged chisel, and a bit more strength to the chisel. I love the old firmer chisels I've acquired over the years.

• **Mortise chisels.** A mortise chisel is even thicker, to provide more power when removing waste from mortises. You only need these if you are planning to do a lot of hand mortising.

Singles or sets?

You can usually save a little money by buying chisels in sets of anything from three upwards. Personally, I think between three and six is enough to start, but only if you get exactly what you require – don't waste money on chisels you don't really need. My ideal set of bevel-edged chisels would include a 3 mm (⅛ in), 6 mm (¼ in), 9 mm (⅜ in), 12 mm (½ in), 18 mm (¾ in) and 25 mm (1 in).

Alternatively, I'd be more creative in my purchasing, bearing in mind that I don't use either the 3-mm (⅛-in) or 25-mm (1-in) chisels very often, and I do use the 19-mm (¾-in) chisel most of the time.

So if my budget was limited, I would start off by buying a couple of chisels: a 6-mm (¼-in) bevel-edged chisel for awkward jobs and an 18-mm (¾ in) bevel-edged chisel for general paring and cleaning up. I would then plan to buy, at a future date, 9-mm (⅜-in) and 13-mm (½-in) firmer chisels for mortising and other chiselling.

Most of my chisels have wooden handles, but I'm not a purist on this subject, and as long as they are comfortable, plastic handles are just as good (if slightly less friendly to the environment). Eventually, you can make your own handles with a lathe (see Basic turning, page 248).

Three bevel-edged chisels: (top) 6 mm (¼ in), (centre) 13 mm (½ in), (bottom) 25 mm (1 in).

How to use a chisel

Developing skill with a chisel takes time and really is a question of touch, though the job is always made easier with a sharp tool. There are various ways of using a chisel.

1 For paring Hold the handle with your stronger hand, using this for the power, and then guide it by cradling or covering the blade with your other hand, a bit like a snooker player holds a cue. Sometimes you'll use the thumb of your weaker hand to push the chisel.

2 **With a mallet** For more power, and sometimes more control, tap or hit the chisel with a mallet, usually holding the chisel by its handle. You can position the chisel bevel up or down. With the bevel facing downwards, you raise the handle for better access and potentially a deeper cut, but it is slightly less easy to control this way.

Jargon busting

Paring with a chisel

When you come to cleaning up the cheek of an end lap, for instance, you pare, using the flat base of the chisel to guide the edge that you push gently by hand. Paring is often done in a sweeping motion to keep the shavings very thin and to cope with the changing grain.

Make a holder for the oilstone so that it can be held in a vice.

When is a chisel blunt?

A chisel is blunt when it doesn't cut as well as it did before. It is blunt when you carefully rub your thumb across (but not along) the edge and it doesn't feel any resistance. It is blunt when you can see the edge, rather than it blurring into infinity.

Initially, woodworkers fear sharpening chisels, often seeing it as a waste of valuable woodworking time, and become anxious that they'll ruin the edge of a new chisel. I've always believed it's a good idea to assume tools are blunt when they arrive, so any sharpening will improve them. It's important to believe that you can improve anything you buy (from a kettle to a shirt) and don't have to rely upon someone else's design and production.

Sharpening a chisel

It's best to assume the angle of the chisel's bevel is about right, so doesn't need regrinding, unless you dropped it while taking it from the box. I recommend that you buy an oilstone and honing guide to start with, possibly as a kit. Choose a medium-grit oilstone, since this will always be versatile and you may want to move on to more sophisticated sharpening systems for fine or coarse work (see Waterstones, page 119).

The honing guide I prefer has a roller underneath and clamps on each side designed to hold chisels or plane irons. Use a 152-mm (6-in) rule to line up the bevel and roller, then run it back and forth over the lubricated oilstone. Once the edge is sharp, loosen the guide and raise the bevel a couple of degrees to sharpen a strip about 1.6 mm (1/16 in) along the edge. This is known as the honing bevel and means you have to work only on a small area of steel each time the chisel needs sharpening, until you need to regrind it (see Using a grinder, page 120).

Once the honing bevel is glinting beautifully, polish the chisel back on the oilstone to ensure that the edge is perfect and the chisel can glide smoothly over the wood.

Use a steel ruler to adjust the chisel.

You should see a fine shaving of metal attached to the edge.

Tidy up the back of the chisel on the oilstone, holding it flat.

A honing guide helps you keep the bevel at the correct angle.

Materials

Colouring wood

There are a number of ways to add colour to your work. You can use a stain or pre-coloured varnish, applying it with a brush or cloth.

1 If you want to retain the patterning of wood, you can apply a coloured stain to the sanded surface and then protect it with a varnish once it has dried. Spirit-based stains are really the best because they bite hardest into the wood and they don't expand the fibres.

2 Alternatively, apply a pre-coloured varnish, which will either be water- or oil- based. These are quicker to apply than stains, but the colour tends to lie on top of the surface rather than soaking down into the grain. You may not notice this to begin with, but you will see the difference later.

A third option is to use a normal wood paint, priming the surface first with a primer and undercoat. Make sure it is safe for children and food to be in contact with the paint if you are using it for toys or in the kitchen. This probably gives you the widest range of colours. Milk paints are a specialized solution – these are only available from limited suppliers in a small range of colours, but the effect on wood is superb.

Dealing with knots

Knots in wood are a serious issue for a number of reasons. Some species, especially softwoods, suffer more from them than others. When purchasing timber, the best advice is to visit the timberyard and choose boards for yourself, so you can avoid knots if necessary.

Depending on the project, you might need to buy blemish-free boards or be able to just place the knots carefully in the project's components. In many ways, knots add character to projects, so don't worry about keeping them, as long as they don't undermine the function of the piece. However, there are a few problems with knots that you have to consider. These include the following:

• Knots can seep resin, particularly in softwood species. The effects of this bleeding are most conspicuous when you paint the wood, since a dark mark may show through. The solution is to paint the knot with shellac before finishing.

• Knots can weaken thin components, so you should avoid any such defects on lengths of wood less than 25 mm (1 in) square in section. Moulding is particularly vulnerable.

• Knots may break out, leaving a hole. Loose knots can be glued in place using cyanoacrylate glue or epoxy, and holes can be filled with filler or another knot. (I have a stock of old knots.) If you use filler, make sure it is darker than the surrounding wood so it resembles a knot.

• Knots can make planing very difficult because the grain is deflected in all sorts of directions and tears. Equally, that grain can look superb if you can control the cut.

Shellac seals knots and stops any resin from bleeding.

Project **Towel rail**

A practical bathroom accessory

This towel rail consists of a pair of end frames joined together by rails, and does not have to be very robust. Mark out the positions of the joints and dowels carefully, and the components should fit easily.

A

E

C

B

D

250 mm
(9⅞ in)

180 mm (6⅞ in)

865 mm
(33½ in)

865 mm
(34 in)

305 mm (12 in)

Cutting list

Part		Material	Quantity	Dimensions length, width, thickness
A	Posts	softwood	4	865 x 75 x 25 mm (34 x 3 x 1 in)
B	Bottom rails	softwood	2	178 x 75 x 25 mm (7 x 3 x 1 in)
C	Middle rails	softwood	4	178 x 50 x 25 mm (7 x 2 x 1 in)
D	Connecting rail	softwood	1	865 x 50 x 25 mm (34 x 2 x 1 in)
E	Hanging rails	softwood	4	840 x 25 mm (33 x 1 in)
F	Dowels	softwood	24	50 x 10 mm (2 x ⅜ in)

Shopping list

Tools and materials

Screws: 4 x 32 mm (1¼ in), no. 8
brass countersunk
Straightedge and **try square**
Ripsaw or **panel saw**
Tenon saw
Bench plane and **block plane**
Sash clamps
Dowel pins
Power drill and **bits**
Chisel: 19 mm (¾ in)
Bradawl
Screwdriver

1 Make a template for the posts from spare sheet material — 5 or 6 mm (³⁄₁₆ or ¼ in) MDF is ideal. Draw up the template full size and cut it out. Round off the top of the template and then use it to mark out the wood for the four posts.

2 Lightly clamp the posts together in line and mark the positions of the three end-frame rails across all of them. Mark the end of each rail for a pair of dowels and mark the drilling centres with a sharp bradawl. Drill the holes, which should be slightly deeper than half the length of a dowel. Slot dowelling pins in the holes in the ends of the rails and position the rails against their marks on the posts. Drill out the dowel holes in the posts, making sure that they are only slightly deeper than half the length of a dowel. Apply waterproof adhesive to the dowels and their holes and then assemble the posts and rails to complete the construction of the two end frames. Use sash clamps to hold the frames together until the glue dries. If necessary, smooth down both sides of each join with a bench plane.

3 Mark the connecting rail slightly overlength and shape it to the correct width and thickness with a bench plane. Mark the shoulder lines for the lap joints on the connecting rail. The distance between the shoulder lines should equal the overall length of the towel rail minus the thicknesses of the two end frames. Mark out the lap joints at both ends of the connecting rail and at the two midpoints of the bottom rails on the end frames. Cut the waste from the joints with a tenon saw. Clean up the joints with a 19-mm (¾-in) chisel, and make sure the faces of the joints are flat and square.

4 Next, drill two countersunk clearance holes at each end of the connecting rail and dry-assemble the joints. Make sure the two joints fit together tightly and then mark the bottom rails, through the clearance holes, with a bradawl. Once assembled, drill the holes for the dowel rod. Using screws, fix the connecting rail to the bottom rail of one of the end frames. The connecting rail holds the assembly together, so fix one end first, and only when the hanging rails are ready should you attach the other end of the connecting rail to the other frame. Notice how the connecting rail is notched into the frame rail.

5 With the dowel rails all cut to length, and the connecting rail screwed to one frame, apply glue to the end of the hanging rails and assemble the towel rail. Make sure you remove any excess glue with a damp cloth, and then complete the piece with a waterproof finish, preferably polyurethane varnish.

Lessons learned

- Lap joints may be simple to cut, but the shoulder lines are very visible so they must be cut accurately. As you will discover, mortise and tenon joints may look complicated, but actually the joint is easier to hide.

- It can be very difficult to get dowel to fit well into a hole. Test the fit first. The dowel joint is relatively strong, but can be difficult to line up.

- It is always worth assembling a complicated project like this in sections, one frame at a time. In this case, you need to assemble the end frames individually, and then join them together with the hanging rails and the connecting rail.

Lesson 5
The versatile dowel

Getting started

In the 1960s and 1970s, with the advent of the cheap electric drill and a boom in home improvement, special jigs for the accurate drilling of dowel holes were popular, and the dowel joint was used extensively for the making of home-built cabinets, chests and bookshelves. The revolutionary introduction of the router in the 1980s led to a decline in the popularity of the dowel joint and the dowel-drilling jig.

There was a time when it seemed that every piece of furniture included a dowel joint. Now the biscuit jointer and router dominate, but the dowel shouldn't be ignored, since it can be a very effective means of joining pieces of wood. The key benefit of the dowel joint is its versatility, with the dowel rod employed to reinforce restoration jobs, or as a quick solution to strengthen butt joints. These days there has been a revival of the joint, with some furniture-makers using stainless-steel threaded rod instead of wooden dowel for joints. The challenge is lining up holes for drilling, and if you aren't using a jig of some sort, the problem of the drill bit wandering is always an issue, especially when drilling into end grain.

Using the dowel joint

One of the simplest mechanical joints, for fixing two pieces of wood together, is to use short lengths of dowel rod drilled into each component. This technique has been used for decades, if not centuries, in the mass production

of chairs and furniture. With the right equipment and jigs, it is relatively easy to create this joint accurately and to do so over and over again for repeated joints.

Even though the router has superseded the dowel jig, the joint still has value, especially for reinforcing a simple butt joint, with two boards meeting at right angles. One advantage of the dowel joint is that it is very easy to set out and mark up, and the dowel is a versatile way to strengthen a joint. You can mark up the joint quickly as a one-off, use marking gauges for repetitive setting out, or use a jig to produce many joints quickly and accurately.

The joint itself is relatively strong, and the glue area is pretty wide. One of the problems is finding a balance between using enough dowels and weakening the component. You must also consider that drilling into end grain, as is very likely to happen for at least one part of the joint, is not easy, and the drill bit may wander unless you are using a drill press and the component is held against a fence. Checking by eye using two set squares is possible but tricky, and any discrepancy will severely weaken the joint and make assembly difficult.

Lesson planner

Key techniques	Key tools and materials
• Using the dowel joint • Marking up and drilling a dowel joint • Using dowel-markers • Making your own dowel • Making a sanding block	• Buying and using a scroll saw • Geometric marking tools • Drilling jigs • Dowel rod • Child-safe paints

Marking up a dowel joint

There are a couple of ways to mark up a dowel joint, but the simplest is to use a marking gauge. Let's assume you are planning to joint two identical boards at a right angle, as is being done in the Bookends project this lesson. The plan is to use three dowels to reinforce the joint between the two pieces. It is the best joint for the job, but later you'll find that a biscuit will do this as well. You could screw one board to the other, but in doing that, you would need to screw into the end grain of one board, and screws rarely hold well into end grain, because the fibres split around the screw. Nor can you rely on glue, as end grain never bonds very well. You need some form of mechanical connection strengthened with glue.

1 Lay out the two boards, end to end with the inside face of each facing upwards. Gently mark these as the meeting faces with a soft pencil. Also mark the positions for the holes to be drilled across the width, and offer one board up to the other to repeat this. If you have a number of joints to cut, you could keep one piece as a template and use it for repetitive marking. Set the marking gauge to half the thickness of the board.

3 It's a bit confusing, but you must make sure you place the stock against the correct face when marking across the end grain of the other piece. Although the gauge should be set centrally, there may be some discrepancy, so make sure the stock is against the outside face and not against the inside face that you marked earlier. This positions the line correctly. You can square across the positions for the holes at this stage if you haven't done so already. The two boards should now be ready for drilling.

2 With the stock against the end of the board, mark across one component.

Trade secret

Pin or knife?

The marking gauge we are using here has a sharpened knife to score the line, rather than the pin you often find in cheaper models. The advantage of the knife is that it cuts more easily through the fibres, but it leaves a bevelled edge to the groove on one side, whereas the pin produces a V-groove, which is more suitable for marking out mortises and tenons.

Drilling a dowel joint

Assuming that you don't have a drilling machine, I'm going to explain how to make a dowel joint using a cordless or electrically powered drill. This technique relies upon good marking up and the ability to drill accurately and squarely into the two components.

1 Mark up the two components as described on page 55. In my opinion, there is greater risk of inaccuracy when it comes to drilling into end grain, so I would do that first. If necessary, you can then adjust the drilling of the second piece. It is often difficult to keep the drill bit still when starting the cut into end grain, and there may be a tendency for it to be deflected by the grain. Some people use a very thin drill bit first to guide the larger bit, but if the pilot hole is too large, the proper one will not sit accurately, so practise first.

3 Dry-assemble the joint first to check the fit. Then apply glue to the dowels and tap them into one component with a hammer. They should be a snug fit, with some glue oozing out around the edges through the grooves. Bring up the other component and tap home using a rubber mallet. Check for squareness and wait for the glue to dry. It should not need clamping, which is another benefit of this joint.

2 Hold the second piece on the bench, ideally over some scrap, and held down with a toggle clamp or similar. You can use a bench hook for this, but only if you don't mind the board being ruined by drill holes. You will need to use a depth stop to ensure you don't drill right through the timber.
TIP: It's a good idea to countersink all the holes a little, as this will help guide the dowel rod into place when you assemble the joint.

4 There's a good chance that you'll need to tidy up the outside of the joint. Ideally, you want the end grain to protrude, as this is easier to plane back than having to reduce the thickness of the other piece. Use a block plane for paring back the end grain, but be careful that you don't split the end of the board. By clamping a piece of scrap against the end, you can reduce the risk of this happening.

Using dowel-markers

A quick way to mark up a dowel joint is to use dowel-markers. These fit into a drilled hole and have a point for marking the partner piece. They are superb for one-off jobs.

1 Mark up and drill one set of holes in a component – it doesn't matter where, just as long as they are drilled in straight.

2 Fit the dowel-markers in the holes and bring the piece up to its partner or vice versa. You may want to hold the piece with the dowel-markers in a vice, otherwise the centres might fall out as you bring the piece up.

3 Once you are satisfied with the alignment of the two pieces, gently push down to make the marks. Ideally, you need to get this right the first time, so make sure all three marks have been made. Now you can drill the holes as you would normally.

Making and grooving your own dowel

You can buy pre-grooved dowel rod cut to length, bevelled at the ends, and grooved to let the excess glue escape. Without the grooves there is a risk that the excess glue will get compressed at the bottom of the hole and then force the joint apart when you remove any pressure or when your back is turned.

With screws scoring the dowel, you can adjust the grooves that will allow adhesive to escape from the joint.

With a steel dowel plate you can produce your own dowel.

Knock the dowel through the jig using a medium hammer.

If you don't have any pre-grooved dowel, it is easy to make your own by drilling an appropriate hole in a piece of scrap and inserting nails or screws through the side of the hole to make the grooves. Screws are best, since they can be adjusted more easily. Tap the dowel rod through the groover, cut to length, and bevel the ends for easy insertion.

You could also make your own dowel by drilling appropriate holes in a piece of mild steel or by buying a dowel plate. Harder steel will produce a better surface, but desperate situations require desperate measures. Some people even use a very hard species of wood for the dowel plate, but it isn't as effective and can 'polish' the surface of the dowel rod too much and reduce its adhesion.

Cutting out shapes

Toys make great projects in the early stages of woodworking. One of the most popular approaches is to cut out shapes using a scroll saw and make them into mobiles, bookends, or just animals to play with. There are many books with scroll-saw patterns, or you can use a copier to enlarge or reduce images you come across, though don't ignore the copyright laws if you start selling your work. The simplest technique is to stick copies to the workpiece with spray adhesive, but be sure that you do so in a well-ventilated space or outside, since the fumes can irritate.

Trade secret

Making a sanding block

However well you plane a board, everything can be ruined by turning over the corners with uneven sanding at the end. The best solution is to use a sanding block for finishing. This spreads the pressure and reduces the risk of sanding too much away around the edges or in dips. Though you can buy various types of sanding block, with the abrasive held by pins or by Velcro, a quick and cheap solution is to make your own.

Find an offcut block about 89 mm (3½ in) long, 63 mm (2½ in) wide and 38 mm (1½ in) thick, around which you can fold paper- or cloth-backed abrasive. Bevelling the edges of the block can help facilitate the folding process and increase the lifespan of the abrasive.

Tools

Buying a scroll saw

The scroll saw wouldn't be the first machine I'd buy, as I'd always favour a band saw, but many woodworkers get going with this versatile tool. It can't be used for cutting up boards, but the scroll saw is ideal for beginners who want to dabble with toymaking and create jigsaw puzzles and other gifts.

Essentially, the scroll saw is no more than a mechanized coping saw, with a table to hold the timber you are cutting. Though there are varying designs, the blade always cuts on the down stroke, and because it is so thin, you can cut tight corners and curves to produce shapes. By stacking thin boards one on top of the other, you can create multiple designs. Some scroll saws will cut material up to 51 mm (2 in) thick, but there is a tendency for the blade to wander and bend at these extremes, with a loss of accuracy.

There aren't many things to look out for when buying a scroll saw, and the amount you pay depends on how much you expect to use it. Some scroll saws have a longer throat than others, so check the distance between the blade and the back of the frame. Others have variable speeds, which is useful, but to be honest, I've never used it on my machine (which is always set on 'fast'). The table will invariably tilt, but this only needs to be one way. Check out the extraction facility before you buy. Some have nozzles that blow the dust away from the line of cut, but personally, I prefer those that suck up the dust rather than blast it around.

A further issue is the blade-holding device and tensioning mechanism. Test out a few of these first, since some are more awkward than others and you may end up using this feature.

Tips for using a scroll saw

Fixing the blade in the frame is an important part of preparing the scroll saw. Make sure the blade is centred in the holders; otherwise it will be pulled off-line as you tighten the frame and you'll shorten the life of the blade. Test the tension by flicking the blade with your finger (obviously with the saw turned off) until it sings. Experiment until you find a tension that suits your work.

My dislike of scroll saws has always been based on the tendency for the workpiece to jump and clatter on the table if you don't hold it securely. Small pieces are particularly susceptible. You can buy hold-down devices, but I prefer to use my hands and just remember to maintain the pressure. A magnifier and light can make cutting much easier.

Internal cuts require a piercing hole, through which the blade is fed for cutting. Some scroll saws are supplied with a flexible drive and drill for drilling this tiny hole as you sit at the saw. This is a good option if you are planning to do a lot of complicated cutting with lots of internal cuts, but personally, I rely on a cordless drill or drill press.

Choosing blades

The thinner the scroll-saw blade, the more likely it is to break, and you will go through a fair number. The best idea, when you start scroll-sawing, is to buy a multipack of blades of different sizes and tooth configurations. On most blades all the teeth face downwards, but more modern configurations have a few teeth pointing upwards for a finer cut. I prefer the simple blades, since I've found they give me better control. Whatever you do, make sure that you make a note of which blades you like for particular tasks. Then buy a bulk order of them and clearly label them so you know which is which.

Drilling jigs

Some years ago I threw away my last drilling jig for making dowel joints because I so rarely use this technique. It coincided with the purchase of a drill press. However, jigs can be very useful in the manufacture of cabinets, such as kitchen cupboards, and there are some very good ones on the market.

One extremely useful drilling jig that I do use regularly is the pocket-screw jig. This device guides a special stepped drill bit to produce an angled hole in the side of a board, which you use for attaching screws to another piece. Effectively a reinforced butt joint, it isn't the strongest joint, but it is good enough for many quick jobs.

Marking out shapes

If you get into scroll work and start designing your own shapes, you will want to buy a few geometry marking tools. These include plastic sheets of circles or other shapes, rubber rules that you can bend to a specific shape, and the French curve, which has an ever-increasing radius to suit whatever shape you want to produce. Many of these can be bought at a stationer's and are often provided in children's pencilcase kits. I've been using a pair of the cheapest compasses for years to scribe curved lines on shelves to fit into alcoves or against awkward walls.

Materials

Dowel rod

Buying dowel rod can be one of the most frustrating tasks for a woodworker. Rarely are the diameters consistent, and any variance will result in a sloppy joint or unexpected tightness that splits the wood. The most common dowel rod is made from softwood, but you can also purchase hardwood dowel from various species.

Personally, I prefer to make my own dowel using a dowel plate I bought some years ago at what seemed like a high price for seven holes drilled in a piece of steel. It has proved to be invaluable, since I can now produce whatever dowel rod I desire.

Child-safe paints

If you are making toys, it is important to check that any finishes are child-safe. This should be displayed on the label, and if it isn't, you'd better use something else. When making toys, it is also important to remember that small parts can be swallowed.

Project **Bookends**

For their favourite storybooks

These teddy bear bookends are a good introduction
to the world of scroll-sawing and to the challenges
and benefits of the dowel joint. Though these are
made from softwood, you could use plywood or
another, more exotic wood.

160 mm (6¼ in)

130 mm (5⅛ in)

A

125 mm (5 in)

C

200 mm (8 in)

30 mm (1⅛ in)

140 mm (5½ in)

40 mm (1⅝ in)

19 mm (¾ in)

19 mm (¾ in)

70 mm (2¾ in)

B

Cutting list

Part	Material	Quantity	Dimensions length, width, thickness
A Bear	softwood	1	159 x 130 x 13 mm (6¼ x 5⅛ x ½ in)
B Base	softwood	1	140 x 140 x 19 mm (5½ x 5½ x ¾ in)
C Upright	softwood	1	203 x 140 x 19 mm (8 x 5½ x ¾ in)

Shopping list

Materials

Screws for attaching the bear: 2 x 38 mm (1½ in), no. 6
Dowel rod: 10 mm (⅜ in) in diameter

1 Copy the bear shape to fit and fix it to the board with spray adhesive.

2 Cut around the outside with a scroll saw or with a coping saw. One of the advantages of a scroll saw is that it gives a superb finish that usually requires very little extra finishing. Try to keep the piece moving steadily with as few jerks as possible, and don't panic if you wander off the line. Your mistakes are unlikely to be noticeable later once the pattern has been removed.

The base (**B**) and upright (**C**) are made from rough-sawn boards 150 mm (6 in) wide and 25 mm (1 in) thick, planed to 140 mm (5½ in) wide and 19 mm ¾ in thick. Cut the pieces to length and clean up the ends with a block plane to make sure they are square. It is particularly important that the end of the base that joins the upright is square for the joint to work.

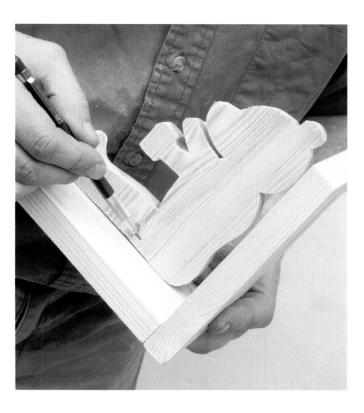

3 Mark up and drill three holes in the end of the base for dowels, using an appropriate bit. Check the fit of the bit and the dowel in waste end grain and long grain first.

Using three pointed dowel-markers, transfer the position of the dowels from one piece to the other. Drill the holes, using a depth stop.

Glue the dowels and knock the joint together, having first drilled pilot holes for screws in the base. Once dry, clean up the joint, paying particular attention to the underside where the end grain of the upright is unlikely to be entirely flush with the bottom of the base. Use a block plane to clean up the joint.

4 Sand and finish, rounding over any edges and corners. Then screw the bear in place.

5 Paint the surface of the wood with high-gloss paint and add any final decorations to complete the bear.

Lessons learned

- If you learn anything from drilling holes for dowel joints, it's that you can rarely overcome mistakes made in drilling the holes at an angle or in the wrong place. They invariably end up sloppy if you try to rectify problems, though you can resolve some errors by inserting a dowel in the hole and starting again.

- I hated using scroll saws initially, but plenty of practice has improved my technique. The wood doesn't jump so often, and I can cut to the line accurately. In fact, I often find cutting can produce a more flowing line than a pencil can, and I often leave the original mark when a better line presents itself.

Lesson 6
Planing as preparation

Getting started

The plane is no more than a chisel held within a metal body, with various adjustments to help control the cut. Understanding the principles of planing, and developing the dexterity to handle a plane effectively, are the foundations for most woodworking and probably the most important skills you will learn. After all, almost every woodworking task and project requires flat, mating surfaces, and any inaccuracy is punished when you come to assemble the piece.

When it comes to successful planing, so much depends on developing what's sometimes referred to as muscle memory: It used to be called practice. The way you hold the plane, the way you stand, and the way you transfer weight and pressure determine how easily you achieve the results you expect.

There are many types of plane to choose from. In this lesson we'll discuss some of the options, what to look for, and why I'm recommending a bench plane. This is likely to be the most expensive tool you will have bought so far, so it's worth investing in something that will last and is versatile.

The moment you start planing, you discover the true challenge of working with wood, for you have to understand and deal with the way wood grows and the effect grain has on your work. I will be outlining some of the principles of wood technology and introducing some of the most common hardwoods.

Lesson planner

Key techniques	Key tools and materials
• Holding a bench plane • The way to stand • All about pressure • Holding the wood • Flattening the edge • Planing to thickness and width	• Bench planes • Setting a plane • What is grain direction? • Is texture an issue? • Some common hardwoods • Simple abrasives

Holding a bench plane

Once the plane is sharp and set up properly, it's time to give it a go. There is nothing finer in woodworking than the sound of shavings hissing from a plane, curling their way off the bench and scattering across the floor. To plane successfully, you need to hold the plane firmly but not too hard: you certainly don't need white knuckles.

Hold the rear handle with your stronger hand, extending your index finger along the side of the cutter, just as you do with a saw, and for the same reasons. Your other hand holds the knob at the front or in some cases actually clasps the side of the plane, but we will look at this later. Your rear hand does most of the pushing, with the front one adding power, guiding the plane, or being used for downward pressure (see Holding a saw, page 13).

Get your weight well over the plane, with pressure applied at the front.

Extending your index finger around the plane iron gives you more control.

The way to stand

Whether you are using a bench plane or a surface planer (see Using a surface planer, page 157), the principles of stance are pretty much the same. Place the workpiece in the vice so that it is horizontal and free from obstruction. Assuming you are right-handed, position your right foot near the start of the board and your left foot a comfortable step forwards, but pretty much in line with the board, so that your shoulders are twisted parallel to the board.

The planing starts pretty much level with your body, which feels natural, and you then extend the plane as far as you can. If the cut is longer than you can reach comfortably (and planing is all about finding what works for you), move your right foot up to your left and then take another step forwards with your left foot.

All about pressure

In theory, a plane can cut with no downward pressure. The flat sole should keep the plane level, with the cutter engaging the wood and the weight of the plane maintaining the cut. More often than not, though, you will need to press down to keep the cut going and ensure you produce a flat surface. There is a tendency to remove more wood at the start and end of the cut because the back of the plane will tend to dip at the beginning and the front will drop as it leaves the board.

To avoid this, you need to compensate by pressing down on the front knob at the start until the length of the plane is on the board. Then you can spread the pressure to both handles until you reach the end of the board, when you must push down at the back a bit harder. The only way to learn this is to experiment on some softwood, producing loads of shavings.

Practice planing

To practise planing, you need a piece of wood at least 610 mm (2 ft) long, but no more than 914 mm (3 ft), to give you a good length of stroke without having to overextend. The best board for this is about 38 mm (1½ in) wide, to give the plane good lateral support. It is often more difficult to learn on narrow pieces, since the plane tends to tilt one way or the other and then it mysteriously stops cutting. Wider boards are just plain hard to work. (Please forgive the pun.)

A piece of softwood will do, but make sure it is free from knots. You are looking for something without conspicuous growth rings and with a fine, even texture. Some hardwoods are worth trying, like cherry, whitewood and hickory. The grain pattern will guide the direction of planing. Imagine they are contours on a map, and you are planing downhill. It can help to look at the edge of the board to see which way you should plane, as if you were stroking a dog to smooth its fur (see What is grain direction?, page 69).

Notice how the plane is following the grain (shown by a 'V').

On this board you would plane from left to right to prevent tearing.

Holding the wood

Assuming your workbench is a portable one, put the wood in the jaws, making sure the pressure is even along the length. One of the problems with these benches is that the jaws can damage boards. This doesn't matter when you are practising, but to make a project, you will need to check the jaws for sharp edges and pimples. It is a good idea to replace the existing jaws with softwood jaws 25 mm (1 in) thick if you intend to use the bench for woodworking over a long period of time.

Of course, anyone who has a solid workbench can hold the piece in the bench vice, parallel to the front edge. Make sure the jaws are lined with softwood so as not to damage the workpiece. Hold the board so that it is parallel to the bench top (and presumably the floor), with the top edge high enough above the bench so that your plane doesn't hit anything, but with enough in the vice for good support.

Flattening the edge

Before you plane, check the straightness of the board by looking along its edge. This is done to choose which face of the board to plane first. Ideally, start with an edge with high ends and a hollow at the middle. This way, the plane cuts at the beginning and end of the stroke, and then gradually the cuts increase towards the centre. When the high point is at the middle, the plane will tend to rock and it is much more difficult (though not impossible) to fashion a level edge. You'll know the edge is flat when the shaving is uninterrupted from start to finish. You'll also know that you can plane.

By planing the concave 'hollow' edge, you will remove the ends first and work into the hollow.

Sight down the board to find out which edge is concave and which is convex.

If you try to plane a convex edge, the plane is likely to rock and you won't achieve a flat surface.

Trade secret

Guiding the plane

It is one thing to flatten the edge of a board along its length but quite another to ensure that the edge is square to the face. To stop the plane from tilting to one side or the other, hold the front of the plane with your thumb behind the knob and your fingers curled underneath, running against the board. This has the added advantage of keeping the plane centred on the board, which is important because the cutters on many planes are sharpened with a very shallow curve along the edge to cut a fraction deeper at the centre. Do be careful, though, to keep your fingers away from the blade and make sure there are no protruding splinters in the wood. (See Setting a plane, page 68, Using a grinder, page 120, and Fettling a plane, page 122.)

Planing wide boards to thickness

Most woodworkers will end up planing wide boards to thickness by machine or buying ready-measured timber from the timberyard. In my opinion, planing a wide board to thickness by hand is not a skill that's worth spending time perfecting in the early stages of woodwork. You have to learn how to move the cutter around the board, often using angled strokes to find and level the high points. (This reduces the friction on the cutter and improves the cut, though you should always finish parallel to the grain.)

Planing a board to width

Given that the board is thicknessed, smooth on both sides, and one edge is planed square to the best face, you will need to plane the second edge to produce parallel edges. Ideally, you need to have cut the board roughly to width before planing, but if the edges are far from straight, you may need to straighten one edge first. The best way to mark up a board for width is with a marking gauge, which is very similar to a mortise gauge, but with only one point and not two (see Marking out a mortise, page 99; Mortise gauge, page 101).

Set the stock to the width of the board you want. Holding the stock against the best edge, use the point to mark both the best face and the other side. Use a couple of light runs with the marking gauge rather than trying to push the pin in hard once. Now you can plane the edge, working down to the tiny grooves. You will notice the shavings narrow a fraction just as you hit the groove, and this is your clue that you've reached the right level.

If the edge isn't flat, move the plane over towards the 'high' side and remove narrow shavings until the edge is level.

Use a marking gauge once you have planed one edge.

As you reach the scored line, you will notice the shaving narrows.

Jargon busting

Face and edge

Almost all woodworking starts by creating two adjacent surfaces at 90° or, as we say, square to one another. As most components have one side wider than the other, these are known as the face and edge. Sometimes referred to as the best face and best side, these are the surfaces you plane first. You start by planing the wider side, or face, until it is flat. This can be very slow work and is more often than not done by machine these days. At this stage I'll assume it has already been done at the timberyard. In the future, you can do this by using a surface planer (see Using a surface planer, page 157).

Once you have chosen the best face, you need to identify it with a pencil mark. You do this by also determining the best edge, which is usually the one easiest to plane first, with the ends higher than the centre. I make a small V-sign on the face, pointing towards the best edge. Once the edge is planed, I mark a corresponding sign on that, pointing towards the best face. This face and edge have become the reference for most future work on the project and are normally the sides that are seen.

Tools

Bench planes

I've made do with two planes for the last ten years, using a powered surface planer and thicknesser to do most of the planing and thicknessing. I love planing by hand and occasionally will make a project without machines for fun, but surfacing isn't a job that I enjoy enough to do by hand. Bench planes are defined, more often than not, by their length, with nomenclature depending on where you live.

My favourite bench plane is a jack plane, sometimes referred to as a No. 5 bench plane. It is about 356 mm (14 in) long, with a 51-mm (2-in) cutter. It is the ideal compromise for planing edges, and occasionally the face, without being too short or too long. You can spend as much or as little as you like on this, but I'd probably look to pay about £60 to get something that will last and which you will enjoy using.

Setting a plane

To get a plane to shave well, you need more than just a sharp blade. As you set the depth of the cutter, the edge will protrude through the mouth. Look along the sole to watch it arrive. Use the lateral adjustment to get the blade level with the sole, and away you go. Drop the cutter farther if you need to remove more wood, and then check that the shaving isn't getting caught in the cap iron.

Loosen the chip-breaker nut and remove from the cutter before sharpening.

Look down the length of the plane sole to check that the cutter is protruding and level.

The curved part of the chip-breaker directs the shaving out the plane mouth.

It is important that the plane is free of any dirt or dust when you put the cutter back in position.

Materials

What is grain direction?

Just as stroking a cat is easier in one direction than the other, planing is easiest when it is done with the grain, with the fibres either parallel to the sole or pointing downward. Fibres pointing up towards the plane are more likely to tear.

Unfortunately, you can't guarantee that even in the most ideal situation a board will be cut from the tree with the fibres all flat. More often than not, the grain isn't entirely straight, with some species having notoriously spiralling or interlocking grain that can suddenly veer off in all directions. Around knots and defects, grain will often wander and make planing especially difficult.

The grain direction is usually indicated by the patterning of dark and light bands (growth rings) that is common to most species, though to a much lesser and greater extent depending on the type of tree and local conditions. It is almost absent in some species. The lighter bands signify the growth in springtime, when the fibres are used to carry nutrients and moisture to the growing tree. The darker, denser late wood is added over the summer and supports the new growth. The contrast in density of late wood and early wood can further challenge the woodworker trying to plane against the grain.

Is texture an issue?

The texture of wood varies greatly from one species to another. Oak, for instance, has a coarse texture. When it is planed, open pores are exposed. This can be seen as an asset by people who like the tactile effect or as a nuisance by those who like their finish perfectly flat. Wood with a fine texture is usually more easily smoothed, though this doesn't mean that the grain direction isn't awkward and that the fibres won't tear.

Nor is texture consistent within wood. Those species that have an even or uniform texture, whether it is coarse or fine, tend to be easier to work than those that are described as being uneven. Generally speaking, woodworkers prefer grain that is straight in direction and even in texture. These are certainly the best species for beginners to try.

Some common hardwoods

It won't take a new woodworker long to want to work with hardwood and sample its amazing range of colour, texture and patterning. Here are a few of the best hardwoods to start off with because they are relatively easy to use and widely available.

Cherry (*Prunus serotina*) Described as black cherry in the US and American cherry in the UK, this timber is now ubiquitous, offering many of the qualities of mahogany. It has an even texture, a straight grain, and is good to work.

White oak (*Quercus alba*) Straight-grained and with few defects, white (or American) oak is good and hard and will produce sharp corners and details. It has a coarse texture, full of character, and great patterning.

Red or soft maple (*Acer rubrum*) Easier to work than its hard cousin (hard maple, *Acer saccharum*), soft maple has more interesting colour but a fine and even texture.

Simple abrasives

The best abrasive for woodworking, at least initially, is cloth-backed aluminum oxide, which can be bought on rolls (so you can tear off what you need). When you sand, start with a coarse grade and, grade by grade, work down towards the finest grit size. You can get by with rolls of 120-, 220- and 320-grit. I also recommend that you buy some flexible abrasive pads (or take them from the kitchen, where they are used for scouring). Though you can buy all sorts of block systems for holding abrasive, wrapping it around a simple wooden block is pretty good and will help you to keep it flat.

Project **Knife block**

For your kitchen knives

If you buy planed boards to make this knife block –
and I suggest that you do unless you already own a
surface planer and thicknesser – you will need a
plane only for cleaning up after assembly. The
construction is simple. Take three boards, cut knife-
shaped slots in two sides, and then glue them all
together (see Using a surface planer, page 157).

Detail showing slots

200 mm
(8 in)

255 mm
(10 in)

A

B

A

75 mm
(3 in)

200 mm
(8 in)

Top plan

Knife slot

Outer piece

Middle piece

Outer piece

Cutting list

Part	Material	Quantity	Dimensions length, width, thickness
A Outer piece	hardwood	4	305 x 216 x 25 mm (12 x 8½ x 1 in)
B Inner piece	hardwood	2	305 x 216 x 38 mm (12 x 8½ x 1½ in)

Shopping list

Tools

G-clamps: you'll certainly need two and ideally four

1 Cut the parts to length, with a little excess on each. Don't worry about cutting the angles yet.

Check how well the boards fit together by clamping them together without glue and by checking their flatness with the straight edge on your combination square. Unless there are bumps on the surface, the clamps will probably draw up any gaps, but it's good to test first.

If you have to plane the surfaces flatter, do so very carefully: only take a very little off each time, and always check to see that you are removing just the high points. It is as easy to cause more problems than you'll solve with this sort of flattening, but it is also a good test of your ability to use a plane and to identify where a problem lies.

2 Mark out the knife slots on the central or outer piece, depending on how you buy your timber.

Chop down vertically around the knife slots, but not too deeply. The slots won't be seen but will be visible where they are cut across the top, so try to be as tidy as possible there. Perhaps leave that section till last when you have learned some lessons on how the grain is behaving and how it's best to work.

Chisel out the slots using a mallet and chisel, with the bevel facing downwards if you find it easier. Notice how chiselling in different directions is affected by the grain direction, with tearing more likely one way than the other.

TIP: When your bench plane is not in use, it is sensible to store it on its side to prevent damage or blunting.

3 Do another dry assembly with clamps to check the fit and get the clamps right; then spread waterproof wood glue on the mating surfaces and assemble.

Once the glue has set (probably overnight), remove the clamps and tidy up the edges with a bench plane. Leave the ends for the moment.

Mark the shape of the final block on one face and cut with a hand saw. One day you'll have a band saw to do this! Holding the block in the vice, tidy up the ends. If you can, use a block plane, since this is suited to working with end grain (see Band saw, page 109 and Planing plywood and end grain, page 24).

4 Chamfer the edges with a plane, then use abrasive around a small piece of wood to clean up the block. Finish with a vegetable oil such as Salad Bowl Oil, which is safe to use on items that will be in contact with food and available in woodworking catalogues. Alternatively, use olive oil.

TIP: When planing a block that has been glued up from boards, first chip away any excess adhesive, since this can damage the edge of the plane's cutter.

Lessons learned

- You can clamp up boards tightly to overcome some gaps, but if they are too great, you will never resolve the problem and you will need to do further planing.

- It's very difficult to align components when you are gluing up with clamps. A dry run helps, but the glue still changes the situation, especially with parts more likely to slip. A good tip is not to overtighten the first clamp and use that only for positioning. And don't expect to get it exactly right – you're better off expecting to do some tidying up afterwards.

Lesson 7
The dedicated mitre

Getting started

One of the first tools I tested as a young journalist on a woodworking magazine was a Nobex mitre saw. I'd previously relied upon home-made mitre boxes, which guide a standard tenon saw in grooves cut at angles (usually 45° or 30°) to the fence, against which the wood is held. I'd always found cutting accurate mitres something of a challenge and was intrigued to see how a dedicated mitre saw might improve my joint-cutting.

The measure of the tool's excellence is that I still have it and use it somewhere in the grey zone between regularly and occasionally. No powered option has come near to its accuracy, and that is what the mitre joint demands. There is no hiding from inaccuracy when you cut a mitre. Even the tiniest of slip or misjudgment is amplified when it comes to assembling the frame. I consider it one of the most difficult joints to cut and am often amazed that so many woodworking books place it as one of the earliest techniques. I would have liked to introduce it later, to be honest, but I just couldn't hold off any longer!

The mitre isn't a particularly strong joint, with end grain meeting end grain, but it is tidy and quick. It is invaluable when it comes to joining moulded profiles, and for many of the decorative additions you may want to add to your projects. The mitre can't be avoided, so you'd better practise the techniques thoroughly.

Lesson planner

Key techniques	Key tools and materials
• The mitre joint • Marking out a mitre joint • Cutting a mitre joint • Assembling a mitred frame • Reinforcing a mitre joint	• The mitre saw • Buying and using a mitred frame • Mitre clamping systems • Glues for mitres • Moulded profiles • Glues • Velcro-backed abrasives • Cork tiles

The mitre joint

Accurately cutting a mitre joint requires a fair amount of practice and will doubtless involve many mistakes along the way. Done well, it is a beautiful joint, with a neat line at the corner and the profiles or mouldings meeting at the joint and then gracefully moving on. In fact, the line of the joint can help to emphasize the shape of a profile or moulding.

Unless reinforced with wooden splines across the corner or metal staples in the back, it isn't a strong joint. In fact, normally the mitre depends on glue, and therein lies the problem because the joint is almost end grain to end grain – the most unsatisfactory arrangement in woodworking. The glue doesn't have long fibres to grip when applied to end grain, just as it's difficult to pick up a match by its tip.

The basic four-sided frame employs 45° cuts as mitres, with more sides lowering the angle. Mitres tend to be used for joining relatively thin stock, like picture frames, but are also chosen for box-making and interior trim using wider boards. However, the longer the mitre, the more opportunity there is for a mistake and for gaps to appear in the join line. However, the mitre is a very clean solution for boxes, since there's no end grain to disrupt the lines of the design, and it is excellent for making frames of more than four sides.

Marking out a mitre joint

Mitred frames are generally easy to mark out, since you need do little more than cut the pieces to length. It is, however, easy to mess up by cutting a profile the wrong way, producing an external mitre when you need an internal one. I've wasted many lengths of picture framing doing that. It is for this reason that I often, unnecessarily, mark up all mitre joints even when I'm using a jig, just to remind myself which way to make the angled cut.

More often than not, mitres are cut in some form of jig, so you won't usually need to square the whole way around each piece. If you are doing a lot of them, it might be worth buying a mitre square for 45° angles, but I have one and rarely use it, picking it up occasionally to set the angles on machines.

Having cut mitres on one piece, use it to mark off the cut on the next one.

If you are cutting without a mitre saw, use a combination square to mark up.

Hold the moulding against the fence when using a mitre box.

Mitre angles

The angle of mitre you cut depends on the number of sides to the frame. The simple calculation is to divide 360° by twice the number of sides.

Four sides	45°	Seven sides	25.7°
Five sides	36°	Eight sides	22.5°
Six sides	30°	Ten sides	18°

Cutting a mitre joint

Though you can obviously make an angled cut by following a line, most woodworkers quickly learn the benefits of using a guide of some sort to hold the workpiece and direct the saw. The simplest version of this is the mitre box, but there is much benefit in buying a dedicated mitre saw.

The mitre box is very simple to make yourself, either with a single fence at the back, as I have, or with one at the front as well. The saw runs in slots cut across the box. Unfortunately, with time the grooves widen, though it helps if you use Japanese saws or those without a kerf.

The slots in a mitre box usually wear after a few years and lose accuracy.

There are countless ways to cut a mitre, all of them based on the principle of the timber being held against a fence. Either the fence or the saw moves to cut the mitre. Bench disc sanders can also be used effectively to produce very accurate mitres.

Assembling a mitred frame

Another of the challenges of using mitred joints is assembling the frame. Though I will later show you how to cut a locked mitre joint, the main problem is that the mitres will tend to slip, especially once you've applied glue.

Picture framers have special clamps to hold each corner while a special staple is inserted in the back of the joint. For less specialized woodworking, the best approach is to use one of the many frame-clamping systems developed for the purpose.

Obviously you must do a dry run first, and it is particularly important, with the mitred frame, to have a flat surface. It is a good idea to keep a plywood board, say 25 mm (1 in) thick, that you use for assembling frames. Polish and wax it so that dried glue can be knocked off easily.

The slightest inaccuracy in the length or angle of cuts can put the frame out of square, so you must check it before gluing up. The simplest technique is to use a pair

of thin offcuts, each pointed at one end, to check the diagonals. If the diagonals are the same, you can be sure the frame is accurate. Overlap the pointers, extend them into the corners across a diagonal, and mark one of them. Try the other diagonal and see if the pointers line up on the mark again.

If the diagonals are wrong, it may just be that the frame is slightly skewed, and a nudge to one corner will put it right. Otherwise the chances are that one component is longer or shorter than its matching one and you may need to start again. If they are all the right length but the angles are wrong, you should be able to get the diagonals right, but there will be gaps in the joints. Solution: cut the mitres again!

TIP: If you find the mitres are difficult to align and keep falling over, a simple trick is to lay them out in a line with the mitres facing downwards. Then stick them together temporarily with sticky tape, ideally a type that comes off easily later. You will then be able to assemble the frame with ease. This works particularly well for wider mitres – say, for making boxes or drawers.

Reinforcing a mitre joint

Modern glues are often sufficient for a mitred frame. Picture frames will often survive this way, and boxes with mitred corners are sometimes supported by the top and bottom and the internal framework.

A quick way to reinforce a mitre is to cut thin slots across the joint and insert veneer splines or thicker wooden keys. You can do this with a contrasting species for good effect, and it can be done before or after the joint has been glued, but I think it's easier with the mitre glued, unless you are prepared to make a special clamping device to hold the joint while you make the cut.

With the frame clamped, use a pair of pointed battens to check diagonals.

You need only a piece of plywood with a 90° corner to make a jig.

Fix the plywood block with glue to a larger piece to make a holding jig.

Making a simple cutting jig to reinforce glued mitres is very simple. To a piece of plywood or timber fix a smaller block, the corner of which you know to be 90° (or whatever is appropriate for the frame). Hold this in a vice, and rest the joint on the block so that you can cut the spline slot. Cutting can be a little tricky, since you will be working against the grain, so be steady and use a fine saw. Practise first.

Once the slot is cut, insert one or more pieces of veneer with glue and tap home. The grain should run across the joint. Once the glue is dry, pare back the veneer spline with a chisel. When using mitres on boxes you can use a series of splines and angle them to mimic dovetails.

If you don't want to see the splines but need reinforcement, you are going to need to insert a loose tongue, dovetail or spline inside the mitre joint. This is not very easy to do by hand and tends to be used for larger mitres on cabinets, for which the biscuit jointer is a good option.

You can use veneer for the splines, the number of pieces depending on the width of the cut.

Hold the mitre on the jig to cut the slot for a spline.

Trim back the veneer spline after the glue has set.

Try using a contrasting spline for added effect.

Tools

The mitre saw

For many years, until I bought a band saw, my mitre saw was the only guided saw I owned. These are extremely useful for cutting mitres, naturally, but also for cutting any piece of timber to length. The finish can be excellent, and when used carefully, they are very accurate. The best ones can cut slices of wood so thin they are translucent when held up to a light.

Check that the rear fence is at 90° to the table or bed of the saw on which you rest the timber. In the past, I have lined both the fence and the table with plywood, thinking it would give a better cut, but I'm not convinced it helps and it certainly reduces the depth and width of cut. One

benefit of a wooden lining is that it supports short lengths better. Another is that you can add stops for repetitive cutting more easily, and the lining protects the workpiece.

Some mitre saws have end stops you can adjust for repeat cuts. I've never much favoured these since they tend to get in the way and the sharp point of the mitre is so delicate that it's easy to align it incorrectly, but I have often used the integral clamps that come with some saws. Most of the time I keep a versatile 24 tpi blade on the saw for speed and reasonable finish.

Using a mitre saw

A good mitre saw should have stops for the most common angled cuts. You will use 45° and 90° most often, but the others will be useful. Make sure these are accurate to the

You can set a stop on some mitre saws for repetitive cutting.

I have in the past fixed a wooden fence to my saw, but it can restrict the cut.

Use a piece of scrap ply to support a picture-framing profile.

You can even adjust the depth of cut on good mitre saws.

saw. There may also be a clamping device that holds the blade to its set position. A depth stop should ensure the blade doesn't cut into the table and should also allow you to make stopped cuts if, say, you are using the mitre saw for cutting through housing joints or housings.

It is important that the saw is held firmly in the folding bench, or is clamped to a worksurface, since it will tend to wander as you cut. Line up the cut with the marked line and cut gently, holding the workpiece tightly against the fence. Clamp the timber to the fence or table if you can, otherwise it can easily move halfway through the cut.

If you are cutting mouldings for picture framing, you may need to support the rebate with a piece of scrap to stop the piece falling over and ruining the cut. Plywood is good for this job, and in fact, you can use the same pieces to adjust a router for cutting the rebate if you are making your own profile.

Mitre clamping systems

One of the most common systems for clamping mitres is the string or band clamp that envelops the frame, with blocks at the corners tightening the joints. These can be

You will often need to support the parts of a frame during assembly,

The string frame clamp is simple but very effective and easy to make.

Another popular clamp uses a threaded rod and corner blocks.

bought or made. With an L-shaped block at each corner, you simply tighten the string with a tourniquet, but I think the shop-bought version I'm using here is difficult to beat, especially for small frames.

An alternative system is to use a threaded rod instead of string to draw the blocks together. The Veritas version of this works well because the blocks sit so firmly on the worksurface, though I've found you often need to raise thinner stock off the surface to get even pressure. It is also a good idea to place a false board in the centre of rebated frames so that they don't collapse inwards as you assemble the components.

Materials

Glues for mitres

On site, carpenters tend to use a two-part adhesive for gluing mitres quickly before fixing in place. These combine a cyanoacrylate liquid and spray catalyst that speeds up the bond. They are amazingly strong, but tend to be brittle, so can't be relied upon for long-term strength. The two-part mitre glue is just one of many specialized adhesives.

Special cyanoacrylate adhesive can quicken the bonding process.

I always have some contact adhesive ready for sticking down fabric covering or tiles, and slow-dry cyanoacrylate for quick fixes. This is much more useful, I find, than normal superglue, since it is slightly thicker for a stronger bond, and you have about 45 seconds to make the joint.

Mouldings

DIY stores sell many types of applied mouldings and profiles in softwood and hardwood. Ideally, you should look out for hardwood mouldings that are certified as being supplied from a sustainable source. They are extremely useful for woodworkers who are looking to add some decoration to their work; however, once you have a router table up and running, there won't be as much need to buy mouldings because you can make your own. Most applied mouldings are flat-backed, but some are already rebated, especially if you go to a supplier of picture-framing products.

Doors can be improved with creative use of applied mouldings, mitred at the corners. The best way to attach profiles is with finishing nails and glue, using a nail set to tap the nail heads below the surface. Tidy up with filler.

Velcro-backed abrasives

Increasingly, abrasives are attached to power tools, sanding blocks and sanding machines with Velcro. I always keep old discs and sheets because a used coarse abrasive can become a perfectly good fine-grade one once the grit has been dulled. You must watch out, though, that wood grains embedded during sanding don't scratch the surface.

Old pieces can also be used to make small sanding blocks for curved surfaces, or for getting into awkward spots. You can buy self-adhesive 'hooks' and stick them to whatever you like for sanding. I once made a detail sander this way from a mechanized toothbrush.

Cork tiles

The Noticeboard project in this lesson features cork tiles as the surface for pinning notices to. Cork is a superb material and we should be encouraging the use of it, because it is produced sustainably. Producers have suffered terribly in recent years with the move to plastic stoppers for wine bottles, which may be recycled but are unlikely to be from a sustainable source. I refuse to call such items 'corks', as it's an insult to the cork woodlands that have an uncertain future.

I believe woodworkers have a special responsibility to our forests and woodlands, depending as we do on timber to fuel our hobby or career. I would encourage everyone to question the source of the materials they use and support the development of sustainable forests that maintain biodiversity and protect a proportion of old-growth forests until new specimens mature to the age of the veteran trees that are so difficult to replace.

There are various types of cork tiles. Some have a peel-off back for quick fixing, and the tiles are available sealed or unsealed. Cork is easy to cut and a pleasure to use.

Project **Noticeboard**

For notes and photographs

The mitred frame on this noticeboard is actually no more than applied decoration and requires no reinforcement, but it sets off this useful project very well. Don't be fooled by the seeming simplicity of the mitre: it is a difficult joint to cut accurately.

Cork tile

Mirror plate

Dimension to suit

MDF baseboard

B

A

D

C

Dimension to suit

Dimension to suit

Cross-section of board

Dimension to suit

Softwood front moulding

MDF packing strip

Countersunk clearance hole through base

Cutting list

The size and shape of this project rely on the dimensions of the cork tiles you can find, though of course you could cut larger ones to size or build them up from smaller tiles. The thickness of the packing pieces (**C**) sandwiched between the moulding (**B**) and base (**A**) must match the thickness of the tiles (**D**) and be 6 mm (¼ in) narrower than the moulding you choose. The packing piece can be made from MDF, plywood or timber. With so many potential variations, we are not publishing a full cutting list, though as a guide, our noticeboard is 711 x 1016 mm (28 x 40 in), and the base is made from 10-mm (⅜-in) plywood or MDF.

Shopping list

Materials

Two hanging brackets
Contact adhesive

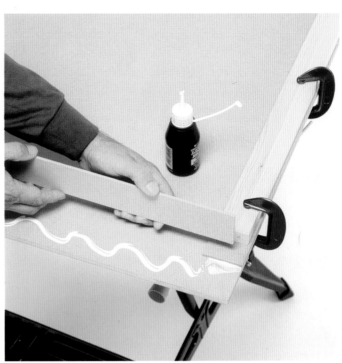

1 Start by laying out the cork tiles (**D**) on the base (**A**), with the base about 25 mm (1 in) smaller so that you can trim the cork to size once the tiles have been laid. Fix the tiles in place with contact adhesive, following the manufacturer's instructions for both safety and application.

Overlap the moulding (**B**) on the tiles by about 6 mm (¼ in) and measure the size of the base. Cut accordingly with a hand saw or band saw if you have one. I tend not to use a jigsaw for this job, since I get a better finish cutting by hand.

2 Instead of using a packing piece between the moulding and base, you could buy rebated moulding to match the thickness of the cork tiles. Most picture framers will supply lengths of profile. It is actually a neater solution.

Glue the packing piece (**C**) around the outside of the cork tiles, ideally mitred at the corners for the neatest result, though with MDF or ply, a butt joint (shown in the illustration) will hardly be seen.

3 Plane the edge of the base and packing piece, and check the diagonals to ensure the frame is square. Drill countersunk holes through the base and packing piece to attach the moulding.

Cut the mitres on the moulding and glue in place on the packing pieces using carpenter's glue.

4 Clean up the joints and paint or varnish the mouldings; then screw hanging brackets to the base and hang in the kitchen, hallway or a child's bedroom.

Lessons learned

- Mitres aren't as easy to cut and assemble as you might imagine. You need care to cut them well and a few little tricks to make accurate frames.

- The approach you take to the making of a project depends so much on the tools you own and the materials you can buy. By using rebated mouldings to make the noticeboard, you can save a couple of stages and produce a better piece.

Lesson 8
Making panels

Getting started

Making up panels from narrow boards can be one of the most rewarding of woodworking jobs. Not only do you produce more stable boards, but you are also able to produce wide panels from narrow stock – often an economic approach. Should I ever be employed in a furniture-making factory, it's the job I'd be happy doing all day. Having previously worked largely with softwoods or as a woodturner, I remember thinking that I'd become a proper woodworker the day I made my first oak panel.

One of the surprises of this operation is that it can be very quick. The boards need only to be rough sawn, with the edges planed straight and square. Then you have to juggle the boards to arrange the grain in a stable and attractive manner. This seems a very suitable end to the first term of woodworking, and it opens up all sorts of horizons for anyone wanting to become a self-sufficient woodworker, unrestrained by the restrictions inadvertently imposed by the normal supply of timber and tools.

In many ways, the first steps into woodworking are a lesson in what you do and what you don't need to do to make some simple projects and some progress. So far, the investment has been extremely low by way of machinery and tools, and there's no reason why that shouldn't continue. I find that the more woodworking I do, the fewer tools I need, mainly because I find which tool is best for specific operations and I don't bother buying tools that only have a vague purpose. And as my skills have developed, I've been able to discard some equipment, though I've rarely thrown out a clamp of any sort, and it is clamping that we will be discussing this lesson.

Making panels

It's quite possible to cut very wide boards from a single log. In fact, my desktop is made from a single slab of cedar of Lebanon 1219 mm (48 in) wide, and it hasn't moved a jot. Sadly, it no longer has the delicious aroma of a fresh-cut plank. More often than not, such boards will crack and cup, and quite possibly twist and bow as well. As woodworkers, we have to tame that beast while working with wood's natural forces and beauties.

The simple solution is to use a series of thin boards to produce a broader one, just as you can buy softwood stripwood, and many worksurfaces are made from short lengths of beech, maple, cherry or walnut. Even if you've bought boards surfaced, this will still be a necessity if you want to make solid wooden doors or tabletops. The ability to construct thin panels to fit inside a frame, for instance, enables you to cut thick boards into thinner stock and then reassemble them as panels. This is economical, but you will need a band saw at least.

Arranging the boards into a panel is a skill in itself. The first lesson to learn is that panels generally look best when comprising an odd number of boards. However good your assembly, the join lines are likely to be visible, if only to the subconscious, and the same stern judge will automatically be drawn to the line that often bisects a panel comprising an even number of boards. Three, five or seven are good options. If the strips you use are too narrow, the join lines will be obvious. If they are too wide and you use too few, the panel is likely to be unstable.

Once you have chosen the boards you need, study the end grain to alternate the growth rings for maximum stability. Check the edges for knots and conspicuous

Lesson planner

Key techniques	Key tools and materials
• Making panels	• Sash and other clamps
• Assembling a panel	• Random orbit sander
• Planing bevels	• Foaming adhesives
• Marking angles	• Buying hardware
• Working with short grain	• Stains, varnishes, dyes, oils

Note the unnatural strippy effect (left) and the attempt to match darker parts (right).

grain patterns that will show up if they are on a join line. You are trying to achieve something natural, just as you'd expect in natural wood. In the photos (page 84) of three strips of ash, you can see that in one permutation the darker band of grain narrows to an unusual point. I would not arrange the boards like this, since it looks wrong. The other way looks better. Once I'm satisfied with the order, I draw a large triangle across all three boards so that they can be reassembled with ease when it comes to gluing up.

Some woodworkers plane boards to be butt-jointed into a panel in pairs, planing the meeting edges at the same time. Then they flip them over to ensure any angle on the plane matches. Personally, I prefer to do one at a time and make sure the edge is straight and true. I like to build up a muscle memory and get all the edges right.

Assembling a panel

To produce a large panel, say for a tabletop, it is a good idea to insert biscuits, dowels, or a loose plywood tongue to strengthen the joints. More importantly, it helps to align the boards so that they all lie level, and you won't have to waste wood and time planing both sides flat. Dowel rod is probably the simplest with the tools we have so far, but the biscuit jointer is the ideal tool for the future. Use a marking gauge to show the centre-line on the edges of each board; then clamp the boards together and mark across pencil lines with a set square to show the positioning of the dowel holes. You need a hole every 457 mm (18 in) or so.

One of my best decisions ever was to ask Santa Claus for sash-clamp stands one year. These support your sash clamps and can transform them into holding devices for all manner of routing operations. Do a dry run assembling the panel so that the clamp heads are

Keep some wooden cauls for distributing clamp pressure along a board.

positioned correctly and you are sure about the arrangement of the boards. By habit, I use a caul to protect the wood from the clamp heads and hopefully even out the pressure a little. I use an old chisel to clean glue off these cauls: in fact, I always keep a semi-blunt chisel on the bench ready for doing the sort of tasks that normally ruin an edge. It happens to be an old, long paring chisel, so it also has good reach.

Make yourself an area for clamping up panels.

Use a wedge and alternating sash clamps to inhibit any bowing.

Spread glue along one edge of each butt joint and gently tighten the sash clamps. You should see small bubbles of glue appearing along the join lines; otherwise there might not be enough glue if there is a dip (which you should have already found when you did a trial run). You can use only a certain amount of pressure before the sash clamps start to bend and the boards start cupping. In fact, it is a good idea to alternate the clamps, and you can use wedges to stop the boards at the centre from pushing upwards. There may be some tendency for the boards to buckle if they are positioned above the centre-line of the clamp screw.

Once the glue has set, you can plane the panel flat. If you have a workbench, you'll find this easiest against a benchstop, or even quicker with a surface planer and thicknesser. Final sanding can be done with a random orbital sander, though the portable belt sander is useful for cleaning up large panels or tabletops.

Planing bevels

The Wall Cabinet project in this lesson requires a fair number of edges to be bevelled. This is typical for any project that incorporates angles. The technique is relatively simple as long as you are methodical. Mark up the bevel carefully, and be sensitive to the fact that the plane won't be flat on the edge, and you will need to get used to using it at an angle.

1 Once the board has been planed to thickness and width, score a line a fraction in from one edge using a marking gauge. It is tempting just to plane the point of the bevel to the existing edge, but the trouble with that technique is that you never quite know if you've planed any of the edge away. By planing down to a scored line, you know when you have reached the mark.

Use a protractor to set your adjustable square to the correct angle, in this case 45°.

2 Mark the bevel across the end grain and then set the marking gauge to the bottom of the bevel. This is when it's useful to have a couple of marking gauges – one set for the top of the bevel and the other for the bottom.

Trade secret

Improving clamps

An important refinement for sash clamps is to make pads to protect any wood you are clamping. I've made them here from American whitewood, which is also known as yellow poplar and tulipwood, depending on where you come from, but I have also used plywood, which is less likely to break. These are a fraction wider than I'd normally make them – about 51 mm (2 in) wide and slightly more likely to break, but at least they spread the pressure even more widely. You can glue wood or cork pads to other G- and F-clamps as well, using superglue or hot glue.

3 Having marked the line, start planing the bevel, with the plane held roughly at the angle. Try to keep the planed edge even and straight to give the plane something to rest on. You will notice that you've reached the scored lines when the shaving suddenly becomes a fraction thinner on one or both sides.

When planing a bevel, always make sure that you have marked the line to which you are working.

Tools

Sash clamps

Sash clamps are made to a couple of designs, but the most common is the rectangular-section sash clamp, with the clamp foot resting against a pin that fits in one of a series of holes. The pins take time to adjust.

In the United States these clamps have a round bar, with the clamp foot held by the friction of a clasp of loose steel leaves. This makes it very easy to adjust. The round bars are sometimes painted, protecting them from moisture and glue, therefore reducing the risk of a reaction between oak and iron. When this happens the wood can be tainted with a black mark, though it usually doesn't penetrate too deeply.

You can buy sash-clamp stands, and these are a superb addition to any workshop. Clamp-head protectors are also available.

Other clamps

There are various other styles of clamp you might consider buying. Ideally you need a good combination of types: some small, light ones, some powerful G-clamps, and some good-access, fast-to-set clamps for holding jigs or workpieces to the bench.

The G-clamp. The G-clamp is powerful and can be long, but it doesn't have very good reach and tends to be heavy.

The F-clamp. Also using a screw for pressure, the F-clamp has one fixed end with the other sliding along a bar. These give good access and are very fast to adjust, but don't always give as much pressure as the G-clamp. They are ideal for fixing machines and jigs in place.

The cam clamp. This is based on the same principle as the F-clamp, except that the pressure is exerted by the turning of a cam. Pressure is even less than that of the F-clamp, but they are very light and manoeuvrable, and superb for sensitive fixing.

The pump-action clamp. A refinement of the 'guns' used for distributing silicone, these offer speed, power and lightness, and are very useful to have around the workshop.

Random orbital sander

One of the most successful power tools to have surfaced in the last 20 years is the random orbital sander. An amalgamation of the disc sander and the orbital sander,

this provides the fine finish of the latter with the power of the former. Because the sanding disc spins in an oscillating pattern, it leaves few marks and yet can remove a significant quantity of waste.

The random orbital sanders also produce clouds of dust. Not only must you wear a dust mask or respirator, but I suggest you start collecting old vacuum cleaners and hoses for fitting to power tools to remove the dust at source. The tool comes supplied with a bag, but I find that dust extraction is a far better option.

Marking angles

As your collection of tools and equipment grows, you will be tempted to buy all sorts of gadgets for marking out. Personally, I favour having very few and have grown to love the versatility of the combination square I've been using to make some of the projects for this book. Most of the time I use a simple protractor for marking out angles, but I do love the plastic angle templates that can be used for setting an adjustable square or perhaps a machine. I was given them as a going-away present when I moved on from editing one of the British woodworking magazines some years ago, and I think they are made by Richard Kell.

The sliding bevel is ideal for marking out angles.

All about wood – short grain

In the best of all best possible worlds, to paraphrase Voltaire, the grain in a board is straight and true. But often enough it curves away and in some cases becomes a line of weakness, especially when the piece is load-bearing for table or chair legs. In the case of a chair leg, you're looking out for lines of grain running at an angle across the workpiece. The wood is most likely to split where the grain line runs from one side to the other. Sometimes you can use this grain to your advantage, especially if the component is shaped, but watch out that you aren't creating a future fault.

Where the grain runs at an angle across a board, there may be short grain that can easily be split off (shown here by a chalk mark).

Materials

Foaming adhesives
Once you get into making panels of your own, you will discover the challenges of cleaning up dried adhesive. My solution is to use a foaming polyurethane glue for assembling panels, since it is very easy to clean off with a chisel and won't dent a plane's cutter. Other dried adhesives are likely to chip a plane's iron. These foaming adhesives react with the moisture in the wood, and you can buy them in slow (a couple of hours), fast (30 minutes), and superfast (5 minutes) types.

Buying hardware
DIY stores usually have a good stock of hardware, including locks, doorknobs and hinges. Poor hardware can really undermine the quality of your work, so it's worth paying a little extra and finding a specialist supplier of solid brass fixtures. Though coated hinges and handles will do for some projects, try to find quality hardware to complement your efforts when it matters. The best

furniture-makers will also spend some time cleaning up hardware to remove rough edges and will check that the slots in their screws are all in line.

Water and pigment stains
Often suspended in water but also in solvent, pigment stains comprise relatively large particles that can fix themselves only into the open pores of coarse-textured woods like oak and ash. They give the wood a wash of colour that is highlighted by variations in the grain. The water content also raises the grain of the wood, which can cause problems in finishing. You need to wet the surface first, sand it back, and only then apply the stain.

Stained varnishes and oils
You can easily buy varnishes that are ready-coloured, particularly for antique pine or mahogany. The trouble with these is that the colour sits on the surface rather than soaking deep into the fibres, and you can always tell that the wood has been stained. Also, when the varnish starts to degrade, the blisters will reveal unstained patches.

Dye stains
The best stains, though only available in a limited range of colours, are dye stains. These are made from much smaller particles of colour and soak deep into the wood. You can almost see them biting into the surface. They are usually dissolved in spirit or alcohol, and don't raise the grain. Apply them with a brush or cloth.

Project **Wall cabinet**

For glasses or cups

Simpler to construct than you might imagine, this
wall cabinet needs good planing skills and introduces
the challenge of hanging a door on hinges.

Cornice

H

Front elevation

553 mm (21¾ in)

Wall batten

570 mm (22½ in)

Door frame strip

D

Shelf

Door stile

B

C

F

G

Bottom panel

A

A

Door panel

Shopping list

Materials

Butt hinges: 1 pair of 51 mm (2 in) hinges with screws
Screws and dowels to join the top and bottom to the uprights
Doorknob

Cutting list

Part	Material	Quantity	Dimensions length, width, thickness
A Top and bottom	softwood	2	571 x 292 x 32 mm (22½ x 11½ x 1¼ in)
B Shelf	softwood	1	552 x 241 x 32 mm (21¾ x 9½ x 1¼ in)
C Front upright	softwood	2	559 x 190 x 32 mm (22 x 7½ x 1¼ in)
D Rear upright	softwood	1	559 x 114 x 32 mm (22 x 4½ x 1¼ in)
E Door frame strip	softwood	2	559 x 70 x 32 mm (22 x 2¾ x 1¼ in)

Part	Material	Quantity	Dimensions length, width, thickness
F Door stile	softwood	2	559 x 44 x 25 mm (22 x 1¾ x 1 in)
G Door panel	plywood	1	559 x 279 x 19 mm (22 x 11 x ¾ in)
H Cornice	softwood	1	400 x 79 x 32 mm (15¾ x 3⅛ x 1¼ in)
I Wall battens	softwood	2	229 x 38 x 32 mm (9 x 1½ x 1¼ in)
J Internal support	softwood	3	Softwood offcuts to fit

1 Glue up the boards for the top, bottom and shelf (**A** and **B**), using sash clamps if you have them or foxed wedges otherwise.

While the glue sets, cut the front uprights (**C**) and rear upright (**D**) to length. Don't fall for the temptation to plane the bevels at this early stage: you'll find it easier to drill the dowel joint holes before the bevels are formed. Also cut the door frame strips (**E**) to length.

When the glue has set, plane and sand the panels; then cut them to shape. Make sure the top and bottom are identical and that the back edges of the shelf match those of the top and bottom. Notice how the front edge of the shelf is set back a little to accommodate the door. It is also notched for the door-frame strip.

Drill the dowel holes in the three uprights. Notice how there are two dowels at the bottom to stop the uprights from twisting. Using dowel-markers, offer each upright to the top and bottom to mark where to drill the corresponding dowel holes. Drill and countersink the screw holes in the top and bottom. Drill the holes in the top to fit the cornice.

2 Plane the bevel of each front upright and glue the door-frame strip to the inside face of each upright. Tidy up that joint with a jack plane once the glue has set.

3 Attach the shelf supports to the front and back uprights, and then assemble the uprights and the top and bottom, remembering to insert the shelf at this stage, since it might not fit later. Add glue to the dowel rod, but use the screws to bring the joints together. This is a good solution for anyone who doesn't have many sash clamps and is perhaps using ready-prepared stripwood for the top, bottom and shelf.

Glue the door stiles (**F**) to the plywood panel (**G**), measured carefully to fit the opening in the cabinet. You could use a solid piece of wood or even tongue-and-groove boards. Then cut the hinge recesses in the door stiles and uprights.

4 Cut out the curved cornice (**H**) with a coping saw, scroll saw or jigsaw and screw to the top. Then cut and drill the wall battens and fix them to the walls.

Sand and tidy up the cabinet, and apply the finish of your choice. I don't much like the stained effect – which has, however, worked well in this case – as I think it can reduce the impact of the new wood. Use hanging brackets at the top to hold the cabinet to the wall, and add a knob and catch.

 Lessons learned

- It doesn't take much to be able to make your own panels, and this corner cabinet would be greatly enhanced by a solid timber door.

- If you mark up carefully first, it isn't difficult to plane bevelled edges on boards.

Building
Your Skills

What you will find in this section

What to expect

Tools

I am a great believer in building up a toolkit gradually, investing in kit when the need arises, rather than equipping an entire workshop on day one – otherwise you may spend money on machines you will rarely use. You may also be under the impression that new tools will make up for a lack of skill: this does not follow. However, during this chapter we'll be looking at some essential power tools that will transform the way you work, both in speed and accuracy.

Materials

With improved skills and more equipment you can start working with a wider range of timber types, notably hardwood. Hardwoods can be easier to use than softwoods in some ways, and the results are often more pleasing. However, they also put greater demands on your tools and skills, and also require a good understanding of timber technology.

The band saw is one of the most important machines you'll ever buy, but a small one will do you well for many years (see Band saw, page 109).

Liming is just one of many effects you can achieve with some open-grained hardwoods (see Limed finishes, page 123).

A good workbench will transform your work, giving you a solid platform and a place to cut and plane (see Anatomy of a workbench, page 130).

Use contrasting species for dramatic effects, as shown here – a dark bung has been used to hide a screw head (see Making plugs to hide screws, page 131).

With time you will develop the ability to find your own solutions, but always protect yourself from noise and dust (see Fitting extraction, page 159).

Not all hardwoods are easy to use. Yew wood, in particular, has grain running in all sorts of directions and is very difficult to plane without tearing (see Selecting timber, page 161).

Techniques

Every woodworker has to be able to work with wood to cut, shape and join it together. Though there are all sorts of new jointing systems available, learning how to cut interlocking joints from solid wooden boards is an essential skill and will ultimately give you the greatest freedom when designing and crafting your own projects. In this section, we will look at some of the most important joints.

Learn how to mark up and cut a series of mortise and tenon joints (see Lesson 1, page 98).

Though it is valuable to learn how to plane boards by hand, power sanding options can speed up the process of stock removal and finishing dramatically (see Belt-sanding a board, page 118).

The housed rebate joint is just one of many variations of interlocking joints that rely on a good glue line and shoulders for strength and stability (see The housed rebate joint, page 147).

Projects

This section's projects introduce hardwoods and various types of timber, and shows how they can be worked and jointed. Learning the characteristics of timber is a key skill that contributes to an understanding what can be achieved.

Occasional table **p102**

Child's furniture **p142**

Hardwood stool **p112**

Crockery shelves **p152**

Garden bench **p124**

Picnic table **p162**

Workbench **p132**

Plate rack **p170**

Lesson 1
Square hole, square peg

Getting started

Though plenty of projects can be made without an interlocking joint, most woodwork involves some mechanical connection between components. Glues, screws and nails were enough for the birdbox project in the last lesson, but usually these will not provide long-term solidity. The basic and obvious principle of any joint is that a cavity, often known as a mortise, is formed in one or both components, into which fits the other part or a loose piece that joins the parts together. In this lesson we will be introducing the tools and techniques for simple jointing.

Mortises, to use a specific term in its most general sense, come in many different forms, but there are a few types that are more common than others. Learning when to use which particular joint and how to cut it are two of the most important skills a woodworker will ever learn.

The most frequently used joints are the round hole, which takes a loose dowel or round-section component, and the square-sided hole, which is the most usual definition of a mortise. To produce this, woodworkers tend to use a chisel of some sort, and it is this operation we will examining here.

When to use a mortise and tenon

The best way to join narrow sections of timber to produce a frame of sorts – as opposed to using wider boards to make a box or cabinet – is with a mortise and tenon or a dowel joint. Many chairs are mass-produced with the latter, using dowels drilled and glued into each component. There is a great simplicity to this joint, and it is very cost-effective and relatively strong. However, it is surprisingly difficult to produce successfully for four reasons:

1 You need more than one dowel, or the components will twist. With very thin components it may be difficult to find space for more than one dowel.

2 Aligning the holes in both components is awkward unless you have a special jig.

3 The chances are you will need to drill into the end grain of one component. Doing so is far harder than drilling across the grain, and the drill bit is far more likely to wander unless the component is locked into some sort of jig.

4 Both ends of the dowel have to be glued into a hole. With modern adhesives this isn't a problem, but it does raise the risk of the joint breaking at some time in the future, as glues are more likely to deteriorate than wood.

With the mortise and tenon, on the other hand, you fashion a male tenon where you would need to be drilling a dowel into end grain. It has the integral strength of the wood and reduces the risk of breaking because only one part of the joint (the tenon into the mortise) is glued. Cutting a rectangular or square mortise in the other part is slightly more difficult than drilling, but there are simple marking tools and chisels for making the task easier.

Matching the mortise and tenon

To understand how a mortise and tenon is cut, the following terminology describes the components:

The width of the mortise = the thickness of the tenon
The length of the mortise = the width of the tenon
The depth of the mortise = the length of the tenon
Mortise sides = tenon cheeks
Mortise ends = tenon sides
Mortise bottom = tenon end

Types of mortise and tenon

The simplest style of tenon is nothing more than a male

Lesson planner

Key techniques	Key tools and materials
• Marking out a mortise • Using a chisel • Cutting a mortise	• Mortise gauge • Rubber mallet • Wooden mallet • Making a cutting list • Developing a bill of materials

component fitting into a similar hole. This is used in chair-making, often with round tenons in round holes. To give the joint more strength, you can cut shoulders to reduce the risk of pivoting. This doesn't increase the gluing area, but it improves the mechanical fit and hides the mortise from view. These shoulders can be cut on one, two, three or four of the sides of the component. In this lesson we will be using barefaced tenons, with a haunch (see Foaming adhesives, page 89).

Marking out a mortise

Once you have some machines and jigs, you will be able to cut mortises and tenons accurately without having to mark them up individually, but for the moment you will need to mark up each joint. An accurate fit depends on good marking. The mortise gauge is an essential tool for this.

The width of a mortise should be roughly one-third the width of the component to provide the greatest strength. But the actual width should be determined by the chisel with which you will remove the waste from the mortise. It is this width that you set the mortise gauge to mark. First, though, mark the length of the mortise on the component, using a square to mark the lines across the surface. These lines don't need to go around the piece unless you are cutting the mortise through the wood and want to cut from both sides. Once you have marked the length of the mortise on one component, you can use this to repeat the mark on other components. This not only speeds up the process but also guarantees that the joints are

When marking up mortises, avoid any knots that might weaken the joint.

Adjust the mortise gauge to suit the chisel you will use to chop out the waste.

Marking up the mortise is easiest with the workpiece held in a vice.

Trade secret

Holding a mortise gauge

It's good perceived wisdom to plan the components so well that you hold the stock of the mortise gauge against the appropriate face for both the mortise and tenon. However, in my experience, this takes too much planning in the early stages of woodworking, and it's better to adjust the mortise gauge accurately so that you can use it against either face.

Cutting a mortise

Seeing that the width of the mortise and thickness of the tenon is governed by the width of the appropriate chisel, the best place to start cutting is with the mortise. The tenons can then be cut to fit them. The challenge, when cutting the mortise, is to remove the waste without damaging the sides and ends of the hole, which determine the strength and accuracy of the joint. There are various ways of removing the waste.

With the bevel downwards, make feathering cuts along the mortise.

1 Using just a chisel, first cut the edges of the joint with the chisel held vertically. Then knock down the ends deeper (vertically), initially a fraction inside the marks, since you can trim the joint accurately at the end. To remove the waste this way, work your way down the mortise, alternating between vertical cuts down the sides and ends, and feathering cuts to take out the wood. This is best done with the chisel bevel facing downwards for better access. You'll usually find you have more control over the chisel if you tap it gently with a mallet rather than trying to force it by hand.

2 A faster solution is to remove the waste with a drill first, but this can also lead to inaccuracy. Once you have the machines, this can be done simply enough, but for the moment you will need to use the electric drill you have around the house, ensuring that the holes are cut vertically or the joint will be angled. You are better off using a narrower drill bit and trimming later with a chisel (see Using bearing-guided cutters, page 138; Getting started, page 178; Tools, page 270).

Trade secret

Keeping the horn
Often, but not always, a mortise will be positioned at the end of a component. It is important to leave some waste on the end of the component, since there is a danger that the wood will split during cutting or assembly of the mortise. This excess wood is sometimes referred to as the horn, and can be cut off later, after the glue has dried and the joint is secure.

Tools

Mortise gauge
This device enables you to mark up mortises and tenons. It comprises two pins, one of which is adjustable, and an adjustable stock. The best mortise gauges have a threaded adjustable pin, and this type is worth buying because it is the easiest to adjust and there should be no reason to buy another in the future. (Mine has lasted years.)

Other tools to buy

Rubber mallet. Buy a heavy one that can be used to thump components together. It is equally useful for dismantling failures!
Wooden mallet. This is usually made from beech and should last you for years. Check the comfort of the handle in your hand, since you may be using this for many hours, and you don't want to develop blisters.

Materials

The success or failure of a project relies not only on your skills and tools but also on the materials you acquire to make it. One of the most common mistakes is not buying enough timber or buying it in the wrong dimensions. Learning how to plan the materials you need is a vital part of woodworking, though the build-up of offcuts from mistakes has its benefits.

Making a cutting list
With every project it's important to make a list of all the components you need. This is known as the cutting list and shows exactly the length you need for each piece, not forgetting the joint. The cutting list relates closely to any drawings or plans you make for a project.

On the cutting list, mark the number of components, the type of wood, and then its length, width and thickness. This should be a simple extension of the drawings, and you should already have considered the available board sizes in relation to the making of the parts.

Developing a bill of materials
When you go to a timberyard, you need a bill of materials, which describes exactly which boards you require at the start of a project. From these boards, the individual pieces that make up the cutting list will be cut. In most of the projects in this book, we don't show the bill of materials, because this very much depends on the available stock and on any adjustments you want to make. Bear in mind that the timberyard may not have the intended size in stock, so it's always worth taking the cutting list as well to work out an alternative solution. However, some yards won't be willing to work out an entire conversion there and then, and will expect you to have a reasonable idea of what you need.

To develop a bill of materials, you need to know roughly what boards are available and in which lengths, widths and thicknesses. Length may be determined by what you can carry in the car! Look through your cutting list for parts that complement one another when it comes to board dimensions, though once you have a surface planer and thicknesser, you'll have more freedom to mill timber to the sizes you need. Remember that you can make boards wider or thicker by gluing them together, but it's very difficult to make them longer. Length is very often the determining factor when it comes to creating your bill of materials. Remember when you make the bill to leave a bit of excess on the end of each component for mistakes and natural wastage (see Lesson 7, page 156).

Project **Occasional table**

A table of many uses

Though we have explored more complicated mortise and tenon joints in the lesson, this occasional table employs just about the most simple of them – the barefaced tenon. It has a shoulder on the top edge, known as a haunch, and the rails are connected by what's known as a centre lap or cross-halving joint.

50 mm (2 in)

110 mm (4⅜ in)

C

50 mm (2 in)

1/3

2/3

12 mm (½ in)

Haunch

610 mm (24 in)

A

1 in. (25 mm)

B

230 mm (9 in)

90 mm (3½ in)

90 mm (3½ in)

Chamfered edge of birch-faced plywood

Cutting list

Part	Material	Quantity	Dimensions length, width, thickness
A Top	plywood	1	610 x 610 x 25 mm (24 x 24 x 1 in)
B Leg	softwood	4	230 x 90 x 90 mm (9 x 3½ x 3½ in)
C Rail	softwood	2	620 x 140 x 38 mm (24⅜ x 5½ x 1½ in)

This project has been designed specifically with commonly available sizes of softwood, so the design and cutting lists were determined by what can be bought easily. Therefore, deciding what we need is relatively easy. Remember that the thicknesses quoted here are rough-sawn sizes and relate to how they are sold in the yard, rather than the thickness and width of the board you take home.

Shopping list

Bill of materials

Top: 25 mm (1 in) plywood, 1 piece, 610 x 610 mm (24 x 24 in)

Legs: 102 x 102 mm (4 x 4 in) PAR softwood, 1 piece, 1016 mm (40 in) long, allowing about 25 mm (1 in) on each leg for wastage

Rails: 50 x 150 mm (2 x 6 in) PAR softwood, 1 piece, at least 1295 mm (51 in) long, allowing 25 mm (1 in) or so on the end of each piece for wastage

Tools and materials

Steel brackets: 4, to fix the rails to the top

This table can easily be assembled with a rubber mallet and held in place by screwing the frame to the top while the glue sets. You should consider buying some 1 m (36 in) sash clamps. (See also Making foxed wedges for clamping, page 129; Advanced clamping, page 180.)

1 Cut the legs exactly to length. Mark out a mortise on one leg.

2 Lining the legs up together at the bottom, use the first mortise to mark up its position on the other legs; then use the mortise gauge on each to mark the mortise. Remember to mark the depth of the haunch on the top.

Use a drill with a 25-mm (1-in) or 32 mm (1¼-in) flat bit to remove as much waste as possible.

3 Notice that the tenons will be too wide to be determined by the width of your widest chisel. Instead they must match the exact width of the rails. In some ways this makes the joint more difficult, since the edge of the mortise won't be hidden by a tenon shoulder, but at least the joints will be right under the table and hard to see. Trim the mortise sides and ends with a chisel. Cut the rails to length.

4 Mark up the tenons on the ends of the rails and use a tenon saw to cut the notch for the haunch.

Positioning the centre lap joint is a bit tricky. The best way is to find the centre of each rail along the length and then measure away from the point half the thickness of the rail – 18 mm (¾in). Draw squared lines down each side at that point, then measure down half the width of the frame and mark across there. You can use a marking gauge for this (see Using a marking gauge, page 44).

5 To remove the waste from the centre lap joint, cut down each side, making sure you keep to the waste side of the drawn line. It is worth doing this accurately, since it is difficult cleaning up the end grain with a chisel.

Chop out the waste from the joint with your widest chisel, working from both sides so as not to split the wood as your chisel exits.

Use the cut joint to mark up the second rail, ensuring that you position this one on the opposite edge of the rail. If it's not in the right place, you'll have two joints cut in the lower or upper edge and they won't fit together.

Cut out the top, or just clean up the edges if you've bought it ready cut. You can bevel the edges with abrasive or a plane if you own one already (see Lesson 6, page 64).

6 Dry-assemble all the joints and screw a bracket to each rail. Take the components apart and apply wood glue to the tenons, spreading it across the joint. There's no point gluing the centre lap joint, since the end grain won't adhere well enough for it to be worthwhile – this joint should be tight anyway and need no glue.

Lessons learned

- If the mortise sides aren't chopped out squarely, the leg will be forced into an angle. You may be able to get away with this on a heavy project such as this one, but on more refined work, pieces won't go in well and the fit will be poor.

- The tolerance between the centre lap joint being too tight and too loose is very fine, and though it doesn't make much difference here, sometimes this will be critical both for looks and strength.

7 Knock the legs onto the rails, then screw the rails to the top to hold the assembly while the glue sets.

Lesson 2
The ubiquitous tenon

Getting started

Dovetails might be challenging to cut and a conspicuous example of woodworking skill, but no joint is as important as the tenon. In learning when and how to use the tenon, the woodworker develops techniques and abilities that can be used in many situations.

There are so many ways to cut this joint, from the simple tenon saw and a chisel to various jigs, templates and guided cutters. It doesn't really matter which technique you end up choosing. Whether your choice is determined by the equipment you own, by speed and accuracy, or by the enjoyment of cutting joints by hand, nothing is sweeter than slotting home a neat-fitting tenon.

Though the joint is hidden, defects or inaccuracies in the cutting of a tenon can have significant consequences for both the structural integrity and tidiness of the job. That's what makes the marking up, and the setting of fences and guides, so important. The tenon can be cut quickly and accurately, and is very easily reproduced in batches if the preparation is done properly.

Marking out a tenon

Although it's not the case with this lesson's project, the Hardwood Stool, the key measurement for tenons is usually the distance between the shoulders, since you will often have a tenon at each end of the piece. Mark up the first shoulder, working your way round from the face and edge marks with a pencil and set square. Once you have the shoulders marked up on one piece, you can copy them

across on to the other components (see also Cutting in pairs, page 75; Marking up with a rod, page 180).

Next, use the mortise gauge you set earlier for the mortise, to mark up the tenon. I tend to do this with the component angled up and away from me, resting on the top of one leg or in my stomach, but you might want to start with it held in the vice. Ideally, you will want to run the stock against the face mark you made earlier and be consistent with all components. That is certainly the safest way to position the joint accurately, but you will have to learn how to hold the mortise gauge in both hands, which is a skill worth developing anyway.

Cutting a tenon

The fit of the joint also relies upon the accurate cutting of the tenon.
- The tenon cheeks and ends must be parallel and at the correct angle.
- The shoulders around the tenon must be level, or the joint will pivot as it is clamped up.

I prefer to cut the tenon cheeks and sides first and then the shoulders. If you cut the shoulders first, you lose the control the wood offers as you near the end of the cheek cut and the waste begins to break away.

1 Hold the wood in the vice at about 45°, with the tenon facing away from you. Cut down the marked line, which I often make more conspicuous by running a pencil down the groove, keeping the tenon saw to the outside. Do the same for the other cheek.

Lesson planner

Key techniques	Key tools and materials
• Marking out a tenon • Cutting a tenon • Cutting tenons on a band saw	• Band saw. Many people use nothing more than a band saw for cutting tenons. If you're searching for a mechanized version of the tenon saw, look no further.

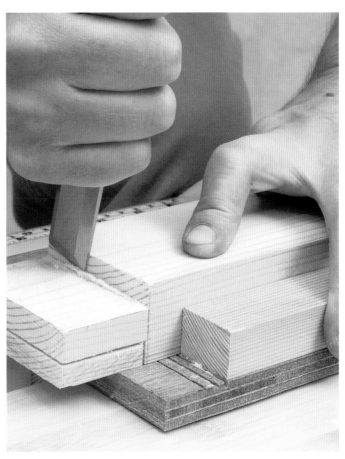

3 Clean up where the cheek and shoulder meet using a chisel on an angle, with gentle strokes towards you.

Test the fit in the appropriate mortise, trimming the tenon to fit. For softwoods the fit can be quite tight, as the wood has some give, but for hardwoods it must be more accurate. It can help to bevel the end of the tenon with the chisel to guide the tenon into the mortise.

2 Turn the piece around and repeat the cuts. Then position the piece vertically in the vice and cut down to join up the angled cut. Do the same for the sides, if your tenons have them. Cut the shoulders with a tenon saw using the bench hook.

Trade secret

One tenon fits all mortises

One bit of early discipline to learn is to ensure that any tenon can fit any mortise when you are assembling a frame. To do this, the mortises must be identical, which will certainly happen once you start mechanizing your processes. Then when you cut the tenons, test them in one mortise. If you don't feel confident about this, make sure you clearly mark which tenon fits well in which mortise, though this takes a lot of thought and can go wrong. (See Common tasks for the table saw, page 221.)

Cutting tenons on a band saw

The band saw is ideal for cutting the tenon cheeks and ends because it cuts along the grain so well. This is also a good introduction to repetitive cutting and illustrates how machines can reduce the amount of marking out.

1 Mark out a tenon on the end of a board, possibly an extra piece that you can experiment with but which is exactly the dimensions of the others.

Use these markings to set the band-saw fence to cut the cheeks, making sure the cut is to the outside of the drawn line.

You don't need to cut the full length of the tenon for the moment, just 3 mm (⅛ in) or so on both cheeks. Cut away the waste and test the fit in a mortise you've already cut. Adjust the fence accordingly and keep testing until it's right.

2 You can now set a stop to ensure that you cut exactly the right length, stopping just short of the shoulder. To do this, the components for tenoning must first be cut to exactly the right length. Cut a sample tenon to the shoulder mark on one piece, stop and band-saw and clamp a piece of scrap wood to the fence to act as a stop.

Now you can cut all the pieces; then cut the shoulders by hand. The band saw isn't ideal for cutting the shoulders, as they need to be even more accurate, though it can be done using the mitre guide to push the piece and the fence to act as a stop.

Tools

Band saw

It's time to buy your first machine. You could carry on with a jigsaw, hand saw and coping saw and make superb pieces, but woodworking will become a new experience once you own a band saw. A small one is inexpensive to buy and can be used for many jobs:

- Cutting boards to make them thinner and narrower
- Cutting sheet materials
- Cutting curves
- Cutting tenons and some other joints

You will no longer be governed by the dimensions of stock sold in the local timberyard or DIY store, though you will still need a hand saw and sawhorses for cutting boards to length. Band saws are quiet, take up relatively little space and cause very little dust, especially if they're hooked up to a workshop vacuum, and last for years. These vacuums are relatively inexpensive and better than a household vacuum as they can handle high levels of sawdust.

Self-lubricating guides are also available to direct the blade more tightly.

The blade's teeth should protrude over the front of the rubber tyre on the top wheel.

Get a feel for the blade tension. Most blades need about 12 mm (½ in) of travel.

Attach a workshop vacuum to the band saw to achieve dust-free cutting.

Anatomy of a band saw

A band saw has two wheels, around which travels an endless blade, driven by a motor attached to the lower wheel. Most of the blade is guarded, but for a short section it is open, and it is here, above the lower wheel, that a metal table is positioned to support wood during cutting.

● Band saws are defined by the diameter of the wheels and by the size of the motor. The smallest band saw is a 300-mm (12-in) model, with a motor of ½ hp.

● Guides above and below the table ensure that the blade runs vertically so that you can make accurate cuts.

● A shop vac can be attached to the extraction port at the rear of the band saw to keep dust to a minimum.

● The top wheel can be adjusted in two dimensions, to tighten or loosen the blade and ensure that the blade runs on the wheel correctly and doesn't spring off the front.

The ideal alignment is to have just the teeth protruding over the solid rubber tyre that protects the wheel.

● The table usually tilts to 45°, but only to one side for cutting on an angle with the grain. This can be very useful.

● There is usually a groove in the table for sliding a guide to make cuts across the grain at 90°, or an angle of your choice. But band saws aren't known for their accuracy for cuts across the grain, and there are better tools and machines for this job. A band saw will, however, do the job, especially if you take care setting it up (see Cutting a mitre joint, page 75).

Choosing a band saw

In my opinion, you can't go wrong buying a band saw, even if you buy the smallest, cheapest model. That's what I did ten years ago, and it remains my main cutting machine. Given my time again, I might just go for the next size up, a 356-mm (14-in) model with a motor of 1 hp or 1.5 hp, and a 381-mm (15-in) table, but the most important thing is to set it up properly and keep the blade sharp.

Some of the features you'll be asked to consider are:

1 Table size (see point 4).

2 Motor size (see point 2).

3 Depth of cut, between the table and the upper guide. The depth of cut is more often than not limited more by the size of the motor than by the available space.

4 Width of cut, determined by the distance between the open and closed sections of the blade. Though you can cut sheet materials on a band saw, the table isn't big enough to cope with large, broad pieces, so a more significant issue is the distance you can achieve between the fence and the blade. Though the throat is about 178 mm (7 in) on my band saw, I can only get 90 mm (3½ in) between the blade and the fence, which limits what I can do.

5 Minimum and maximum blade width. I generally have a 6-mm (¼-in) blade in the band saw and find this ideal for most uses, but also sometimes fit a 12-mm (½-in) blade. I wouldn't want a band saw that couldn't cope with either end of this range.

Setting up a band saw

The critical issue with a band saw is to have the blade running smoothly and vertically, without any tendency to twist. There are a few key tricks to achieve this:

1 Keep a stock of new blades. As they lose their edge, band-saw blades will tend to pull to one side and won't cut parallel to the fence. Make sure the join in the blade is smooth, if necessary filing it a little if it is catching the guides.

2 Set up the guides well. The blade should run vertically without the guides, and it's then just a case of gently tapping the guides within a credit card's width of the blade to prevent twisting. As long as the blade is sharp, it should cut straight and true.

3 Some people file the back of the blade to round it. Do this very carefully with the saw unplugged and then rotate the wheels by hand while using a metal file to remove the edge from the back of the blade. This also helps when it comes to cutting curves.

Trade secret

Band saws that don't run true

Often a band saw won't cut parallel to the fence, but you don't want to change the blade. Draw a line along a board and start cutting. You will automatically find the angle the blade wants to cut. Now place the fence at that angle, and the blade will cut parallel. It's not a long-term solution, but it will work for a while. By the way, when buying a band saw, make sure that you can position the fence at an angle like this on the table.

Materials

Band-saw blades
Joined with a soldered scarf joint, band-saw blades are defined by the width of the blade, the number of teeth per inch, and by the shape of the teeth. You also have to tell your supplier the length of blade you need, since all machines are slightly different. I tend to buy 10 tpi regular-form blades, 6 mm (¼ in) wide, for detail-cutting, and 6 tpi skip-form blades, 12 mm (½ in) wide, for ripping boards to width.

You can make your own blades by buying blade stock on a large roll and bevelling the ends with a file or grinder. Then join the ends with silver solder, heating the blade with flux and a blowtorch. When the blade has cooled, file back any excess solder. This is certainly an economical approach, once you have gained some experience in making the blades.

14 tpi   10 tpi   6 tpi (skip)   4 tpi (skip)   3 tpi (skip)

For fine cutting with a band saw, you need a blade with as many teeth per inch as you can get. A blade of 6 tpi is a good compromise, however.

Project **Hardwood stool**

For perching

This three-legged stool looks simple to construct.
To make it well, you need accurate jointing and good
planing skills, but the result should be a superb piece
that will display what you've learned so far. Oak is used
here, but other hardwoods, such as cherry or walnut,
will work just as well.

355 mm (14 in)

40 mm (1⅝ in)

3 mm (⅛ in)

32 mm (1¼ in)

6 mm (¼ in)

3 mm (⅛ in)

C

40 mm (1⅝ in)

30 mm (1⅛ in)

46 mm (1⅞ in)

3 mm (⅛ in)

40 mm (1⅝ in)   25 mm (1 in)

32 mm (1¼ in)

3 mm (⅛ in)

B

A

3 mm (⅛ in) shoulder

400 mm (15¾ in)

Cutting list

Part	Material	Quantity	Dimensions (length, width, thickness)
A Top	hardwood	3	381 x 127 x 32 mm (15 in x 5 x 1¼ in)
B Leg	hardwood	3	430 x 75 x 38 mm (17 x 3 x 1½ in)
C Wedges	hardwood	3	25 x 35 x 6 mm (1 x 1⅜ x ¼ in)

Shopping list

Tools

Jigsaw If you haven't bought a band saw, you will need a jigsaw to cut the round top. The tapers on the legs can also be cut on the band saw or by hand with a hand saw. Using a hand saw will take longer, but there will be less cleaning up than if you cut with a jigsaw.

A pair of sash clamps These will help you glue up the top, but this can be done with the dogs of a portable workbench if it's wide enough or with wedges.

Router Later you'll discover how a router can be used for shaping the top.

1 Cut three lengths of hardwood to glue up for the stool top. Check that the edges are straight and square, and align to check they mate well and to see how the grain matches. Once you are happy with the arrangement, draw a large triangle across all the boards so you can reposition them when it comes to assembly. Although you won't necessarily be able to notice where you've glued up boards like this to make a larger piece, always do so with an odd number of pieces since it looks better to have a board (rather than a joint) running down the centre.

There will be no give when it comes to clamping up, so there must be no gaps. Plane the edges if you are in any doubt, making sure you don't remove more from the ends than the centre.

Glue up the boards with sash clamps or the dogs on a portable workbench, or try using foxed wedges (see Making foxed wedges for clamping, page 129). Try to keep the boards level to reduce the amount of cleaning up later.

2 Once the glue has set, plane the top smooth on both sides. It is easier to do this before you cut the circular shape. Set the plane to cut very thin shavings, since there is a risk you will tear the grain, especially as you can't guarantee that the grain direction is consistent between the boards. For that reason you may need to work across the grain or at an angle if there is a lot of planing to do.

Find the centre of the board and draw a circle 356 mm (14 in) in diameter. Cut around this with a band saw or jigsaw, being careful to keep the cut as smooth as possible to reduce the amount of cleaning up later. The edges of a hardwood circle can be very hard work to smooth using a block and abrasives. A router will speed up the process (see Lesson 5, page 136).

Mark up the top for the mortises, dividing the circle into three. Use a set square to mark around the edges and then join up on the other side so you can mark up the mortises on both sides.

3 Chop out the mortise from both sides, with the top splayed for the wedged tenon. Take great care not to split or damage the top side, since this will be visible and difficult to clean up unless you have a portable belt sander, which you could rent for the job (see Belt-sanding a board, page 118).

Lessons learned

- Do everything you can to reduce the amount of cleaning up you will need to do with a plane or abrasive. Thinking ahead and cutting carefully will save you time later.

- Planing a taper is much easier one way than the other!

- End grain is harder to clean up than long grain.

4 Cut the legs to length, not forgetting the tenon, which you should leave about 1.5 mm (⅟₁₆ in) overlong, since it can easily be tidied up after assembly. Mark out the taper. Cut the taper and clean up, making sure the tenon isn't tapered. Bevel the bottom of each leg with a block plane.

5 Mark out the shoulders for the tenons. Because the shoulder is the same 3-mm (⅛-in) width the whole way around the tenon, it is probably easier to use a marking gauge than a mortise gauge to mark up the cheeks. Work on a trial piece first to be sure that the tenon will fit snugly in the mortise.

Cut the cheeks and then the shoulders, and then cut down into the tenon for the wedges, stopping short of the shoulders. Don't make the cut for the wedges as wide as it looks on the drawings: it should be one tenon saw-cut wide.

6 Do a dry run, testing the wedges but not tapping them home. The fit must be good because there is no going back once the wedges are tight.

7 Spread glue around the tenon on one leg and knock into place with a rubber mallet. Then glue in the wedges and tap them home so the tenon expands tightly. Do the same for the other legs, either immediately or once the glue has set on the first leg.

Clean up with fine abrasive and apply a finish – oil would be ideal.

Lesson 3
Perfecting the surface

Getting started

So far we have really only used the bench plane for truing edges and tidying up joints. Planing a board to thickness by hand is one of the most challenging skills for the woodworker, and for this reason many people prefer to buy a jointer and thickness planer for quick, accurate results. I can't say I'm a purist in these matters, personally favouring this approach more often than not, but to ignore the technique would be a dereliction of duty.

There used to be a maxim – and many tutors and craftspeople probably still follow this rule – that the only way to learn woodworking is to build up hand skills first and only then move on to machines. Though I can see why someone who had spent years learning skills would want future generations to follow his path, I consider it a myopic approach that must put off many potential converts. So I sympathize with those beginners who buy a few machines to get going and only later are engaged by the beauty and enjoyment of working by hand.

Whenever I've done woodworking demonstrations at a home-improvement show, the crowd is always most engaged when I'm planing. Planing with a sharp bench plane is certainly one of life's treats. There's no dust, just the hiss of shavings spilling off the bench and the revelation of a smooth surface with a lustre that cannot be matched by any machine. Sycamore is a superb wood to practise planing, and with a well-tuned tool you can remove shavings less than 1/1000th of an inch thick. However, you'll soon want the challenge of taking on oak and other more awkward hardwoods.

Lesson planner

Key techniques	Key tools and materials
• Planing a board • Belt-sanding a board • Smoothing boards • Sharpening a plane	• Bench planes • Using a cabinet scraper • Waterstones; Slipstones • Bench grinders

Planing the face of a board

Planing a board to the correct thickness by hand is a laborious procedure that requires a sharp cutter and plenty of patience, whether or not you are starting with rough-sawn timber or a pre-planed board that is just too thick. There will be times when the timberyard won't be able to supply the exact thickness you need.

To illlustrate the technique, I've chosen a piece of black cherry, which has a fine texture and a benign grain that is usually straight, so you won't suddenly tear the surface. Black walnut is similar, as is white oak, but ash will tear if you plane the wrong way and is hard to work. Just to show it's possible, the photographs show me planing on a folding bench, with the workpiece held against stops using foxed wedges (see Making foxed wedges for clamping, page 129). To be honest, though, it is not an operation I'd recommend, since you have to put most of your weight on the bench to stop it jumping about. This sort of planing is best done on a proper bench (see Lesson 4, page 128).

I prefer to place a cupped board with the concave side down and then plane the convex surface. This contradicts the advice you'll be given for planing with a machine, which demands that you machine the concave surface first. In planing a convex surface, there is a risk that the plane won't sit flat on the board and you'll end up with a tilted surface that wastes thickness. However, when working by hand, the rigidity of the board is the most important consideration and using wedges to chock up a convex surface can be time-consuming.

Whichever technique you choose, your first strokes will be to find the high ground. Gradually work your way down, watching as the planed surface grows. Keep an eye on how this is happening to ensure that you don't remove too much in one spot and always try to keep the plane flat. Remember to press down on the front knob at the start of the stroke and on the rear handle at the end to keep the tool level.

Once the surface is nearly level, you can start angling the plane to plane in all directions. This will also reduce the risk of tearing – on hardwoods that are tearing whichever way you plane, you can acually do some of the planing at right angles to the grain direction.

Once you have one face planed, you can use a marking gauge to mark the thickness you need along the edges and across the ends. Use the same procedure for planing to thickness, watching out for that moment when the cutter hits the scored line and the shaving narrows fractionally.

With the plane at an angle to the board, you can gradually remove the high points of a board.

Using a cabinet scraper

When grain is awkward and you can't get a perfectly planed surface without tearing, you may need to turn to a cabinet scraper for finishing. Some woodworkers don't like using abrasives because they believe the grit dulls the surface of the wood, whereas the cutting action of a scraper or plane leaves the fibres fresher. It is certainly true that a scraper can remove stock more quickly than sanding by hand (see Making a sanding block, page 58).

Generally, you use a cabinet scraper once the project has been assembled for finishing, but it can be employed on components earlier, especially if you want to apply a finish before gluing up. Hold the scraper in both hands, with your thumbs at the back and fingers around the front. By pressing with your thumbs, you bend the scraper slightly, so that only an inch or so of the edge is in contact with the surface. You can then push or pull to cut with the minuscule cutting hook that you form along the edge.

Take care not to scrape grooves in the wood as you work. You'll soon learn that you can scrape in almost any direction, but watch out for scratchmarks in the surface caused by a poorly sharpened edge or a piece of dust caught in the scraper.

Though diagonal planing will normally do, you may sometimes need to plane at right angles to the grain on really awkward timber.

By curving the cabinet scraper, you can adjust the depth of cut, but you are always aiming to produce shavings rather than dust.

Belt-sanding a board

To get the feel of planing a board, you could use a portable belt sander. I've always rented these, usually when I have a tabletop to smooth – they make quick work of awkward grain and are used in the same way as a bench plane. You have to be even more careful, with a belt sander, that you don't dip at the corners or ends and remove too much, and the addition of a skirt accessory helps with the levelling and stops the dust from escaping. I always attach the sander to an old vacuum cleaner, ever since the day I forgot to check the dust bag, which got clogged up and overheated the motor.

Belt sanders can be used to plane boards, but they are fairly difficult to control because they can remove stock very quickly and are often heavy and unmanageable. Make sure that dust is extracted at source. Notice how the board is held in a portable workbench with wedges.

Frames can be fitted to some belt sanders for better control. Brushes give some flexibility but also a firm base.

Tools

Buying cabinet scrapers

Along with rectangular cabinet scrapers, you can buy versions incorporating one convex end and one concave end. There is even a French curve version with an ever-decreasing radius. The quality of scrapers does vary, though as a general rule, the thicker ones are probably better. The only way to test them is to see how well they hold their edge and how easy they are to sharpen.

Sharpening a cabinet scraper

So much has been written about the sharpening of cabinet scrapers that some woodworkers are frightened off, believing it to be a dark art they dare not try. Actually, it is very simple. The scraper cuts with a hook that is turned over during the sharpening process by filing and by friction.

2 Use a burnishing tool (or the shaft of a screwdriver) to turn the hook over, initially at right angles to the scraper and then at an angle of about 20°, but you should experiment to find an angle that suits you.

1 Start by using a metal file to clean up the edge, to remove any vestige of the previous 'hook' and to straighten the edge. Filing along the edge also helps get the new hook going.

3 Feel for the hook along the edge: I find the tip of my middle finger is the most sensitive.

Trade secret

Improvising a cabinet scraper

You can make your own scrapers from a hacksaw blade, and Rolf Harris, the Australian performer/artist, once introduced me to the idea of using broken glass for scraping. (Remember to use tape on three sides to protect your hands.) Using a cabinet scraper is hard on the hands, and the metal can become very hot, so there are various jigs and devices for holding the scraper.

Waterstones

Long ago, I gave up on oilstones and turned instead to Japanese waterstones. These are relatively soft but can produce the most superb edge. You can also dress them with ease so that any dipping can be flattened. I have two stones: a 3,000 grade for reshaping edges and a 10,000 grade for honing.

The stones can be stored and used in a special pond with holders that invert the stones in water when they are not in use. The pond top is made of glass, to which you can fix wet-and-dry abrasive sheets for dressing the stones or for fettling the sole of a plane.

Slipstones

For smaller jobs, like touching up router cutters, you need slipstones, which are available for all types of stone. Experiment with different types to see which one gives you the best edge. I often use a diamond slipstone because they fold away neatly and you can buy them in coarse, medium and fine grades. I rarely use waterstone slipstones, but I do have a teardrop ceramic slipstone. These were all the rage a few years ago, and they are lubricated with a little water or saliva. You either love them or hate them.

Using a grinder

To sharpen bench planes, you will need a grinder. Any one will do, but there are a couple of refinements to make. It is a good idea to fit a custom-made tool rest that is wide, flexible and easy to adjust to the angle you need. Touch is so important when it comes to sharpening, and with a good tool rest you don't need so much pressure and can feel how an edge is sharpening against the stone. In time you will also want to buy quality stones from a specialist supplier.

It takes time to build confidence in using a grinder, but once you've mastered the skill, you'll be amazed by the neatness of the bevels. Some tool rests come with jigs to hold the cutter in a plane, but you'll soon find doing it by hand is quicker. Be particularly careful not to overheat the corners, which will go blue if they are too hot, and will become too brittle to hold an edge and

The corners of plane irons are particularly vulnerable to overheating, when the steel blues and the temper is lost.

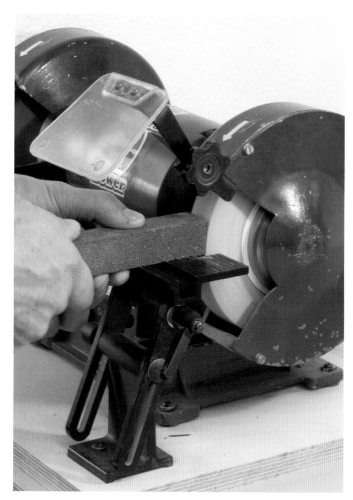

It's a very good idea to replace the manufacturer's tool rest on most grinders with a custom-made one that gives you a better platform and wider range of angles.

Redress the wheels on a grinder when the grit fills with debris.

therefore impossible to sharpen. Keep a jam jar of water beside the grinder for cooling the edge. Don't remove the guards from the grinder, and always wear safety goggles or glasses. When the stone has a glossy look and doesn't cut well, you can use a dressing stone to flatten the surface.

Sharpening a plane

The process of sharpening a plane's cutter with waterstones is pretty much identical to the technique used on an oilstone. With a bench plane, as opposed to a block plane or chisel, most people round the corners after grinding the angle using a small file to stop sharp corners from digging into the wood. You should also work a very shallow curve along the edge of the cutter so that it cuts a fraction more at the centre than at the edges, but only a tiny amount. Aim to have a mirror finish on the honing bevel and on the back of the cutter along the edge.

Using waterstones in a special pond is a tidy solution to a messy but effective method of sharpening.

Japanese waterstones need to be flattened regularly on a piece of wet-and-dry abrasive that has been stuck to glass.

Watch for the way the water cascades over edge as a sign of a well-sharpened blade.

Hone the back of the cutter until it shines like a mirror.

Flatten the sole of a new plane on wet-and-dry abrasive that is glued to a sheet of plate glass.

Fettling a plane

While you are learning, you won't know which of the frustrations you encounter using a bench plane are because of your lack of skill or because the plane is poorly set up. If tools were sold perfectly set up, the first stages of woodworking would be much easier. The approach you take depends on your character, so don't worry if you want to get going quickly and only later level the sole of the plane and make sure that the cutter is held flat and tight on the frog. Once you feel confident, take the plane apart completely, tidy up all the parts, and check that the ground surfaces are all flat. Then reassemble it in a better fashion.

Specialized planing tools

There are a few specialized tools and gadgets that will make planing boards by hand easier.
- **Winding sticks.** You can make these yourself. Use to check boards for twist (see Flattening the edge, page 66).
- **A long steel rule.** Use this for marking up and for testing the trueness of an edge or face.
- **Try planes.** These longer bench planes help in the levelling of a board, as their length keeps the plane flatter, the wider cutter removes more stock, and the substantial weight gives you more power. All of which adds up to greater expense.
- **Surface planer.** An alternative to both the belt sander and bench plane. This is very useful for cleaning off old finishes and for very rough boards, since the blades are disposable and easily replaced. But they are quite difficult to use accurately.

Materials

All about wood – sap and gum

Black cherry (*Prunus serotina*) has become one of the most popular species for woodworkers. It has an interesting grain pattern, colour that can be used naturally or stained to match mahogany, and an even texture and high lustre. And you can buy it from certified sustainable sources. Not surprisingly, it's becoming more expensive. But it's not without its faults. It usually contains some sapwood and can have black gum streaks or pockets that are difficult to avoid and give a dirty appearance, though many woodworkers like that natural feel. Unlike knots, the dark streaks are often difficult to see on rough-sawn boards and can suddenly appear. If it is a concern, make sure you buy more timber than you need to build wastage into your estimates.

Watch out for sapwood along the edge and dark gum lines on woods like black cherry.

Sanding grades

Abrasives for belt sanders are supplied in varying widths and lengths. The lower the grit number, the coarser the abrasive. The grade you use with a belt sander is usually much lower than you would use by hand. So while you might choose 120-grit for rough hand-sanding, you'd use 60 for rough belt-sanding. You won't find many sanding belts finer than 180, but you will certainly want to use 320 or finer for final sanding by hand.

Limed finishes

Woods with an open grain pattern, like oak or ash, look superb when they are limed. This process involves the rubbing of a wax/chalk paste into the grain to emphasize the pattern. For added impact, stain the surface with a coloured water-based stain (see Colouring wood, page 49).

1 Roughen the surface of the board with a brass wire brush to open the pores. Don't use a steel brush on oak because any loose metal fibres could get contaminated and stain the wood.

2 Rub liming paste into the grain using a woven plastic scouring pad. These are available in coarse, medium and fine grades, and are much easier to use for applying wax than steel wool, since they tend not to shed their fibres so readily and are cleaner to use. They are never, however, as hard-wearing as the coarsest steel wool.

A soft brush is ideal for burnishing a wax finish.

3 Before the paste dries, rub off as much excess as you can with a cloth. The harder you work, the more subtle the effect will be.

For a subtle effect, rub liming wax into the grain and then rub off the excess.

Project **Garden bench**

For the patio or garden

As an introduction to working with hardwoods, this garden bench is both dramatic and easier than you might expect. We used beech, which has a very subtle grain so that the design details aren't lost, but you could use oak or one of the more rot-resistant softwoods, like western red cedar. The dimensions of this bench are very flexible and will almost certainly be determined by the boards you can find. We used beech for all the components, but this is a matter of choice, though for outdoor furniture we recommend wood that is naturally resistant to rotting.

413 mm (16½ in)

1525 mm (60 in)

A

75 mm
(3 in)

45°

B

Seat

12 mm
(½ in)

B

C

Leg component
(the components
are glued
together during
assembly)

335 mm
(13¼ in)

Top inside edge of leg
component bevelled to
throw off rainwater
(optional)

C

320 mm (12½ in)

75 mm (3 in)

Cutting list

Part	Material	Quantity	Dimensions length, width, thickness
A Seat	beech	2	1525 x 203 x 76 mm (60 x 8 x 3 in)
B Support block	beech	4	419 x 108 x 76 mm (16½ x 4¼ x 3 in)
C Leg	beech	2	337 x 317 x 76 mm (13¼ x 12½ x 3 in)

Shopping list

Tools and materials	Extra tools for the job
Dowel rod for fixing seat to support blocks: 10 mm (⅜ in) in diameter. Cut dowels 25 mm (1 in) in length **Screws:** 12 x 75 mm (3 in) no.10 flat-headed screws	If you don't feel happy about planing with the bench plane we've been using to this point, you will need a surface planer, belt sander, or a planer-thicknesser.

1 We have assembled the legs (**C**) from two boards, glued together with a butt joint. Plane a length of wood about 711 mm (28 in) long, and 159 mm (6¼ in) by 76 mm (3 in) in section. This is a good length for planing by hand, since you won't need to move much as you work from the beginning to the end of the stroke. You will need to prepare two of these lengths, then cut each one in half.

2 Plane and thickness the board for the support blocks (**B**). This needs to be about 1626 mm (64 in) long, though you can save wood by alternating the diagonals when you come to cut them up.

Cut the support blocks to length, then tidy up the angled cuts with a block plane and a sanding block.

Once the glued leg components are set, you will need to clean up the joint and level the surfaces, since the butt joint is rarely perfect.

TIP: One way to resolve any inaccuracies in joint lines is to make a feature of the joint line by bevelling the edges before you glue up the components.

3 Mark up the lap joint between the support blocks and legs, leaving the top of the legs flush with the top edge of the support blocks. Cut down the shoulders with a tenon saw, remove the bulk of the waste with a coping saw, and then tidy up the end grain with a chisel (see Cutting a lap joint, page 45).

4 Cut the little bevelled notch from the centre top of the legs so that rainwater runs off this exposed area of end grain.

Drill holes in the support blocks for the screws and dowels.

5 Plane the seat boards. These are quite long for hand planing, and you will need to shuffle along as you stroke the plane along the board.

A band saw (see Band saw, page 109) or table saw (see Lesson 4, page 218) is the ideal tool for cutting the waste off the bevelled sides of the seat. Otherwise you will have to do this with a bench plane. Bevel the ends first, by cutting with a hand saw, and then tidy up with a block plane. Then you can bevel the sides, as we did for the uprights in the corner cabinet project a couple of lessons ago (see Planing bevels, page 86).

6 Use dowel-markers to transfer the dowel holes in the support blocks on to the underside of the seat. Drill these holes (see Using dowel-makers, page 57).

7 Assemble the legs and support blocks, then screw them to the seat. Clean away any excess glue (which should be water-proof) with a damp cloth and clean up once set. Finish with oil.

Lessons learned

- Planing and thicknessing a board really does rely on a plane that has been well set up and sharpened.

- Hardwoods can be easier to use than softwoods because they bruise less easily and their texture and grain pattern is often more uniform.

- Planing needs a solid platform, so the sooner a woodworker has a good bench, the sooner he or she can do more ambitious work.

Lesson 4
The workshop

Getting started

There is a common maxim among woodworkers that you can never have enough clamps. In contrast, you only need one workbench, but the irony is that to make your own bench, you might be expected to need a selection of long bar clamps to assemble the under-frame. Fortunately, there are various techniques and fittings to help you build the project for this lesson, the Workbench – that most important part of any successful workshop.

I have to admit that I bought my own bench from a company exporting bubinga benches from Africa. It's far from the biggest bench in the world, and for a while I covered the tool well to give myself more space for woodworking, as I considered the tool well to be merely a dust-catcher. Nowadays, though, I have a good assembly area that provides a flat space for constructing projects, and the workbench has the dedicated task of holding timber for planing, shaping and cutting.

For that purpose the best benches are heavy (or held down firmly) and flat. If you can't hold the workpiece without wobble, you've little hope of planing it accurately, and I've found myself perpetually improving and renovating the vices and holding devices as my woodworking skills and expectations have developed.

Draw-boring

If you look at old oak furniture and wood-framed buildings, you may notice the ends of pegs holding mortise and tenon joints in place. While certainly performing this function, the pegs are also used to tighten the joint in the

1 Drill holes through the mortise with a false tenon to stop splitting.

2 Matching holes are drilled in the tenon, nearer the shoulder.

3 Cut lengths of dowel, longer than you need.

4 Sand off the dowel edges to make it easier to insert through the mortise and tenon.

5 Cut off the ends of the dowel rod and sand.

Lesson planner

Key techniques	Key tools and materials
• Draw-boring • Drilling into end grain • Making plugs to hide screws	• Anatomy of a workbench • Vices • Using a tape to measure • Add-ons for a workbench

absence of long clamps to do the job or, in the case of buildings, the impossibility of doing so. This is called draw-boring and is a particularly neat trick.

Cut the mortise and tenon joint just as you would normally. Once it has been cut, drill a hole at right angles to the mortise, usually placing a piece of scrap wood in the mortise as a fake tenon to stop the inside face of the mortise from splitting. With the hole drilled, remove the scrap and insert the real tenon. With a sharpened dowel the diameter of the hole, mark the centre of the hole on the tenon. Pull the rail out and then drill a similar hole through the tenon, positioning it a fraction nearer the shoulder than the mark you made.

When you reassemble the joint using glue, you can push a dowel through the holes and it will pull the tenon into the mortise. There are a few golden rules for this to work.

Drilling into end grain

Drilling into the end of a board is surprisingly difficult. You'll find that the bit wanders, creating a sloppy hole

that won't hold a dowel or direct a bolt. For this job you might try using a drilling jig, which is held against the board and helps to guide the drill bit. I'm not too keen on this, because I don't like dowel joints. They are difficult to position, and I don't like drilling into end grain, but they are useful for this particular job. Don't buy an expensive jig, but if you are having problems drilling end grain, it is worth a try.

It's very important to make an indentation when drilling into end grain, or the bit will wander.

With time, you will be able to drill vertically just by muscle memory.

Drilling a narrow hole first can help keep the drill bit straight as you drill into end grain.

Trade secret

Making foxed wedges for clamping

If you don't have sash clamps for assembling the stool top, you can make your own with what are known as foxed wedges. To a piece of chipboard or similar, 18 mm (¾ in) thick, screw and glue two lengths of 51-mm (2-in) rough-sawn softwood about 406 mm (16 in) apart. Now cut four wedges from offcuts the same thickness as the stool top – make them 100 mm (4 in) long, and tapered along one edge from 25 mm (1 in) thick down to 6 mm (¼ in). The wedges work in pairs, overlapping to push the boards for the stool top together tightly.

Tools

Anatomy of a workbench

The workbench performs differing tasks in all workshops, depending on what woodworking is being attempted, though there are a few basic principles that apply. Many workshops will have at least two benches – one for planing and forming joints, and the other for assembling components. Then there are the many worksurfaces used to support machinery and equipment.

The basic bench is built on a frame with legs and shelves, either open or enclosed with doors. All that matters is that it is heavy and won't move as you plane. The bench top is usually made from thick hardwood, a dense variety like maple, and must be flat as a reference for anything you are working on. Other features include two vices (shown below) and a tool well (above right).

1 A vice at the right-hand end – often used to clamp timber against dogs that fit into holes along the front of the bench.

2 A second vice to the left-hand end of the front, used to hold boards on edge for planing and for many other holding jobs.

3 Some benches have a trough at the back called the tool well, into which you can put tools and bits below the surface.

Using a tape to measure

Spring-loaded, flexible steel tapes are useful in the workshop, especially because they can measure internal and external measurements. The hook on the end slides in and out by the thickness of the hook for that purpose. However, usually no two tapes are the same, so once you start using one, stick to it.

The hook on a retracting tape can be used over and against a workpiece. However a steel rule is more accurate.

Add-ons for a workbench

Many manufacturers produce sophisticated gadgets for the workbench. You don't need them all, but some are very useful.

The hold-down. An L-shaped device that fits into a hole in the bench top and clamps down boards to further reduce the risk of movement.

The bench stop. A hinged metal plate with teeth along the front edge, against which you hold a board for planing.

Home-made panel stop. Designed as a stop against which you can plane wider boards or panels without them pivoting.

Bench vice. Many woodworkers favour adding an engineer's vice for holding odd-shaped components. These can also give you better access around the workpiece.
Board support. I have a hole drilled into the front edge of the bench for a peg to support long boards in the vice when planing the edge or cutting mortises.

Positioning the workbench

It's worth taking some time working out how to lay out your woodworking space. The direction of cut on some machines will regulate how the space is used, but a key criterion is the siting of the workbench. You must leave plenty of space around the bench, especially at the right-hand end, which you will be using for holding boards in the dogs. But you also need to be able to plane beyond the vice on the front at the left. If that's a problem, you could position the vice towards the middle of the front edge, but this isn't ideal.

Assembly table

If you have the space, a table for assembling projects is a good idea, with overlapping edges so that you can use clamps around the edges. This lesson's project is ideal for this purpose and for storing tools or timber. The table doesn't need to be as sturdy as the workbench.

Materials

Making plugs to hide screws

A good way to hide the use of screws as fasteners is to drill a wider hole for the screw head to sit in (known as counterboring) and then fill the hole with a plug. Using a special cutter in a drill, you can cut your own plugs and then glue them in place. Cut the plug back with a flush-cutting saw, and then pare it with a chisel. One of the key skills is to pare across the grain of the plug so that you don't tear the grain. Finally, sand it smooth.

The best plug-cutting bits produce tapered plugs for the tightest fit.

If at all possible, keep the grain of the plugs in line for a neater finish.

Tap the plugs home with a smear of adhesive.

Take care when paring back the plug, as the fibres can easily tear.

Project **Workbench**

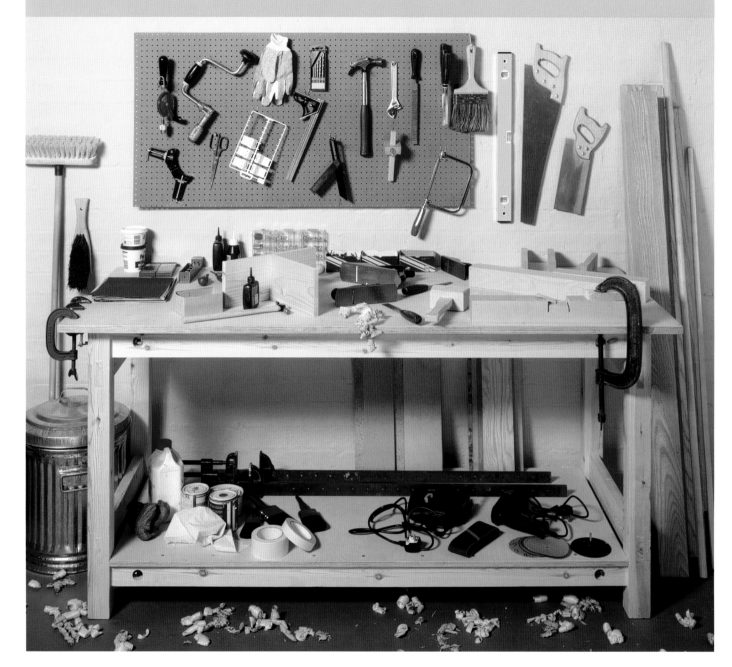

For the workshop

A portable workbench is ideal for many jobs, and
I still use mine around the workshop and whenever
I work on site. But a permanent, solid bench not only
gives you a better, bigger base for working, it also
allows you to add various holding devices and gives
you a space to store tools. Don't be put off, though –
just because it's large doesn't mean it's difficult to
make. This bench is made entirely from prepared
softwood, direct from the timberyard or DIY store.

Worktop

Long rail

900 mm
(35½ in)

End frame

660 mm
(26 in)

1725 mm (68 in)

1800 mm (71 in)

750 mm
(29½ in)

D

F

**Stub tenon should be half
the width of the rail**

A

E

Housing

B

C

**Bottom
shoulder**

**Tenon is half the
width of the rail**

Leg

Cutting list

Part	Material	Quantity	Dimensions length, width, thickness
A Leg	softwood	4	876 x 89 x 89 mm (34½ x 3½ x 3½ in)
B Long rail	softwood	4	1594 x 89 x 38 mm (62¾ x 3½ x 1½ in)
C End rail	softwood	4	660 x 89 x 38 mm (26 x 3½ x 1½ in)
D Worktop	birch ply	1	1803 x 749 x 25 mm (71 x 29½ x 1 in)
E Shelf	birch ply	1	1613 x 648 x 25 mm (63½ x 25½ x 1 in)
F Fixing block	softwood	6	127 x 19 x 19 mm (5 x ¾ x ¾ in)

Shopping list

Tools and materials	Extra tools for the job
Coach bolts: 8 x 178 mm (7 in) with nuts and washers **Countersunk screws** for fastening the blocks and the shelf: a box of 38 mm (1½ in) no. 8	**Wrench** for tightening the carriage bolt nut

Softwood parts are listed as planed dimensions, not rough-sawn dimensions. To find the rough-sawn width and thickness to ask for, see page 17.

1 Mark up the positions for the mortises on one of the legs (**A**). Square the whole way around the legs for the through tenons on the end rail (**C**) and just across the inside face for the long rail (**B**) stub tenons. This will help remind you which is which. Once you have marked up the positions on one, use that to copy across to the other legs.

Normally, the mortise should be one-third the thickness of the rail, but in this case, for extra substance, I've gone for tenons half the thickness of the rail: 19 mm (¾ in). You should be able to set the mortise gauge to mark up all the mortises and all the tenons, so make sure it is accurate. Mark up all the mortises.

Glue the legs, using sash clamps, and leave to set.

2 Drill and chop away the waste from the mortises, working from both sides for the through ones.

Cut the end rails (**C**) a fraction overlong so that the tenons will protrude through the legs by 3 mm (⅛ in). Mark up the shoulders at each end on one rail, and then use that to copy across to the others; square the lines the whole way around. It doesn't matter if the length isn't exactly as we've shown, so long as the shoulder-to-shoulder distance is the same for all the rails.

3 Use the mortise gauge to mark up the tenons.

You can use a band saw to cut the tenons, as explained in Lesson 7, but these rails are quite deep, and balancing larger components like this on the small band-saw table can be tricky. It is difficult to tell if you are cutting the workpiece accurately. I'd probably cut these by hand – first the cheeks and then the shoulders. Always cut one tenon first and check the fit in the mortise.

4 Repeat the marking and cutting process with the long rails (**B**), but this time don't leave the rails overlong, since the stub tenons must fit exactly. The important thing, again, is to ensure the shoulder-to-shoulder distance is identical on all these rails. Dry-assemble one set of end rails and two legs to check the fit. If you don't have bar or sash clamps, the best technique to use is the most traditional, called draw-boring (see this lesson's techniques), which uses pegs to pull the tenon into the mortise. You could also use wedges to tighten the joint.

5 With both end frames glued, mark the position for the coach bolt in the top of each leg and drill, making sure the hole is true by lining up with a square or by asking a friend to eye it for you. There is a trick you can do with a pair of mirrors, but I've never tried it, because a square and a bit of luck seems to have worked for me. Use a drill bit a fraction larger than the coach bolt so that there is no scope for movement when it comes to locating the nut in the rail.

6 Drill out the recess in the long rails for the nut using a flat bit, measuring it carefully so that the bolt protrudes from the nut by about 6 mm (¼ in) once the joint is tight.

Dry-assemble the bench frame, and mark the positions for the holes in the end of each long rail by tapping the drill bit you've just used into the end grain. You can do this joint by joint without assembling the whole frame.

Drill into the end of the long rails, aiming to hit the nut opening dead centre. One day, when you're a professional, you'll have a horizontal borer for this job, but for now you'll have to do it by eye. Do this for all the long rails.

7 Assemble the end frames and long rails, and secure with the bolts. You might need a friend again to help support the ends. Screw the attachment blocks along the top edge of the long rails, with clearance holes drilled for screws into the top.

8 Cut the shelf to size and screw it to the bottom rails; then cut out the top and screw that up from below. You are ready to discard the portable workbench.

Lessons learned

- The recesses for captive nuts in the end rails are easier to work with if they aren't just drilled, but a flat side is chiselled so that the nut has better grounding and there is more space for the wrench.

- Check exactly what overlap you want on the top to suit any vices you plan to add. Check also that the height of the bench suits you.

Lesson 5
The router: a flexible tool

Getting started

If there is one tool that sets the woodworker apart from the home improver, it must be the router. With an ability to cut joints and add decoration, the router is versatile and flexible but requires dedicated cutters, fences and jigs to maximize the opportunities it offers.

Holding for routing

One of the most significant challenges when routing is how to hold the workpiece without the holding mechanism interfering with the router's travel. On a proper workbench this can often be achieved between the end vice and a dog, though more sophisticated products use either the suck of a vacuum cleaner or just friction. Whichever you choose, the timber must be held firmly, since any movement is likely to lead to slips and mistakes.

Routing safely

Some people consider the router to be a dangerous tool. In theory it certainly is, but with the plunge router, the cutter can be disengaged and retracted faster than on any other power tool. By using guides and jigs, you control the router, and you should obviously change cutters only with the plug pulled from the socket. For safe cutting, you should always work in the opposite direction to the cutter's rotation, just as pedestrians walk against the flow of traffic on country roads. Never use the router hand-held with any cutter that is designed for use in a router table, as will be stated in the catalogue, and keep the depth of each pass to a minimum.

Lesson planner

Key techniques	Key tools and materials
• Routing with the side fence • Routing across the grain • Using bearing-guided cutters • Using a biscuit jointer	• Buying a router • Buying a biscuit jointer • Router cutters • All about wood – MDF

To rout across the grain, simply clamp a straightedge across the workpiece.

The router is one power tool where I don't necessarily recommend sucking away the shavings at source, since any hose can inhibit manoeuvrability and potentially make the router more dangerous. That said, I would always use extraction at source if routing MDF or any of the timbers that irritate the skin or affect breathing. I have added clear plastic to the base of my routers to improve visibility and keep the base level. Always use a dust mask or respirator, goggles or safety glasses, and ear defenders.

Routing in steps

It is tempting, but invariably counterproductive, to make every routed cut in one pass. Not only are you likely to burn the wood, but there is a risk that the cutter will loosen in the collet and drop into the wood. So take it in small steps. This is one of the real advantages of the plunge router (as opposed to the fixed-base router), because you can normally set three depths that you can return to time and time again if you have more than one cut or workpiece to rout.

Routing with the side fence

The side fence, which comes with almost all routers, is a useful accessory for routing along the length of a board, whether that's to rout a rebate or profile on the edge or to cut a groove farther in. You can also use a side fence to rout across the grain, but this isn't the best way of doing the job, since the fence will be running against end grain, which tends not to be as smooth as long grain.

An important early step is to add a wooden lining to the side fence, ideally using something fairly hard so that it runs easily. Without the lining, there is often a gap around the cutter, which can lead to awkward jumps at the beginning or end of a cut. You can cut into the wooden lining with the router's cutter and reduce the risk of tearing.

When taking a series of cuts in steps, do so by adjusting the depth rather than the side fence, which should remain fixed once you've found the right setting with some practice cuts.

Routing across the grain

Today's routers, especially the fixed-base models, bear a surprising resemblance to the traditional hand tools of the same name. These are still available, though little used, with a cutter fixed centrally to a metal base to which is attached a handle on each side. These aren't easy tools to use and are mainly employed for cutting housings across the grain. This is one of the key jobs of the modern router, but instead of using the side fence, the best approach is to fix a guide to the timber and run the router against that.

First, you have to measure the offset between the cutter and the edge of the router's base. This will obviously change depending on the diameter of the cutter, but it's the sort of measurement that is worth keeping on a board in the workshop, so you don't have to measure it each

When routing, always be ready to raise the cutter, with your hand on the locking lever.

An acrylic sub-base provides a firmer platform. Measure the offset between cutter and side of the base for routing against a straightedge.

The simplest way to use a router as a hand-held tool is with the side fence.

Trade secret

Too much of a good thing
It is always a good idea to have some extra timber for a project, planed to the appropriate dimensions to set up tools and machines, and in case of mistakes. One saves so much time by having extra timber for such eventualities, since it won't necessarily be easy to set up a thicknesser or marking gauge again to achieve the same result.

time. Make sure you know to which edge of the housing this offset relates.

You can buy marvellous straightedges that clamp to any width of board for this operation. Or, you can make a straightedge yourself, and the one shown here has a guide

fixed to the underside to ensure that the housing is cut at 90° to the edge. With a bit of planning, you can make such a jig to a width that allows you to rout a housing on each side, which is handy for making a series of housings for shelves. One way to hold the jig in place is with a bench hold-down (see Add-ons for a workbench, page 130).

Using bearing-guided cutters

Bearing-guided cutters, whether for cutting rebates, profiles, or grooves, are relatively easy to use, and little can go wrong by way of a catch except at the beginning of the cut. At this point, the cutter can slip the wrong way around the corner, so if possible, do a very light cut to start, or make sure there is excess on the end of the board. Try to keep the stroke steady so there are no hesitations, because you could make an indentation if you stop.

With a bearing-guided cutter you don't need to use a fence to rout a profile or rebate.

Using a biscuit jointer

Though biscuit jointers can be used for various grooving tasks, their prime purpose is to make slots for compressed hardwood biscuits. This can be done just as you might cut a groove with a router, either against a guide bar or by using the fence that is built into the biscuit jointer. It is one of the easiest of power tools to use, designed for forming joints at corners in cabinets, where the side fence can be employed for both cuts and doesn't have to be moved. A routed housing is probably an easier joint to cut for dividers or for shelves that aren't at the corners of the cabinet. Joining two pieces of ply is simple with a biscuit jointer, and great results can be achieved in a few steps.

1 Line up the two pieces and mark the positions of the biscuits.

2 Adjust the biscuit jointer to cut roughly at the centre of the workpiece. This is done by moving the side fence, then fine-adjusting the blade itself with the knurled knob that moves the blade within the body.

Set the depth of cut. Good biscuit jointers have settings that relate to the standard sizes of biscuit.

Fixed-base routers do not plunge so easily, and the depth is set by screwing the body down into the base. This works well for edge routing when you need only one pass rather than a series of deeper cuts, but generally the plunge router is easier for the beginner to use. It is also safer because the cutter springs back up above the base the moment you release the lock.

Routers are sold in different sizes, defined by the power of the motor and the size of the collet that holds the cutter. The best router to start with has a 6-mm (¼-in) collet and is of medium size, with variable speed, so you can adjust the speed according to the diameter of the cutter. Even the most economical router will provide a good introduction to router use, but check which accessories can be fitted, since its versatility derives from its ability to use a system of templates, guides and jigs.

3 Cut the groove in the edge of one piece. Notice how much dust shoots out without extraction being fitted.

Now make the corresponding cuts in the face, with the marks lined up through the hole in the fence. It is a good idea to fit a dust extractor.

Insert the biscuits and do a trial run. Once you've applied glue to a biscuit, it expands and you will never get the joint apart.

Tools

Buying a router

There are two types of router. The newest designs are what's known as plunge routers, with the motor sliding up and down two steel columns, inside which are heavy springs. Push down on the handles, and the rotating cutter plunges into the wood for simple cutting of stopped housings and mortises. Release the locking lever at the end of the cut, and the router springs back up again. An advantage of the plunge router is that you can pre-set depth stops on a rotating column so that you can make a series of deeper cuts that can be repeated from one piece to the next.

Router features to look out for
• Routers with a spindle lock only need one collet wrench or spanner for fitting cutters.
• Check the position of the locking lever and switch. You need to be able to use these quickly and with the least movement of your hands or fingers.
• Ask how far the collet plunges below the router's base. This becomes an issue when fixing the router in a router table, because the depth of cut is restricted by the thickness of the table (see Using a router table, page 146).
• Some medium-sized routers have collets for both 6 mm (¼ in) and 3 mm (⅛ in). This makes them more versatile because larger cutters are supplied with a 12 mm (½-in) shank.
• Base shape. Plunge routers will usually have a base with curved ends and two straight sides. This is ideal for running against a guide. Other routers may have a round base, with the cutter accurately centred.

Router accessories

Most routers will be supplied with a side fence – which is used most frequently for cutting rebates and profiles along an edge – and some will have other accessories. Even if they are not supplied with the router, check what accessories are available for your model.

● Fine depth adjuster. This effectively converts the plunge router into a fixed-base router, with a very simple mechanism for adjusting the depth of cut. You'll want this feature if you expect to use a plunge router in a router table.

● Some side fences can be fitted with a fine adjuster, which is incredibly useful because fences can be tricky to set accurately otherwise.

● Guide bushes are screwed to the router's base and follow a shaped template that is fixed to the top of the workpiece. You can use the template for cutting out apertures or making shaped pieces.

● Jigs for cutting joints. These can be bought to cut specific joints, like dovetails and mortises, or made in the workshop for specific jobs.

Buying a biscuit jointer

Unless you intend to do a lot of cabinet-making from sheet materials or joint up large panels for tabletops, you probably won't need to use a biscuit jointer very often. More expensive models will be a bit more accurate, but the most basic one will do for most home woodworkers. Do check, however, that the blade is tungsten-tipped and that you can fit on an extractor.

Biscuit jointers produce an accurate joint quickly and simply, and the compressed beech biscuits expand when in contact with the glue to form a very strong bond. You can also buy various hinges and plastic biscuits so that you can dismantle a joint if needed. In addition, there are gluing accessories to assist in applying adhesive to the groove.

The combination plane

One of my favourite hand tools is the combination plane. Along with a set of cutters, you can trench

Even though routers are quick and accurate, there is a certain joy to making beading with a combination plane.

grooves and rebates along the edge of a board, as well as profile with beading cutters and other shaped cutters. I love the way little knives in the nose stop the grain from tearing, and I'm always satisfied when I get it to work well.

Router cutters

The true flexibility of the router is determined by the amazing range of cutters available. The best way to learn what your router can do is to flick through the pages of a routing catalogue and explore the multitude of cutter shapes and purposes. Here, though, are some of the key types of cutter for using the router by hand, rather than in a router table (see Using a router table, page 146).

Straight cutters

The simplest of cutters, straight cutters, are the most frequently used. These are produced with one or two cutting edges (or flutes), or with a spiralling edge for a finer finish. Only the very narrowest cutters have one flute, otherwise the finish is too rough. A wide range of diameters is available, plus long cutters for working with a router table and for cutting deep mortises.

Bearing-guided profile cutters

One of the simplest ways of applying decoration to the edge of a board is to use a bearing-guided cutter, with the bearing following the edge. The advantage of this is that the bearing doesn't spin with the router and so doesn't burn the edge. Many shapes of cutter are available.

Clean up the face of the router's cutter with a slipstone to hone the edge, but take care you don't alter the profile.

However, you can tidy up the back with a slipstone, and soaking them in a cleaning agent can remove any build-up of resin and prolong their life.

Materials

All about wood – MDF

Medium-density fibreboard is my least favourite woodworking material, but it has its uses. It is ideal for building simple chairs and tables, as in this lesson's project, Child's Furniture, but I'd always choose quality plywood first. The advantage of MDF is that you can shape the edges with a router, though this can also be done with the best ply.

Always use extraction and a dust mask or respirator when working with MDF, and watch out for the chips because they can be very sharp and are horrible if they get in your eyes. I would even use extraction for routing MDF because the dust is unpleasant and potentially carcinogenic. Work outside if you can. Expect your tool edges to dull more quickly working with MDF than with probably any other material.

You can change the diameter of the bearing to adjust the depth of cut.

Bearing-guided rebate cutters

With a bearing attached either above or below the flutes, these cutters can be set to cut a rebate along an edge. By using different diameters of bearing, the dimensions of the rebate can be altered.

Trimming cutters

Similar to the rebate cutters, these trimming cutters feature a bearing exactly the diameter of the cutter. Fix a shaped template above or below the workpiece for the trimming cutter to follow and reproduce.

Sharpening cutters

Because most cutters these days are tungsten-tipped, they aren't very easy to sharpen, and there is always a risk that you will change the profile or diameter of the cutter.

Project **Child's furniture**

For the nursery

Biscuit jointed and routed, this child's table and chair is a good trial for making projects entirely with power tools. The process is so simple that we only need explain how to make a chair. These projects are made entirely from MDF or plywood, with small offcut blocks needed to support the seat and top, though this job could also be done with biscuits. Both the chair and table are made from material that is 18 mm (¾ in) thick, which is why the cutting list can be so simple.

600 mm (23⅝ in)
600 mm (23⅝ in)
530 mm (20⅞ in)
86 mm (3⅜ in)
700 mm (27½ in)
470 mm (18½ in)
75 mm (3 in)
75 mm (3 in)
500 mm (19⅝ in)

Corners rounded after assembly

300 mm (11¾ in)
60 mm (2⅜ in)
120 mm (4¾ in)
300 mm (11¾ in)
340 mm (13⅜ in)
200 mm (8 in)
70 mm (2¾ in)
330 mm (13 in)
27 mm (1¹⁄₁₆ in)
265 mm (10⅜ in)
45 mm (1¾ in)
300 mm (11¾ in)

Corners rounded after assembly

Cutting list

Part	Material	Quantity	Dimensions
Table			length, width, thickness
A Top	MDF or plywood	1	600 x 600 x 18 mm (23⅝ x 23⅝ x ¾ in)
B Front and back leg	MDF or plywood	2	530 x 498 x 18 mm (20⅞ x 19⅝ x ¾ in)
C Side leg	MDF or plywood	2	530 x 470 x 18 mm (20⅞ x 18½ x ¾ in)
Part **Chair**			
A Seat	MDF or plywood	1	340 x 298 x 18 mm (13⅜ x 11¾ x ¾ in)
B Back	MDF or plywood	1	700 x 298 x 18 mm (27½ x 11¾ x ¾ in)
C Front leg	MDF or plywood	1	330 x 298 x 18 mm (13 x 11¾ x ¾ in)
D Side leg	MDF or plywood	2	330 x 264 x 18 mm (13 x 10⅜ x ¾ in)

Shopping list

Materials

Screws to fix seat: 4 x 32 mm (1¼ in) no. 8 wood screws
Biscuits: 12 compressed beech

1 On a sheet measuring 1219 x 2438 mm (4 x 8 ft), work out exactly how you are going to cut the components. Some of the leg parts may be able to interlock, to save material.

2 Cut out all the parts, ideally on a table saw (perhaps at the timberyard) so that the edges are smooth and clean. If you go down this route, you probably won't be able interlock the components, and the decision comes down to whether you either want to save time or waste material.

3 Mark up the cut-outs, using the 51-mm (2-in) radius template for the curved corners.

TIP: Design with sheet materials in mind. Often, the way you design a project will have a significant impact on how efficiently you can cut parts from sheet material. For instance, if you build cabinets, sides that are anything over 610 mm (24 in) wide, you are likely to drastically reduce the number of pieces you can extract from one sheet. And don't forget to account for the kerf of the saw, which is likely to be at least 3 mm (⅛ in).

4 Use a jigsaw to cut away the cut-outs. Always wear goggles (and, of course, a mask) when cutting with a jigsaw because it can very easily kick small particles up into your eyes as you watch the cut. In fact, I've had more problems with jigsaws than almost any tool. Cut out the circle in the back of the chair.

Use a belt sander to smooth the internal edges and the curved corners.

Lessons learned

- The router is incredibly versatile. You don't need an expensive one to get going, and you need only a few cutters. Much can be learned from a routing catalogue.

- Routers create a huge amount of dust, particularly when you are working with MDF. You will probably discover that it isn't the nicest of materials to work with, and many woodworkers avoid it completely. Don't assume it is strong because it is heavy: the fibres are actually pretty short, and MDF shelves tend to sag.

- Biscuit jointers are good tools but are not used as frequently as many woodworkers imagine.

5 **Alternative technique** If you are making a series of these chairs and tables, it is worth making jigs to shape the legs with a router, template and trimming cutter. I would make the side, front and back legs the same size so that one template fits all, at least for the chairs.

Line up the components, marking which one matches which, and mark where the biscuits are to be positioned. Cut the grooves for the biscuits.

Use a bearing-guided rounding-over cutter to round the edges, where appropriate.

Dry-assemble each piece, and then assemble with glue, using bar clamps. You can often get away without clamps for a biscuit joint, since the biscuit expands quickly and the joint is so strong.

Glue blocks to the leg assemblies; then drill the seat and tabletop and screw them in place. Alternatively, you could screw a batten along the top edge of the legs, and screw up through that into the underside of the seat or tabletop, so that the screws are hidden.

Lesson 6
The power of the router

Getting started

If buying a router is the seminal moment that elevates the woodworker from home improver to potential craftsperson, making or acquiring a router table is the step that truly maximizes the power of the router. My first router table was no more than a piece of MDF, with the router screwed to the underside. I clamped a straightedge to the table as a fence. It did me very nicely for years, and I've seen professional woodworkers using models of a similar standard.

You soon discover, though, that the router table can easily be enhanced by improving the fence and routing grooves for a mitre guide. If there is an imperative, it is that the table must be flat; otherwise all the benefits of being able to control the cut will be lost in a sea of inaccuracy.

Though any router can be inserted in a router table, some are better suited than others, particularly when you consider the need to change the cutters and raise the router by grappling underneath the table. Fortunately, a few new accessories have improved the ease of cutter-changing and router-raising, to make the router table even more useful.

Using a router table

You work with a router table just as you might a hand-held router, it's just that the timber moves instead of the tool. There comes a time when boards are large and unmanageable, and then it is better to move the router and hold the wood. However, for most small- and

medium-sized components, it is safer and more accurate to use a router table, except that stopped cuts are often easier to make using a hand-held plunge router.

As a rough guide, use the main fence for routing along the grain, just as you would use the side fence on a hand-held router. The mitre guide on a router table is

It's worth having a selection of wooden facings for the fence, each with an opening cut to suit particular cutters.

the equivalent of running a hand-held router against a straightedge to cut a housing or similar. You can also use bearing-guided cutters on a router table, though this can be an awkward operation and it is a good idea to use some form of fence to guide the wood on to the cutter. Otherwise it is very easy for the cutting to catch the end grain and send the timber flying. Some router tables have a pin for this purpose, raised above the surface of the router table.

When you fix a new wooden lining to the fence, you will need to cut a cavity for the cutter. This cavity is ideally wider at the back than the front, to give space for the shavings to be sucked away.

The housed rebate joint

Like one song sung to the tune of another, the housed rebate is effectively two joints in one. It combines the

Lesson planner

Key techniques	Key tools and materials
• Using a router table • The housed rebate joint • The mitre-lock joint	• Making machines of power tools • Making a router table • Accessories for the router table

The housed rebate joint is a favourite for drawers and boxes, as it is simple to cut and offers a large area for gluing.

through housing (or the stopped housing for that matter) with the rebate. The shoulder on the rebate gives the joint more rigidity, and there is plenty of gluing area. It is ideal for corner joints in the making of utility furniture where you'd choose the dovetail for drawer, cabinet and box construction (see Lesson 3, page 206).

This is a simple joint to cut, especially using a router table – though also with hand tools – and once you get the hang of the technique, you'll be cutting the housed rebate joint in your sleep. It is particularly easy to produce repetitively and to set up stops and jigs to reproduce it accurately.

Marking out a housed rebate joint

The simplest way to try this joint is by using material of the same thickness for all the components. By dividing the thickness in two, you can mark up the joint easily, using a marking gauge and a mortise gauge. Of course, once you start using a router table to produce joints like this, you won't need to worry so much about marking up, because it's a case of just setting the cutter and fences.

There are a couple of ways to mark up this joint, and it doesn't matter that much if you start with the housing or rebate, though generally you want to cut the housing first and fit the 'tenon' to that. If you're not that confident with a marking gauge, you can simply measure off the positioning of the housing and square around the workpiece. Or you can set up a mortise gauge and use that to mark out the waste to be removed. You need only a marking gauge to mark up the rebate on the other piece.

Mark out the first joint carefully, and use that to position cutters for making the rest of the joint.

Using hold-downs ensures your fingers aren't too close to the cutter as you push the workpiece across the router table.

Cutting a housed rebate joint

However you mark up the joint, it's a good idea to do a trial run first to get used to the technique for cutting it, because it can be a bit confusing. Cutting a housing with a saw and chisel was one of the first techniques I was taught at school, but the saw is very difficult to control across the width of the board. Follow the three steps pictured below.

1 With the joint marked up, saw down the shoulders of the housing, stopping a fraction short of the bottom. It's safer to do this than to risk cutting too deep. The wood you leave between the housing and the end of the workpiece is likely to be very short and hence is vulnerable. Take care of it.

3 Cut down the shoulder of the rebate and chisel away the waste, first with the grain using a mallet and then across the grain, just with hand pressure, for a smooth finish. Test the fit.

2 Chisel out the waste, making sure you work from both ends so as not to tear the grain. An alternative technique is to hold the workpiece against the fence of a bench hook and chisel towards the fence to reduce the risk of tearing.

Cutting the housed rebate on a router table

You can look at the cutting of the housing in two ways. In one approach, you cut the component exactly to length and work off the ends. This is the easy way and works well enough. You simply use the fence on the router table as a stop and push the component across the cutter with the mitre guide.

The alternative approach, perhaps for making a box or drawer, is to consider the distance between the housings as the critical issue. In this case, you can leave the component about 13 mm (½ in) overlong. Cut the first housing roughly in the right position, but for the second housing, set up a jig, with the first housing dropping over a tongue that is fixed to the mitre guide at the appropriate point. Rout the first housing on all your components and then rout the second one using the jig. This is perfect if you have a series of identical boxes or drawers to make, as is the case for this lesson's project, the Crockery Shelves.

Once the housing is cut, you can rout the rebates on the ends of the other part. Cut this workpiece exactly to length because it has to fit perfectly into the housing. All these parts must be cut neatly to exactly the same length. Then use the mitre guide to push the timber over the cutter. You can cut the rebate with the end against the fence or by using a bearing-guide rebate cutter. Do all the housed pieces first (with some extras in case of mistakes) and then do all the rebates to fit.

When it comes to assembling the joint, there will be extra on the ends of the housed pieces. These are known as the horns. Leave them on at this stage, and then plane or sand them off once the joint has been assembled and the glue has set.

The mitre-lock joint

A neat alternative to the housed rebate joint is the mitre-lock joint. Just as the housed rebate combines two joints, the mitre lock is part mitre, part rebate. It is produced by using a 45° cutter and a straight cutter, and the advantage, once you have set up the router table, is that it is very easy to glue up because the mitre doesn't slide about (see The mitre joint, page 74).

1 Cut the parts to length and rout a 45° mitre across the ends of one part. You could do this with a mitre saw (see The mitre saw, page 77).

2 Insert a straight cutter into the router table and cut a rebate from the mitre.

3 Put the 45° cutter back in the router and gradually raise the cutter and move the fence until it is cutting a stepped shape that is a perfect fit in the other piece.

Tools

Making machines of power tools

The router table is one of the few occasions when I'd advocate the conversion of power tools into machines by fixing them into some kind of stand or table. If you are woodworking on a limited budget or have very limited

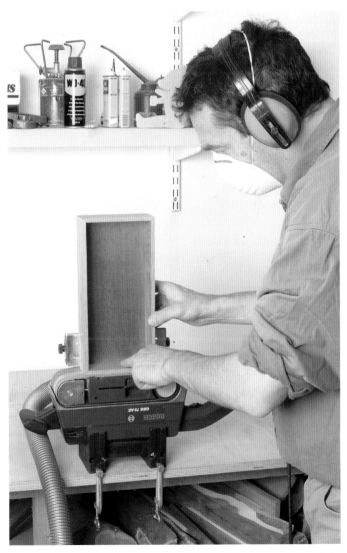

Some belt sanders have a frame and fence for working as a pad sander.

Use a 45° cutter to rout the mitres.

The joint combines rebate and mitre.

space but have plenty of time, there is an argument for buying a workcentre into which power tools may be fitted so that they can either be used hand-held or as machines.

Though some of these work centres are actually very well made – and plenty of woodworkers have startling results with them – I have always found the situation to be a compromise, and I don't like having to waste time changing tools around. I'd rather have fewer dedicated machines and adapt my techniques to suit what I own.

The router table, however, does make a superb substitute for the shaper; indeed, for many home woodworkers it is more than enough. I also use a drill in a drill stand, but only for drum sanding and because I've come to own so many drills. I have a portable belt sander that was supplied with a stand for using it upside down. This has proved very useful for cleaning up joints when a disc sander would mark the wood with telltale curved scratches.

Making a router table

You can buy superb router tables, but they are very simple to make and in the early stages you are well able to experiment with one of your own. Cheap router tables are not hugely accurate, and you may find them more frustrating than one you make yourself. Only by learning what makes a good or bad router table will you come to realize what you need to buy and understand what an invaluable piece it is.

1 The table must be flat. Probably the best material for this is a dense plastic, known commonly as Tufnol. Tufnol is available in a thickness of 13 mm (½ in) or 16 mm (⅝ in), which should be sufficient, though you can reinforce the underside with ribs. Drill the table to suit the holes in the router's base and screw in place.

2 For a fence, you can simply clamp a straightedge to the table. This will do for a while. As your skills grow, you will want a proper fence, which you can adjust easily and finely. These can be bought on their own. The fence must be able to take a changeable wooden lining, which will have to be replaced from time to time.

3 You must be able to fix some sort of extraction behind the fence, using hose or plastic pipe. Otherwise the cutter will get clogged with shavings and won't perform very well.

4 By routing a groove along the table, you can make a mitre guide with which you can push timber across the cutter. This makes for steadier progress.

5 To cope with router cutters of varying diameters, you can cut an access hole where the cutter protrudes. The trick is to have a rebate on the top face of this circular aperture and then make rebated rings that fit inside this hole, level with the table surface.

6 Featherboards work as springs to hold the workpiece against the fence and also as a ratchet to stop the timber from kicking back towards the operator. You can buy these to fit in the mitre-guide groove or to clamp or screw to the table. You can make one yourself by creating a series of angled cuts in a piece of hardwood that has some flexibility.

The featherboard pushes the workpiece against the fence and reduces any risk of kickback.

The mitre guide can be useful for making routed cuts across a board, but make sure that the main fence is at right angles to the mitre fence first.

Accessories for the router table

Remote switch. It is a good idea to buy a remote switch for the router table so you don't have to search for the router's switch when you need to turn it off in a hurry. The router is plugged into the back of the switch instead of directly into the power supply.

Collet extension. Whatever material you use for the router table, you will lose some depth of cut, even if the router's collet protrudes through its base. A solution to this is to buy a collet extension, which fits into the existing collet. Some of these have the added benefit of needing only a single allen key to tighten and loosen the cutter, which makes access under the table far easier.

Router lifter. There are now various gadgets that help you raise the router in the table from above. This makes fine adjustment easier and improves the whole experience.

Miniature brass sash clamps. Few miniature tools are particularly useful, but small brass bar clamps are well worth their low cost. They are ideal for assembling small boxes and drawers.

A collet extension improves the depth of cut by raising the cutter.

With a device for raising the router, you no longer need to fiddle underneath the table to set the depth of cut.

Trade secret

A router for the router table

Though it is a good idea to buy a small- or medium-sized router for hand-held operations, a table-mounted router has other qualities to look out for. Fixed-base routers, for a start, are good for router tables because they incorporate fine height adjustment. Choose a large router, and one that can take 13-mm (½-in) cutters, because the router table enables you to use far bigger cutters than for hand-held operations.

Do consider, however, the method of changing the cutter. Under the router table you will have much more limited access, and fiddling around with two wrenches can be very awkward.

Project **Crockery shelves**

For the kitchen or dining room

This introduction to making drawers uses housed rebate joints rather than dovetails. The sides and shelves of the unit are held together with wedged tenons. The length of the shelves and drawer dividers does not include any excess beyond the through tenons. The excess can be pared and sanded back flush after assembly.

578 mm (22¾ in)

84 mm (7¼ in)

55 mm (2¼ in)

55 mm (2¼ in)

100 mm (4 in)

315 mm (12⅜ in)

990 mm (39 in)

315 mm (12⅜ in)

86 mm (3⅜ in)

100 mm (4 in)

160 mm (6¼ in)

19 x 21 mm (¾ x ⅞ in)

86 mm (3⅜ in)

178 mm (7 in)

10 mm (⅜ in)

175 mm (6⅞ in)

A B C D E F G H

Shopping list

Materials

Drawer knobs

Cutting list

Part	Material	Quantity	Dimensions length, width, thickness
A Side	stained softwood	2	991 x 184 x 19 mm (39 x 7¼ x ¾ in)
B Shelf	stained softwood	4	616 x 184 x 19 mm (24¼ x 7¼ x ¾ in)
C Drawer divider	stained softwood	2	184 x 86 x 19 mm (7¼ x 3⅜ x ¾ in)
D Drawer front	stained softwood	3	178 x 86 x 13 mm (7 x 3⅜ x ½ in)

Part	Material	Quantity	Dimensions length, width, thickness
E Drawer back	stained softwood	3	165 x 76 x 13 mm (6½ x 3 x ½ in)
F Drawer side	stained softwood	6	175 x 86 x 13 mm (6⅞ x 3⅜ x ½ in)
G Drawer bottom	plywood	3	175 x 165 x 6 mm (6⅞ x 6½ x ¼ in)
H Support bearer	stained softwood	1	161 x 22 x 19 mm (24⅛ x ⅞ x ¾ in)

1 Assuming all the components have been surfaced to thickness, start by marking up the mortises on the sides (**A**) and tenons on the shelves (**B**). Make sure the mortises are marked up accurately, the whole way around each part, so that they can be cut from both sides to reduce tearing.

2 Cut out the mortises first from one side and then from the other. Position the piece over the leg of the bench for maximum stability, and place a piece of scrap beneath the mortise to protect the surface. The mortises should be slightly splayed towards the outside so that the wedges can expand the tenons (see page 113).

3 Cut the tenons, with grooves for the wedges. Make sure the tenons protrude from the mortises by at least 3 mm (⅛ in) each.

4 Stop the grooves short of the end of the tenon so that it can't be seen once the unit is assembled.

Do a dry run for the shelves (**B**) and sides (**A**), and mark up the position of the drawer dividers (**C**). This is a bit tricky and has to be carefully measured. You can go for even gaps for drawers or have the outer drawers narrower or wider than the central one.

Lessons learned

- A router table is really useful and can transform a woodworker's life, but it must be set up accurately to work well. Any ridges or bumps will be amplified when they knock the timber off its course.

- Practice makes perfect when it comes to setting up and cutting the housed rebate joint, and there is a great advantage in developing a system that works on the same thickness of timber each time.

- Wedged joints are particularly attractive when done well.

5 Cut the mortises in the shelves for the drawer dividers and then cut the corresponding tenons. Cut the notches in the back of the sides for the bearer (**H**). There are similar notches in the drawer dividers for the bearer.

Rout the groove along the middle shelves for the plates to rest in and then cut the curves on the front edge of the sides. It's best to leave this as late as possible, since you will have found it easier to mark up the mortises before the curves are cut. Make a template of the curves for quicker and more accurate marking.

Clean up the sides, shelves and drawer dividers. You might want to finish the shelves and inside faces of the sides at this point.

Cut out the top, or just clean up the edges if you've bought it ready-cut. You can bevel the edges with abrasive, or a plane if you own one already (see Lesson 6, page 64).

7 Cut yourself a number of small wedges to fit tightly in the tenon grooves. Do a dry run of the assembly, and then assemble using adhesive, holding the unit in place with sash clamps. Make sure you remember to check the diagonals. Before the glue goes off, tap the wedges home, using some glue on each.

When the glue has set, pare back the tenons with a chisel and block plane; then clean up with abrasive. A flush-cutting saw speeds up the paring back of the tenons.

Measure the gaps for the drawers and start cutting out the components to suit. I've heard of woodworkers who make the drawers first and then make the shelves or surround to fit them.

Cut the housings in the drawer sides (**F**) and then the rebate in the drawer front (**D**) and the rebate on the drawer back (**E**), which has to fit in the housing. Groove the sides for the plywood base, with the groove the same depth as the housing. This way, the ply base is the same width as the drawer back.

Clean up, sand and finish the insides of the drawers; then glue up and tidy up the outside.

Finish the whole piece, and attach the knobs.

6 Foaming polyurethane adhesives work well for pre-finishing because the hardened glue just snaps off, but make sure you experiment with it first.

TIP: Finishing before assembly. By cleaning up and applying a finish before assembly, you can save yourself a huge amount of time trying to clean up awkward spots. However, there are risks. If you go down this route, you must be able to remove any signs of adhesive without it smudging the surface. And it is difficult to use this technique when the piece is being stained, because the stain will be vulnerable and tricky to match if you make a mistake.

Lesson 7
Timber control

Getting started

Milling timber is my favourite part of woodworking. I love taking rough boards, finding the best cuts, and planing them to reveal the beauty of the grain, figure and colour.

So much depends on this stage of preparation. Unless the edges and faces are planed straight and square, you will face interminable challenges in attempting to join boards and accurately mark and cut joints.

There are many machines available for woodworking, including surface planers (for establishing planed surfaces on a face and an adjacent edge), thicknessers (for reducing sections to the desired thickness or width) and dual-purpose planer-thicknessers (designed to plane all sides and edges square to each other). I started with the smallest combination of planer-thicknessers. Now I own a surface planer and a site thicknesser, so I can leave them set however I want and don't have to move the tables on a planer-thicknesser.

Using both the surface planer and thicknesser is fairly simple. The important technique, when jointing, is to feel for the face, keeping the board flat on the tables. Make sure it moves steadily and you aren't fighting against the grain. The rest should be simple.

Cleaning rough-sawn wood

It's a good idea to clean the surface of rough-sawn boards before planing, since there is bound to be some dirt embedded in the grain. Such particles, however small, are abrasive and will dull the edges of your surface planer and thicknesser. Using a wire brush also

Brush rough boards with a steel or brass brush to remove any dirt that might blunt tool edges.

helps to reveal the grain pattern to help you decide how to cut up the board to avoid defects. This is a good opportunity to scrutinize the board for any nails, screws or stones that will wreck your tools, though this is very rarely a problem with timber bought from a commercial source.

Converting square section into a panel

The advantage of owning a band saw, surface planer and thicknesser is that you have the control to convert boards however you like. For instance, a piece of 64-mm (2½-in) square-section ash can be made into a panel more than 150 mm (6 in) wide (see Assembling a panel, page 85).

● Study the grain to see which way you want to cut the piece into thinner boards.

A square-section board can be divided into three to produce a narrow panel.

Lesson planner

Key techniques	Key tools and materials
● Cleaning rough-sawn wood ● Converting square section into a panel	● Using a surface planer ● Using a thicknesser ● Fitting extraction ● Selecting timber

• Set the fence on the band saw to cut the board equally. A quick way to check the setting is to make a trial cut with each side against the fence and then measure or just survey by eye the width of the cuts. It is a useful check because band-saw fences aren't always that accurate, and it can be tricky to adjust them just with a rule.

• Make the cuts using the band saw, using a push stick at the end of the cut and keeping the workpiece held against the fence with your spare hand. Make sure the blade guard is set only just above the workpiece.

Set up the band saw to produce even boards to be glued up as a panel.

Use a push stick to keep the board moving through the band saw, but notice how the forward hand is holding the workpiece against the fence.

Once you've cut the pieces for a panel, mark them with a triangle to show how they fit together.

• Reassemble the boards as they were originally (as defined by the triangular mark. Then open up and see how the grain runs before assembling into a panel, as we will in Lesson 8 (see page 166).

Using a surface planer safely

Once the surface planer has been set up accurately, it is a joy to use it to plane one face and at least one edge. (Once you have a satisfactory face and edge, you can thickness the board with a thicknesser.) Because you pass the wood over the cutter with your hands when using the surface planer, there are some important rules for working safely.

1 Always make sure the guard is positioned correctly. For planing the face, this means the guard covers the whole table, above the workpiece. When working on an edge, use the guard to cover the exposed cutter block, and butt it against the workpiece. Some guards have give in them, so that they work like featherboards, holding the timber against the fence (see page 150).

2 If you are not very confident about having your hands so close to the cutter block, use a push block. Use one of these if there is any chance of your fingers slipping, perhaps because they are cold or if the timber isn't running smoothly along the table. Wear earplugs, and possibly safety glasses and a dust mask, though I favour fitting effective dust extraction, which removes any dust and shavings.

Setting up a surface planer

To work properly, the surface planer must be set up accurately, but before you do anything, make sure it is disconnected from the power supply.

1 Check that the outfeed table is flat and level. There should be a 3-mm (⅛-in) gap between the cutter block and the edge of the out-feed table, which you can test with feeler gauges. Use a straightedge to check that the out-feed table is parallel to the in-feed table.

2 Most cutter blocks have simple mechanisms for fitting new blades. You can check if the blade is correctly aligned by placing a piece of timber over the cutter block. As you turn the block by hand towards you, the board should move back by 3 mm (⅛ in). Do this across the board to check that the travel is the same.

3 Routinely check that the fence is square every time you start a planing operation.

4 Spray the tables with a dry lubricant to make planing easier.

Planing the first face

Check the board for defects and metal intrusions, and then decide which face to plane on the surface planer. Traditionally, this should be the best face, since it is the one from which everything else works. (However, thicknessers are so good these days that by the end of the planing operation, both faces could be used.) You are better off starting with the board that is concave along its length or across its width. If the board is bowed badly along its length, you may need to cut it into shorter pieces, since you may be limited in how much usable timber can be processed from the board. Bowing along the length is more difficult to deal with than cupping across the width.

1 Keeping your feet still, push the board forwards with your front hand, feeling for the contact between the board and the table of the surface planer. Once a flat area has been planed from the board, it is important to keep this in contact with the table. If the board starts to wobble, you will find it very difficult to flatten the surface.

2 As your front arm is extended, start pushing more with your rear hand, or with a push block, so that you can bring your front hand back again. It is vital to keep the timber moving or you'll end up with marks, but keep the progress steady. If you push too fast, there is a risk that the cutter block will make ripple marks across the face of the board.

3 Keep going, taking great care to keep your rear hand away from the end of the board as you complete the cut.

4 Check which areas have been planed and continue until the face is entirely flat. After the first pass, check for evidence of chipping, which might indicate that you are feeding the board the wrong way. If you find chips, raise the in-feed table for a finer cut and try planing the other way.

Planing an edge

With one face planed, you can use this against the fence to plane an edge square and true. It is very important to start with the edge that has high points at the ends, though you have to be a bit careful that the first cut of the corner of heavily bowed boards doesn't drop into the gap behind the cutter. Press the board firmly against the fence, checking along the rear edge of the fence that the timber is flat on the fence. Shuffle long boards along with your hands, just as you did for the face.

Using a thicknesser

A thicknesser is easier to use than a surface planer, in that you feed the work in one side and it comes out the other. There aren't many things that can go wrong, and problems are usually associated with trying to remove too much stock in one pass. A common fault is that the timber is torn or chipped, and you may notice pale tear marks, a bit like snakeskin. Adjust the thicknesser to make a finer cut, and these will likely disappear.

It is important to machine components of the same desired thickness at the same time and to the same setting – you may not be able to replicate the setting again. Lay out the parts to be planed, and start with the thickest, gradually working your way down until you are able to thickness all the components on the same setting. Ideally, the final pass should be as shallow as possible for the best finish. A dial gauge is very useful for testing the thickness of the boards as you are working.

Trade secret

Planing thin boards

Whether you choose to use the thicknesser to plane the second edge to width depends on the dimensions of the board. If the board is very thin and quite wide, there is a good chance it will topple over inside the thicknesser. You can rectify this a little by inserting more than one piece at the same time, side by side.

Tools

Buying a surface planer

You can buy surface planers to suit any budget and need. The largest have power feeds and can machine wide boards. For general woodworking, a table and cutter block 305 mm (12 in) wide should be sufficient. Check that the fence is sturdy and that the guard is easy to move into position and effective. Also study the position of the switch and see how quickly you can turn it on and off.

Most surface planers have aluminum tables, either cast and ground or extruded. As a rule, cast tables are the best, since they tend to be heavier and more robust, and cast-iron tables are even better. If you imagine that you will be woodworking for years to come, it's worth investing wisely in a surface planer, because there will be no reason to change it. The small band saw you buy initially will always come in useful for detailed work if you ever replace it with a larger one, but you will never need a standby surface planer, so choose one carefully.

Buying a thicknesser

I use a portable thicknesser; it has a permanent home but can be used on site. When you are using straight, clean boards, you can often get away with using a thicknesser only, however suspiciously you'll be viewed by purists.

A thicknesser has a shorter bed or table than a surface planer, with rollers pressing the timber down while the cutters plane the board. It relies purely upon the integrity of the other face for flatness, though if you only have a thicknesser and no surface planer, wedges can be used to hold a warped or bowed board on a flat board for planing.

These portable thicknessers are ideal for home woodworkers, though they do tend to be very noisy. They can thickness boards up to 254–305 mm (10–12 in) wide. The depth of cut isn't much of an issue. As with the surface planer, check out the accessibility of the switch and the ease with which you can raise and lower the height. Also check the visibility of the depth measure, though I hardly ever use mine, relying instead on a Vernier or dial gauge for testing thickness.

What value the planer-thicknesser?

If you have only a small workshop or a limited budget, there is an advantage in buying a combination machine, a planer-thicknesser. They are cheaper than buying separate machines, and take up less space, but can be time-consuming to use if you have to move one of tables of the surface planer to access the thicknessing component. I prefer having dedicated machines.

Fitting extraction

Both surface planers and thicknessers produce huge quantities of chippings and dust, which are extremely useful if you have a wood-burning stove designed to burn shavings. They must be collected by some form of extraction. Ask your supplier for an extractor designed to cope with your machines, with the important criteria being the capacity of the collector, the volume of shavings it can collect, and the dust-filtration capability. Some systems are designed for storing outside the workshop because the fine filtration isn't low enough.

There are many ducting products on the market for attaching all machines to some form of extraction. I have my surface planer and thicknesser attached to a chip

It is vital that you fit extraction to a thicknesser or surface planer, since both produce mountains of shavings and dust.

extractor that collects the shavings in a bag. On each machine I have a blast gate that can be closed, so the suction is always concentrated on the machine you happen to be using. For saws and other tools that produce more dust than shavings, I use a portable dust collector, which has a finer filter by a smaller collection bucket and only a 51-mm (2-in) hose. You can extend the use of such a small machine by connecting the hose to a plastic dustbin along the route, with another hose leading from the bin to your machines. The dustbin can be made into a cyclone so that the heaviest dust and chippings fall to the bottom and only the finer particles make it to the small, but powerful, vacuum extractor.

Materials

All about wood – studying end grain

You can tell a lot about wood from the end grain; in fact, botanists often rely upon it to identify species. Take the two boards pictured right as an example. The one on the left is ash, with clearly defined growth rings. The contrast is significant between the pale early wood that helps nourish a tree in spring and early summer, and the much darker, far denser late wood that is designed to support the tree and grows later in the summer.

The cherry, on the right, has a much more even series of growth rings, and it's no surprise that it is much easier to use because the texture is so much more uniform through the timber.

Selecting timber

Though many boards are supplied with perfectly straight grain and no defects, others need more careful study to establish exactly what can be used to avoid any sapwood or defects.

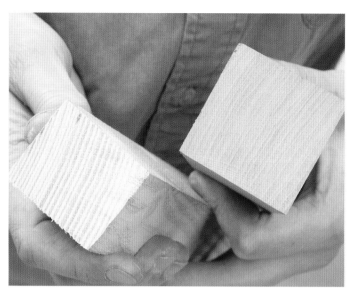

Look at the end grain. Ash (on the left) has a coarse texture, with open pores and distinct lines of grain. Cherry is much more uniform.

1 There is a band of sapwood running down the edge of this sapwood offcut, with the shaded area showing what cannot be used.

2 The sapwood on oak often contrasts dramatically with the heartwood, and though it can be used for effect, it is much softer than the heartwood, so is vulnerable to worm attack.

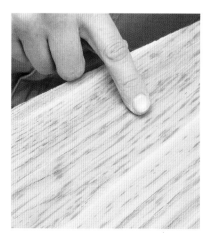

3 On this brown oak board, the grain gently curves diagonally across the face. You will probably want to follow the line of the grain rather than the existing edges when you come to use this board. This will raise the wastage rate; ideally, I should have rejected this board in the first place. Curved grain, however, can be useful for making curved components, like the legs of chairs and tables. The speckles and pale lines on the board are likely to be viewed as a defect by one woodworker and as a feature by the next!

4 Look out for any splits or cracks when working out what to use. Mark and then cut along the line of a check or crack, remembering that there are likely to be more defects in the area, some of which might be hidden.

5 There's nothing much you can do about this major knot in a yew board. Smaller knots, like the one in the top right corner, can be accommodated, but large defects will weaken the piece and make finishing very difficult. Notice the lovely flowing lines of grain in this piece, which make yew one of the most beautiful species but also one of the most difficult to use. Surprisingly, it is a softwood, which is in fact extremely hard and has a contrasting (but soft) sapwood that you can see along the bottom. Wastage can be very high with yew, and it is not a timber for beginners, though it is superb to turn.

Project **Picnic table**

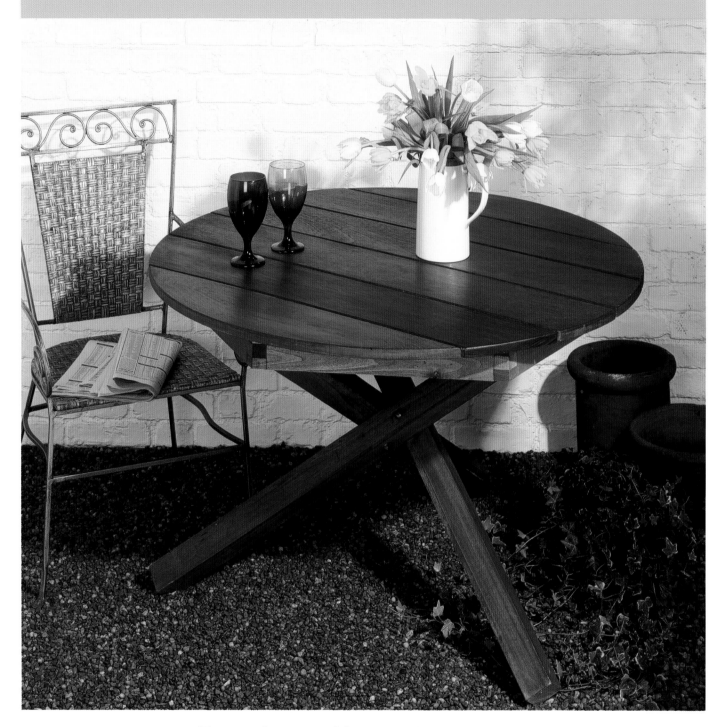

For eating outside

This unusual project tests the woodworker's ability to cut angles and combines the mitre with the tenon joints. You can use either a durable hardwood or treated softwood to make this project. We are assuming that you will make all the components from the same material, though that is not essential.

4 mm (⅛ in)

175 mm (6⅞ in)

70 mm (2¾ in)

785 mm (31 in)

528 mm (20¾ in)

60 mm (2⅜ in)

60 mm (2⅜ in)

60 mm (2⅜ in)

1160 mm (45⅝ in)

Cutting list

Part	Material	Quantity	Dimensions length, width, thickness
A Under-frame rail	Hardwood or softwood	6	527 x 70 x 25 mm (20¾ x 2¾ x 1 in)
B Bearer	Hardwood or softwood	1	787 x 57 x 19 mm (31 x 2¼ x ¾ in)
C Leg	Hardwood or softwood	3	1159 x 60 x 60mm (45⅝ x 2⅜ x 2⅜ in)
D Top	Hardwood or softwood	2	1067 x 175 x 19 mm (42 x 6⅞ x ¾ in)
E Top	Hardwood or softwood	2	1003 x 175 x 19 mm (39½ x 6⅞ x ¾ in)
F Top	Hardwood or softwood	2	787 x 175 x 19 mm (31 x 6⅞ x ¾ in)

Shopping list

Tools and materials	Extra tools for the job
Coach bolts: 3 x 90 mm (3½ in), with washers and nuts **Zinc flat-headed screws** to fix the under-frame to the top: 30 x 60 mm (2⅜ in) no. 8 **Zinc flat-headed screws** to fix the bearer to the top: 10 x 35 mm (1⅜ in) no. 8	**Band clamp**

1 Plane all the components to the correct sections, leaving a few inches of excess on the ends of them all. And make sure you make a couple of extras in case of mistakes.

2 Cut the six under-frame rails (**A**), cutting the 30° angles on the ends. Mark up the depth of the finger joint around each workpiece, with a finger on one end and socket on the other. You can set the marking gauge to the same setting for them all (see Using a marking gauge, page 44).

3 Cut the shoulders with a tenon saw and remove the waste with a coping saw. Tidy up the seat of the joint with a chisel.

Dry-assemble each joint, and then, when you are ready, the whole frame. Number each joint so that you can reproduce the layout with glue. The band clamp is ideal for this construction. Glue the frame and leave to set.

4 Cut the tabletop parts (**D**, **E**, and **F**) roughly to length and arrange. Drill the bearer, and screw it to the underside of the top, with 3-mm (⅛-in) spaces between the top boards.

With the tabletop upside down, fix a routing trammel bar to the centre of the bearer and set the radius for 533 mm (21 in). Using a straight cutter in the router, work anticlockwise to smoothly cut the edge of the top into a circle, taking great care where you jump from one board to the next.

5 Clean up and drill the under-frame; then fix it to the top.

6 Turn the top the right way up and clean the edge of the boards with a sanding block (though it should be pretty smooth if your routing was successful). Now fit a bearing-guided bevelling cutter in the router, and run the bearing against the existing edge to chamfer the top.

7 With the top finished, you can cut the legs to length and drill them for the fixing bolts, as shown in the picture. Sand and finish; then assemble with the bolts and drop the top over the leg assembly.

Lessons learned

- Unless the surface planer is well set up, you won't be able to plane boards effectively and subsequent operations will be undermined by inaccuracy.

- Dust and chippings from machines must be extracted.

- The router is amazingly versatile. The trammel bar, which you can make yourself, is very useful for shaping circles. In this case the trammel will have to be offset from the router because the centre point on the bearer will be higher than the router's base.

Lesson 8
All about cabinet-making

Getting started

Around the home you'll find a plethora of cabinet-making projects, from kitchen cabinets to bookshelves, wardrobes and storage solutions. Sheet materials are ideally suited to cabinet-making, and are easy to work, but great cabinet projects can be made from solid timber, just as the Plate Rack project is in this lesson.

Though modern flat-pack furniture relies on fittings to hold the components together, the housing joint is the traditional joint for joining wide boards together. It inhibits racking movements, especially with shoulders, and also increases the gluing area.

Once again, the router is the ideal tool for cutting both the male and female components of the housing, though the tenon is normally best cut on a router table.

Designing cabinet-making projects

This lesson's project is a typical construction for a book-shelf or rack of some form, as were the Crockery Shelves a couple of lessons ago. With the sides protruding above the shelves, both at top and bottom, it is easy to hide any joints and choose joints that have shoulders to give the piece more rigidity (see How to choose a joint, page 42).

A simple way to make a cabinet with inherent strength is to insert a plywood panel into either grooves or a rebate in the back. This may reduce the depth of the cabinet, but the plywood reinforces the construction. A solid wood back does a similar job, but you have to allow for wood movement and won't be able to pin and glue the panel in place as securely.

Lesson planner

Key techniques	Key tools and materials
• Designing cabinet-making projects • Cutting a stopped housing	• Drum sander • Japanese saws • Buying sustainable timber • Choosing which timber to use

Traditionally, solid wood back panels of cabinets would be a series of vertical boards, probably joined by tongue-and-groove joints without using glue. Each board would be pinned into a rebate, top and bottom, with a single nail, and the tongues would be able to expand and contract within the grooves to allow for changes in moisture levels. Ironically, these days furniture often dries out more during the winter when the central heating is on (see Moisture meters, page 238).

For this reason, anyone making cabinets from solid wood must know the moisture content of the timber in question, especially when it is being used for panels. You can buy a moisture meter to measure this, and for a centrally heated home you need the moisture content to be right down to about nine per cent for it to be stable. If the wood expands or contracts too much, it can easily crack or break joints.

People often want adjustable shelves or dividers within cabinets, and fortunately, there are many shelving systems you can find to make this a simple task. But rigid shelves, jointed into the sides, make cabinets more secure, so it is important to find a balance.

When the joints between sides and shelves are at corners, you will have to consider other joints. The rebate is a simple choice but not very strong. Butt joints can be reinforced with biscuits or dowels, or even more simply with screws. The latter option isn't very attractive, since screws don't hold well in end grain, though you can use pocket screws in the long grain. The dovetail, which some people might consider a furniture-maker's joint, is the strongest of all, and can either be left visible or hidden by some form of cornice or moulding.

Cutting a stopped housing

The housing joint is a great joint to cut for making cabinets, especially when the joints aren't right on the corners so that you can incorporate shoulders to stop movement. The best tool to cut stopped housings is the plunge router, because you can easily raise and lower the cutter at the start or end of the cut.

1 Start by marking up the joint, but instead of marking it out in detail, all you need to do is mark a line, or even

Run the router against a straightedge to cut the housing.

If you use a side fence for cutting the housing, check the offset between the cutter and the fence.

Square up the corners of a routed housing with a chisel.

To hide the joint at the front, cut away a notch from the tenon.

only two points, where the guide will be clamped, taking into account the offset between the cutter and the side of the router's base (see Routing across the grain, page 137).

2 Clamp a guide to the workpiece, and make a mark where you want the cut to end. To ensure that the gap between the housings is exactly the same on both pieces (assuming you are making a two-sided cabinet), you can make a template that clamps to the workpiece. The template is as long as the distance between the housings, minus the offset between the cutter and router base, twice. Rather than the baseplate, you could use a guide bush against the template, but there would still be an offset to consider.

3 Doing it this way means you have to rout from the back to front of the side for one housing, and from the front to the back on the other, because you should always rout from right to left, against the rotation of the cutter. This is why the plunge router is so useful. On the first cut you can start with the cutter extended, but at the end of the cut, when you reach the stop mark, you have to raise the cutter. This is particularly easy using a plunge router,

without having to stop the motor. For the other housing you have to plunge the spinning cutter into the timber at the beginning of the cut.

4 Set the depth of the cutter either by using a depth gauge you make yourself, or a bought version. There are plenty on the market. A simple way to set the depth is to have a few pieces of plywood of set thickness and use them to judge the depth of cut.

5 Having cut the housing, you need to tidy up the rounded end with a chisel, though of course this will be hidden within the joint.

6 For a wide housing, I would use either a hand-held router with the side fence, or the router table with the workpiece running against the fence. When the pieces are heavy, you are probably better off holding the timber and moving the router.

7 Set the cutter to cut both sides of the tenon, testing it first on a suitable piece of scrap. Rout the tenon.

8 Mark off the notch for the front of the stopped housing, cut down the tenon, and chisel away the waste. Clean up with a chisel.

Tools

Drum sander

The best way to clean up curved cuts is with a drum sander. You can buy these as machines, and some of the more sophisticated bobbin sanders (as they are often known) oscillate up and down to prevent scratching. Alternatively, you can make your own by buying a drum-sanding device for a drill.

One design of drum sander is pneumatic, with an abrasive sleeve held in place by the pressure of a blow-up inner tube. These work well, especially if you aim to sand carvings and actually want the drum to have some give. There are similar devices that have a foam core and likewise have some give, which woodturners like. However, my favourite for furniture-making are the solid drums, around which you wrap a length of sandpaper, held in place by a cam. The fact that you can use your own abrasive and don't have to buy expensive sleeves is a bonus, but I prefer them for their more substantial feel.

The challenge of making a drum-sanding machine is dealing with the dust. The solution is to build a cowl around the drum, which catches the dust on the left (sucked away by a vacuum extractor) but is open on the

The drum sander is ideal for shaping curves.

right for access. You will need to raise the workpiece a little at the front of the drum so that you don't run against the bottom edge of the drum. This is a very simple device to make, and it will be useful time and again.

Japanese saws

Some of the finest woodworking tools are made in Japan, and probably the most popular items are their saws. The saw cuts on the push and pull strokes and has no kerf. They cut superbly, but my only concern is that they aren't always as rigid as a tenon saw, and I've found that they can have a tendency to wander. However, I love the feel of them, especially the long handle.

Japanese saws cut on both the push and pull strokes.

Materials

All about wood – sustainability

As woodworkers, we have an important role in promoting the future of the world's forests and trees. We know the value of timber and understand the remarkable nature of wood as a beautiful building material that is strong, tactile, and attractive, and is also renewable. Unless trees are given a value, they will be felled to convert land to other uses, many of which are unsuitable and which will not give us the long-term benefits of forests.

In temperate parts of the world, where many of us live, there are few problems with the sustainability of our trees, though some old-growth forests are still being destroyed at a faster rate than they can recover. In tropical forests,

Even if you make a suction hood to remove the dust from a drum sander, make sure you wear a dust mask and ear defenders.

however, the balance is far more fragile – without the trees, any fertility is soon washed away and regeneration becomes increasingly difficult. We must encourage the use of timber from these parts of the world, but without risking the extinction of some of the rarer or more over-exploited species. That is why the Forest Stewardship Council and other organizations have introduced certification schemes to label timber that is managed and harvested sustainably.

The FSC scheme has been very successful, raising awareness and enabling craftspeople to market their products as having only a beneficial impact on the environment. The only frustration is that the owners of temperate forests have the money to invest in management plans, but certification is a more complicated process in tropical forests. So you can buy all the most famous temperate species with an FSC logo, but very few tropical species. So to make the system really work, we need to experiment with some of the lesser-known tropical species that are plentiful and can be certified as coming from a sustainable source. The *peroba rosa*, which I used to make this lesson's project, is just such a species. Search the Internet for FSC suppliers and you will soon discover sources of such timber.

Choosing which timber to use

Up to now we have only looked at a limited range of hardwoods; most of the projects are made from softwood, which is easy to source and, for a beginner, easy to work. Ironically, as one's skills develop, so the softness becomes less of an issue and more experienced woodworkers find hardwoods with a consistent, even texture (like cherry, walnut and birch) easier to use because the results are more exact and you can work more accurately.

Some softwoods are always going to be useful. Redwood, for instance, is naturally durable, so it can be used for outdoor furniture, while most softwoods can be treated with preservatives more efficiently than hardwoods, which tend not to be porous enough. Softwoods are usually cheaper than hardwoods, so white pine is attractive for interior trim and workshop fittings, while aromatic cedar is favoured for the linings of chests and drawers because its smell and oils repel insects.

The most common North American hardwoods are red and white oak (of which the latter has a more intriguing grain pattern), cherry, hard maple, elm and walnut. These are all counted as quality hardwoods for the making of good furniture or cabinets. For more utilitarian purposes, you might consider birch, hickory, aspen or poplar, which are all pale in colour, relatively inexpensive, and easy to use. These can also be used inside frameworks where they won't be seen.

For a more exotic project there are imported hardwoods from the tropics and other temperate regions. European timbers include oak, walnut, elm and yew – all of which tend to have wilder grain and more defects than the American versions. Tropical hardwoods available from specialist importers of exotic timber include wenge, padauk, zebrawood, purpleheart, various rosewood species, ebony and mahogany. However, some caution has to be paid to these species, and we recommend that you study the lists of threatened species produced by CITES (Convention on International Trades in Endangered Species) and the IUCN (International Union for the Conservation of Nature) to check their status.

Exotic timbers can be bought by mail order. Test the service with a small order first, but there's no reason why you shouldn't use such a method if it works for you. Personally, I prefer to visit a local timberyard to have a good look through their stock, searching for gems.

Timber grades

Softwood and hardwood can be graded to give the purchaser an indication of what they should expect by way of defects as a percentage of a board. The best approach is to check the boards yourself, especially if you think you can make do with a lesser grade that won't cost as much, and to see whether you can live with any defects.

Trade secret

Buying softwoods and hardwoods

Softwoods are sold in increments of 300 mm, with a simple price given for each type or dimension of board. (See Standard sizes of softwood, page 17.)

Contrastingly, hardwood tends to be sold by volume, by the cubic foot. The price is determined by the market, of course, but also by the rarity of the species and sometimes by the width and thickness of the boards.

Project **Plate rack**

For the dishes

Made to take a set of small and large plates, this plate rack isn't designed for wet dishes, but it is flexible enough to suit any chinaware. It was originally made from a lesser-known species of timber, *peroba rosa*, that had been certified by FSC as being from a sustainable source.

603 mm
(23¾ in.)

B

584 mm 23 in. (23 in.)

A

A

C

756 mm
(29 ¾ in.)

A

B

197 mm (7 ¾ in.)

Cutting list

Part	Material	Quantity	Dimensions length, width, thickness
A Side	peroba rose	2	756 x 200 x 22 mm (29¾ x 7⅞ x ⅞ in)
B Shelf	peroba rose	2	603 x 197 x 22 mm (23¾ x 7¾ x ⅞ in)
C Bar	peroba rose	6	584 x 22 x 19 mm (23 x ⅞ x ¾ in)
D Dowel	softwood	26	587 x 13 x 13 mm (23⅛ x ½ x ½ in)

1 Plane all the components. Mark up the stopped housings in the sides (**A**) for the two shelves. The width of the housing depends on what cutters you have for the router, but 10 mm (⅜ in) should be about right.

Rout the housings through at the back of the sides, but stop about 12 mm (½ in) short of the front edge. Square the front of the housing with a chisel.

Cut the shelves (**B**) exactly to length; then rout the tenon on each end. This can be done on a router table against the fence, though each workpiece is quite heavy for this. The shelf is wide enough for you to use the side fence on a router to cut the tenons.

Cut away the notch at the front of the shelves, then tidy up with a chisel.

Make a drawing of the curves for the top and bottom of the sides. The curves are identical; just reversed. I drew them freehand on a piece of plywood and then cut that out and cleaned it up with a sanding block.

2 To cut the curves on the sides, use the template to draw the curves and then cut with a jigsaw or on a band saw. The finish from the saw is likely to be fairly rough, so smooth the curve with a drum sander in a drill, held upright in a drill stand (see Drill press, page 185).

It's a good idea to mark the curve again with the template after cutting, so as to have something to follow with the drum sander; otherwise you won't know how the shape should be. What you can do is draw a second line 1.6 mm (⅟₁₆ in) behind the first line, and make sure that you keep your finished line a consistent distance from that.

Test-fit the sides and shelf. If it's all fine, sand the inside faces, plus the top and bottom of the shelves, and apply a finish. Glue up using sash clamps, and check the diagonals.

Lessons learned

- Housing joints can be difficult to fit. The margin between it being too tight, just right or loose is very fine. Make sure you test the fit on an offcut first.

- Drum sanders create a huge amount of dust, which must be removed at source by extraction.

- Cabinet-making depends on accuracy, both for strength and beauty, so make sure that all the parts are cut to length correctly.

3 Drill the holes in the bars at 41-mm (1⅝-in) intervals. If you have a drill press, this can be done with a special jig to save time (see **TIP**, right).

4 Drill the first hole in the bar and then position-drop that over the dowel stop on your jig. Clamp the jig to the drill press and you can drill hole after hole without having to do any measuring and marking. You can even turn the bar over to drill from both sides to reduce the risk of tearing, especially for the middle bar.
TIP: Drilling jig. With a drill press (see Drill press, page 185) you can drill the holes in the bars without having to do any marking out. Simply fix a fence to a piece of scrap plywood that can be clamped to the table of the drill press. Then drill a 13-mm (½-in) hole 11mm (⁷⁄₁₆ in) from the fence, and tap a short length of 13-mm (½-in) dowel into it.

5 Cut the dowel rod for the racking to length – the mitre saw is probably as good as anything for this, being accurate and neat.
   Dry-assemble and test the fit of the sides and shelf. If it's all fine, sand the inside faces, plus the top and bottom of the shelves, and apply a finish. Glue up using sash clamps, and check the diagonals.

6 Drill through the bars a few times along the inside faces so that you can screw the bars to the dowel. I screwed the bars to the shelves for ease, but to avoid unsightly screw holes or bungs, you could glue them in place.
   Fix the rear set of bars and dowels in place. Use the bars as bearers to fix the plate rack to the wall. Fix the front set in place.

Becoming Self-Sufficient

What you will find in this section

What to expect

Tools

Balancing a reliance upon jigs or workshop devices with the development of one's own ability to create aids to improve efficiency is one of the tricks of effective woodworking. During the final lesson we will look at how machines can improve your work and how jigs can help you repeat operations accurately, but we will also discuss how to make your own systems.

Materials

Learning how to machine your own timber is a key skill, which frees you from depending on the timberyard and means that you can plane and thickness boards to whatever dimensions you require. It is also essential to discover which finishes suit your work best, and to have the ability to use specialist veneers and other skills to decorate your work.

The layout of your workshop must be carefully thought out in order to be able to find tools with ease and keep them in good condition (see page 196).

Oil finishes are simple to apply and give a professional result (see page 187).

There are some brilliant jigs for helping you to lay out projects (see page 237).

A quick option for veneering is to use contact adhesive (see page 239).

Some of the latest jigs enable you to cut strong and accurate joints quickly (see page 273).

With a wider knowledge of adhesives woodworkers can make their joints stronger and longer lasting (see page 261).

Techniques

We have looked at the jointing of wood, largely for strength; during this section we will study how to ensure that those joints are accurate and that the projects are assembled tidily. This is what distinguishes a well-made piece from a brilliantly made item. It is perhaps this part of woodworking that takes the longest to master, as we endeavour to find better ways to improve our skills.

Always make a test fit of any project before using glue (see page 182).

The mortiser speeds up jointing and guarantees accuracy once you've learned how to make the most of your kit (see page 194).

Neat touches, like the lining of a box, can make all the difference (see page 211).

Projects

During this section you will learn how to make panelled doors, a chair, two tables, drawers and much more. Here the vital techniques are put into practice.

Wine rack **p188**

Bookcase 2 **p240**

Sideboard 1 **p202**

Kitchen chair **p252**

Sideboard 2 **p214**

Dining table **p262**

Bookcase 1 **p226**

Shaker cabinet **p276**

Lesson 1
Quicker mortising

Getting started

For many years I made do without a mortiser, relying instead on hand tools, a drill press and my router. Then a friend bought an industrial mortising machine, and passed his hollow chisel mortiser on to me. It changed my life, and I'm beginning to see why he then upgraded, for mortising is all about accuracy, speed and power. With a good mortiser you can cut beautiful mortises to a hair's breadth of accuracy and without the dust and whine of a router.

A mortiser takes skill and time to set up, but anyone who has reached this level will find it easy. It is quiet, businesslike and accurate, and when it comes to assembling a project, nothing matters quite as much as the success of the joint-cutting. Any discrepancies in the joints will be amplified the moment glue is applied and you start clamping up, which is why a test fit with clamps is so important.

When you have as many components as are used in this lesson's project, the Wine Rack, you will soon discover the value of having tested the assembly first.

Designing projects

Creating a design is something of a jigsaw puzzle, with so many pieces coming together to form the complete picture. The woodworker has to consider function, space, shape, colour and ornamentation, not to mention materials, techniques and availability of tools. Normally, though, one or two factors dominate, whether it's the inspiration of a detail you've noticed and want to reproduce, or a specific function that has to be satisfied.

To take this lesson's project as an example, the design of a wine rack is likely to be influenced by the shape of the bottles. Unless you devise a particularly ingenious design, the basic construction will probably replicate the many wine racks that have gone before. So you have to look for other details to add your mark. In this case, it's both the use of metal for the vertical dividers, and the shaping of the uprights, which go some way towards diminishing the standard geometry of a wine rack. The choice of wood is relatively unimportant in this case, though the straightness of the grain in the uprights works well with the curved shape.

Space and style

Obviously you have to consider the space into which a piece fits and take into account the colours, style and size of other fittings and furniture. It's pointless making a table too big for a room and, equally, the table must be able to accommodate the number of chairs you intend to use.

Everyone has his or her own style. Consider the pieces you really like, and look for influences in them that will determine how you might go about designing projects. Look for the shapes, the details, the curves and the proportions. Don't be overwhelmed by dimensions – let your eye determine the proportions of the pieces you design. Some people need to draw them out in detail on graph paper, while others prefer a quick sketch to give them an overall feel, and then they add some detail to confirm the construction of the joints.

There are any number of ways to add ornamentation to a project. The router has become the ubiquitous tool for shaping edges with profiles, but beware the use of predetermined mouldings that will make your projects look like everyone else's. There is a great temptation to pull out a router to add decoration to an edge when it would be more interesting to shape the components, though this usually requires more planning and thought. It all comes with experience and practice. Make a note of what works and what fails, and try to learn from your mistakes as well as from the mistakes and successes of other woodworkers.

Lesson planner

Key techniques	Key tools and materials
• Using a mortiser • Marking up with a rod • Advanced clamping • Routing around a board	• Drill press • Buying a mortiser • Reclaimed wood • Oil finishes

Consult high-quality books on designing furniture and go out and visit exhibitions. Another approach is to restore old pieces. Through my family's furniture-repair business I've seen many failed joints and others that just won't come apart. And you will pick up lines and shapes that look superb, and others that are clumsy.

Using a mortiser

The router may be a great leap forward when it comes to shaping wood, but the mortiser is perhaps one of the most useful tools for quickly producing accurate joints. It is also one of the easiest of woodworking machines to set up and use, and takes away all the pain of cutting mortises by hand. Unlike some machines, the mortiser derives its efficiency through brute force rather than the ability to repeat an operation time after time. In other situations, you can set up a device or jig to produce the same joint or shape with very little input from the woodworker. The mortiser offers a nice balance of user skill and machine power.

The accuracy of the mortiser comes from the setting up of the fence. You do this by marking up a joint with a mortise gauge. Gently lower the hollow chisel down on to the marks and set the fence from that. Then all you have to do is check that the chisel is parallel to the fence, set the depth stop, and lower the fingers to act as a lever to pull the chisel from the mortise. I generally find it safest and simplest to mark lines to show the length of the mortise and copy those to each workpiece for consistency.

One drawback of the mortiser is dealing with the shavings. These tumble from the mortise over the table and against the fence, affecting the accuracy of the machine. You end up having to blow the shavings away from the fence; otherwise the register is poor, and you lose accuracy. A solution is to attach a vacuum extractor hose beside the chisel and remove the chippings at source.

When you fit a wooden face to the mortiser's fence, make sure there is a gap for shavings.

Set the mortise gauge to the width of the hollow chisel for marking up tenons and for your first mortise.

Access to the mortiser's chuck is through a gap in the side.

The mortiser slides up and down a rack and pinion mechanism.

The U-shaped hold-down stops the workpiece from pulling up as you retract the mortise chisel.

Marking up with a rod

To mark up multiple joints, it's a good idea to draw up a full-size rod on a piece of plywood. This simply records the position of every important mark along the length of a component and is used, typically, for the manufacture of doors with all the mortises and profiles to consider. A full-size plan is useful for projects (such as chairs) that incorporate angles. For this lesson's Wine Rack, a rod can be used for positioning the mortises along the uprights.

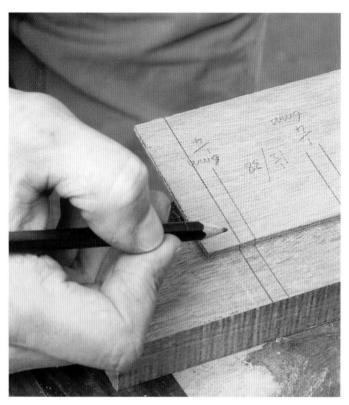

Once you have marked up the critical dimensions on a marking rod, you can use them for all your joint-cutting.

Trade secret

Working to order

A key lesson in woodworking is to device a clear order for making a project. You will often need to start by planing all the components, leaving them overlong, ensuring you have more than enough timber in case of mistakes, and setting up machines or gauges. Don't always follow the obvious course. One might, for example, jump into cutting the curves on the uprights of this lesson's project, since they are such a dominant feature. In reality, cutting the mortises will be far easier without the curves.

Advanced clamping

Almost all clamps are designed for clamping square-edged timber, with the force exerted at 90° to the joint line. When the outside faces are at an angle to the joint you may need to temporarily clamp 'ears' to the workpieces to get the clamp to stay in position.

To assemble a wide mitre, glue an ear to the workpiece temporarily.

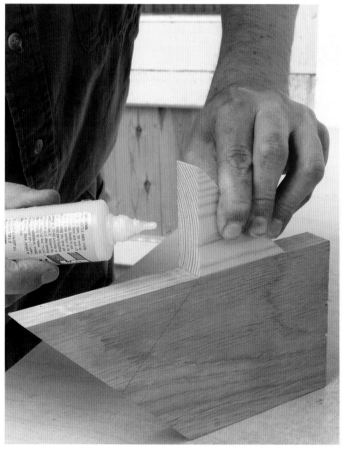

Cyanoacrylate glues are ideal, as they dry quickly, but knock off the excess after use.

Routing around a board

Whenever routing around all four edges of a board, start with the ends and then rout the long grain. This way, any breakout at the end of the end-grain cuts can be tidied up when you rout the long-grain edges.

With an ear glued in place, the clamp can exert pressure across the joint.

Another solution is to stick cork or abrasive pads to the clamp heads to stop them from sliding. When clamping curved work, keep the offcut from the curved cut and use it as a packing piece.

When routing around a panel, rout across the end grain first, as the end of the cut may tear.

Keep offcuts for curved pieces, as they can be used during assembly.

Another important lesson is to only assemble a project bit by bit. Do so one frame at a time, two-dimensionally, so to speak. Only when you are satisfied with each frame should you consider joining them together. Beds, for instance, are always constructed in three stages. First make the headboard, then the footboard, and only when they are done, connect the two with rails.

Rout the long grain after the end grain so that any tearing on the end-grain cut is hidden.

Sash-clamp stands are incredibly useful for keeping everything steady as you assemble the pieces.

Doing a test fit

Just as there's a maxim to measure twice, cut once only, there is also a sensible rule that you should always do a test fit – without glue – of any assembly that involves glue. It gets the clamps set up properly and also checks the quality of the fit. In addition, check the diagonals and fit before applying glue. Inaccuracies are usually caused by an inherent problem that will only be exacerbated in the presence of adhesive. And take your phone off the hook when you start gluing up. One of the best lessons I've learned is to buy a box of latex disposable gloves, which will keep the adhesive off your hands. Make sure your assembly area is clear of any dried adhesive, or your clamps will start rocking. Never use too much pressure with your clamps, as it's bound to knock something out of true. Solve the problem completely during the dry run, and then try it again.

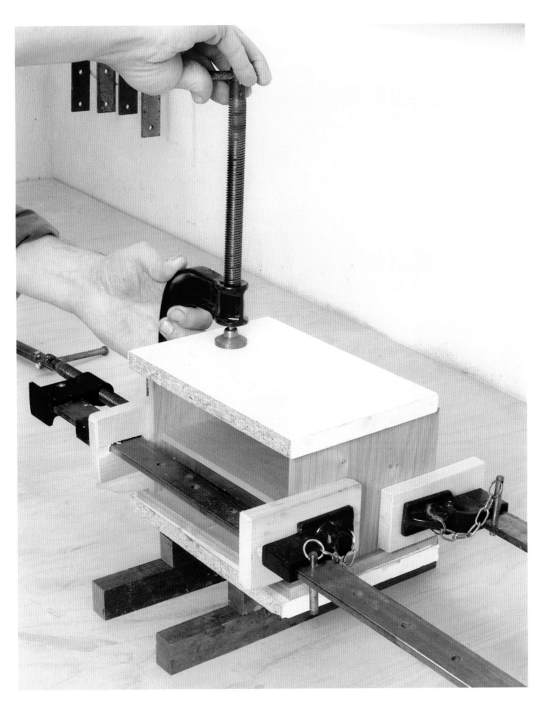

Melamine-faced chipboard is good for assemblies because glue can easily be chipped away afterwards, but make sure it is flat.

Check across the diagonals with a small square during a test fit. Do a test fit exactly as you would if you were applying adhesive.

When attaching a tabletop to a rail, you can use an expanded hole that allows for seasonal wood movement.

Attaching tabletops

Attaching a tabletop to the under-frame should be simple enough, but it is complicated by the fact that a solid timber top is likely to expand and contract with the seasons. These days, a top will often do so against the tide of the seasons, expanding when the central heating is off and the doors and windows are open, and then contracting during winter when the house becomes a blast furnace. It does, of course, depend on the latitude of your home, since the opposite is the case for houses cooled by air-conditioning in the summer.

If the top is fixed to the under-frame too rigidly, something will have to give as it expands or contracts. Even if you ensure the timber is conditioned to the nine or ten per cent that is appropriate for central heating, the wood is still bound to move a bit. There are a few options:

1 Expansion brackets. These right-angled steel brackets have slots cut in them so that the screw can move as the top moves.

2 If you are drilling through a rail into the top, you can either elongate the hole to make a slot, or you can expand the hole into a cone shape. This way you have pressure where the screw head meets the rail, but the hole is much wider where the rail meets the top to allow for movement.

3 Fit turn buttons to the top, and groove the inside face of the rails. The turn buttons are screwed into the top and are tightly fitted into the groove, but the top is still able to expand and contract.

Turn buttons are screwed to the tabletop. Because they are just a tight fit in a groove in the rail, the top can move.

A drill tray is essential for a drill press and attaches to the main column.

Tools

Drill press

You don't need to ask much of a drill press, but it is one of the most valuable pieces of equipment in the workshop. Mine has countless speeds, but I've changed the belts and pulleys only once, and that was when I set it up the first time. It seems to work well enough. You can't go far wrong in buying a drill press, but it is worth selecting one with a simple chuck that you can tighten and loosen by hand. Almost any deficiency can be overcome with a little tinkering, and drill presses are so cheap that they should be right up there as one of the first machines to buy.

The benefit of owning a drill press is that you can guarantee the accuracy of the holes you drill – you just have to hit the mark. They also give you more control when drilling with larger bits, especially Forstner drills and bung cutters. It is, however, worth fitting a wooden table to the drill, and buying an engineer's vice to fit to the drill press can help if you need to drill awkward shapes or small pieces. Investing in a drill tray that fits to the drill press is also a good idea.

Buying a mortiser

Like drill presses, most mortisers are very similar, probably produced in the same factory and just badged with a different brand. You should, however, test the handles for adjustment, since some are very crude, while you may need a allen key on other types.

One of the first things to do when setting up a mortiser is to set the depth of cut.

Set the U-shaped hold-down to keep the workpiece flat and level.

Don't let the auger fall out of the hollow chisel when you undo the chuck.

When the mortiser is sharp it will produce clean shavings instead of dust.

Materials

All about wood – reclaimed wood

The sideboard that we'll be making in Lesson 2 has a lovely old feel to it and could easily be made from reclaimed wood. Even when covered in old varnish or paint, timber is still worth salvaging. I keep a battered old portable thicknesser for just such a job and very rarely change the blades. This way I can quickly remove old finishes without damaging the cutters in my surface planer. I have rescued plenty of antique Cuban mahogany, which bears no resemblance to the stuff we have to use these days, though this material now should probably be avoided for environmental reasons.

Mixed media

We woodworkers often assume that all parts of a project have to be made from timber. Actually, the contrast between wood and metal, for instance, can be amazingly effective, and other materials like glass, stone, and plastic set off timber superbly. I once went through a phase of filling knot holes with epoxy resin and brightly coloured pigment. For another project, I stuck veneer to a sheet of mild steel and then used powerful magnets to produce an alternative type of noticeboard.

Oil finishes

This lesson's project, the Wine Rack, might well be finished with some kind of oil. These finishes are easy to apply and relatively hard-wearing, while providing a softer, less artificial barrier than some of the modern lacquers and varnishes. They vary in hardness – from linseed, which is very soft, to tung oil, which is strong enough to be used for tabletops.

Often, oils are mixed with lacquers and waxes to produce applications that dry faster and are more hard-wearing. When, before the mixed oils, it was a case of using pure linseed oil, there was a maxim that you needed to apply a coat once a day for a week, once a week for a month and once a month for a year. A common theme, still, is that oil finishes are applied with a brush or rag, and any excess is wiped off after a few minutes. In drying slowly, there's plenty of time to dab away any marks and to remove any dust or particles, but it does take a few days to build up an effective coat, which you can leave as it is or go on to wax.

Oil will form a skin in a jar very quickly.

Apply oil liberally with a brush, working with the grain.

After a short while, rub off any excess oil with a cloth.

Project **Wine rack**

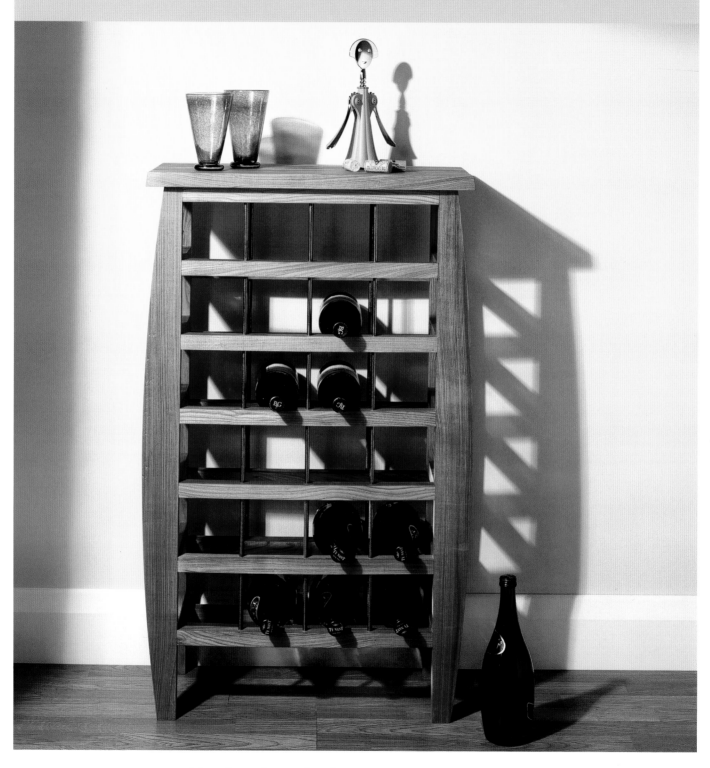

For bottles of wine

A simple design that takes a simple idea and gives it shape and contrast by adding curves to the geometric layout of racking and distinctive vertical dividers made from steel rod.

283 mm (11⅛ in)

560 mm
(1 ft 10 in)

D

32 mm (1¼ in)

790 mm (2 ft 7¼ in)

32 mm (1¼ in)

65 mm
(2½ in)

B

760 mm (2 ft 6 in)

915 mm
(3 ft)

A

100 mm (4 in)

133 mm (5¼ in)

C

25 mm (1 in)

110 mm (4¼ in)

240 mm
(9½ in)

485 mm (1 ft 7 in)

Cutting list

Part	Material	Quantity	Dimensions length, width, thickness
A Upright	cherry	4	914 x 64 x 25 mm (36 x 2½ x 1 in)
B Rail	cherry	14	483 x 32 x 25 mm (19 x 1¼ x 1 in)
C Side rail	cherry	14	241 x 35 x 25 mm (9½ x 1⅜ x 1 in)
D Top	cherry	1	559 x 283 x 25 mm (22 x 11⅛ x 1 in)

Shopping list

Tools

Steel rod: 6 lengths, 762 mm (30 in) long and 130 mm (5⅛ in) in diameter
Flat-headed woodscrews to attach top (**D**): 4

1 Plane and thickness all the parts. Note that many of the pieces are 25 mm (1 in) thick, so you ought to surface boards for those components at the same time. Make sure you have some extra timber dimensioned to the appropriate section for setting up the mortiser and drill press.

2 Cut the uprights (A) to length, though there's no harm leaving the parts a little too long at this stage. But don't think about cutting the curves yet: it will be far easier to do this after the mortises have been chopped out. Whether you use a mortiser or cut the mortises by hand, it is worth marking up the joints using a template or the more traditional rod (see Marking up with a rod, page 180). Cut the mortises in a length of 6 mm (¼ in) plywood, and then clamp this to the workpiece to mark the positions of the mortises.

3 Chop out the mortises by hand or with a mortiser. The mortiser not only removes the chopping stage, but it also means you don't need to mark up each joint with a mortise gauge, once you have set up the fence and depth stop.

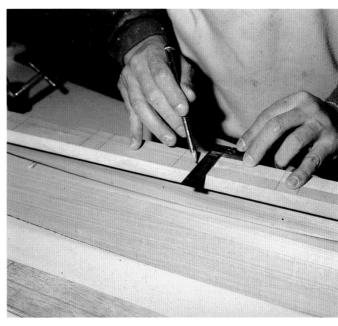

4 There are any number of ways to cut the 56 tenons. The band saw works well for cutting the cheeks and the table saw is good for cutting the shoulders (see Using a table saw, page 218). But you could also use a router table, using the mitre guide to slide the workpiece across a straight cutter.

5 Drill the holes in the rails (**B**) for the vertical rods. If you have a drill press, set up a fence to repeat the operation. Otherwise use a marking gauge to position the holes along the cente-line of each rail. Use a rod to mark the position of each hole along the rails, and square the line around the component so that you can drill from both sides to reduce the risk of tearing.

6 Do a test fit (see Doing a test fit, page 182) of the joints before cutting the curved sides of the uprights. Make a template of the curve from plywood and use it to mark up each component; then cut them with a band saw or jigsaw.

Make sure you keep the offcut, since this can be used as a packing piece when clamping up the rack (see Draw-boring, page 129).

TIP: Always undertake at least one assembly of a project without glue, but clamped up exactly as you would for real. This will get all the clamps set to the right position and ensures that the joints will actually tighten comfortably. Glue, especially the prospect of it going off before the assembly is ready, complicates everything, and a test fit at least eliminates some of the potential complications.

7 An alternative technique for cutting the curves is to make a plywood template, which is stuck to the face of the upright. Work the curve on the upright on the router table, using a trimming cutter running against the template (see Using bearing-guided cutters, page 138). Clean up the curves with a sanding block.

8 Assemble the front or back uprights and rails first. Once these two frames have been assembled and cleaned up, bring them together with the side rails. With so many parts involved, this can be a tricky operation, so be prepared. Test the diagonals at every stage of the assembly, but at the final clamp-up, check that the legs sit evenly on a flat surface.

9 You may be able to find a board wide enough for the top (**D**), but you will probably need to clamp up a panel from three narrower boards (see Assembling a panel, page 85). This will also make it more stable.

10 Having planed the top (though you may want to do this at the start with the other parts), cut it to shape, with gentle curves on the front and back. You can either bevel the edges with a bearing-guided bevel cutter in a router table, or do so by hand with a bench plane, working away from the centre of each curve towards the ends to prevent tearing. Always bevel the ends first, since the grain is likely to break at the end of the cut (see Planing end grain, page 24), and this tear can be removed when you bevel the long-grain edges.

TIP: The holes in the bottom front and back rails for the metal rods must be stopped or the rods will fall out. However, the holes in the top rails can be drilled right through so that the metal rods can be dropped down into position after assembly.

11 Screw the top to the top rails (see Attaching tabletops, page 184). Clean up and apply a finish.

Lessons learned

- When you are dealing with curved components, you have to think carefully about the order in which you work. It is often best to cut the curves after all the jointing has been completed.

- It's worth finding a technique for the repetitive cutting of tenons.

- Make sure any mortises are cut vertically. If a mortise is at an angle, it will be very difficult to assemble the project accurately.

Lesson 2
Cutting tenons

Getting started

A woodworker without a workshop is like a bird without a nest. Once we've found our space to work, we have to piece it together in an endless process that involves perpetual evolution and development. The initial plan is bound to be inadequate within a few years, as the range of equipment grows and ambitions change. But you have to start somewhere, and there is no better place than at the bench.

Siting the workbench is one of the most important tasks for a woodworker. It must be level and ideally in good light. There must be plenty of space around it, especially around the end vice, which is usually positioned at the right-hand end. You'll probably want a shelf and some hanging space behind the bench for nearby tools, but the most critical thing is that the bench top must be flat.

Fortunately, 'flat' is a relative term, and what you initially describe as level will only dissatisfy you once you've acquired the skills to demand greater accuracy. The moment you become frustrated by a workpiece wobbling, you know that (a) the bench top isn't as flat as you'd like, and (b) you're making progress.

Marking and cutting the mitred tenon

Common in chair construction, the mitred tenon is an essential mechanism when two rails or stretchers meet a leg or stile at the same point. To maximize the gluing area and length of the joints, the tenons are mitred at the ends and ideally should meet perfectly to improve the bond.

The cutting of the tenons is simple, carried out just as you would any similar joint, only the ends are mitred. However, chopping out the mortise is a little tougher than normal, since there is a risk of the wood breaking on the inside corner where the two mortises meet. The simple solution is to cut the first mortise and then insert a false tenon before you cut the second mortise.

When cutting the second mortise for mitred tenons, insert a false tenon to stop any breakout where the mortises meet.

Knowing how to make mitred tenons is an important skill that you will need to master in order to construct chairs and tables.

Lesson planner

Key techniques	Key tools and materials
• Marking and cutting a mitred tenon • Identifying tenons • Workshop layout	• Workbench • Assembly table • Machines to fit your workshop • Advanced adhesives

Identifying tenons

While the mortise is, for all intents and purposes, just a hole in the wood, there are any number of different types of tenon. Each one serves a different purpose, though there are elements that are interchangeable. It is important to know the subtle difference between these different cuts, as each has properties making it suitable for a certain kind of join. Here are some examples of the different kinds of tenon you may come across as you gain experience.

Tenon for moulded frame and panel. The frame is rebated and the profile juts out. This will be mitred to match the profile on the post.

A tenon cut from a rebated rail. Notice here that the haunch is angled. None of it is seen, but there is less tendency for the tenon to twist.

The basic haunched tenon. This helps retain some substance at the top of the stile, while keeping some of the tenon full width to stop twist.

A simple full-width tenon. You use this when the tenon is entering a post at the middle rather than the ends.

This is sometimes known as a stub tenon, with shoulders on all four sides. It is the most common tenon and hides the mortise well.

The double tenon is used to increase the gluing area and strength of a tenon when you are using stock of quite small dimensions.

This tenon is often used on the middle rail of panelled doors. The tenon is split so as not to weaken the post. It is wide to stop twist.

A more basic version of a tenon for doors has no shoulders at the ends. This makes the mortises more visible, yet adds strength.

A haunched stub tenon. An example of how various techniques can be combined for a special situation.

I've found that a shelf just behind and above the bench is a great place to store the planes I use most often.

Tools

Workshop layout

I love reorganizing my workshop. At least once a year I'll have a purge and rearrange my machines, worksurfaces and tools, finding new places to store offcuts and equipment I rarely use. Some people happily work in chaos, but I prefer to have a reasonable platform from which to build, without being obsessive about tidiness and order. Though I hate not being able to put my hands on a particular tool when it's needed, that doesn't mean it has to be filed alphabetically: it just needs a logical home.

Here are some of the key features of a well-organized workshop.

Workbench

This needs plenty of space so that you can work at both ends, with no obstructions, when you are planing with the bench vice or working around the end vice. Some woodworkers position the bench in the centre of the room, allowing 360° access.

The bench arrangement and tool storage are matters of taste and need. Not everyone likes tool wells, which can fill with dust and shavings. I've devised a system of shelves behind my bench, with one above the bench level and one below the level. The one above the bench is ideal for placing planes away from the action whilst remaining easy to pick up. The other shelf has holes for chisels and stores tools that are used less frequently. Behind the bench I have a sheet of plywood attached to the wall, into which I fix screws to hold tools, the advantage being that I can move the additional screws around as my needs change. My bench has drawers and a cupboard, the former being particularly useful for storing abrasives, marking tools and other small items.

The screws and glues used most frequently are kept near the bench.

Assembly table

If you have the space, I recommend that you create a worksurface dedicated to assembling projects, though it can also be used for temporary bench-top machines. Store sash clamps near this area, ideally hung from racks on the wall and within easy reach. A metal tube or thick piece of dowel rod can accommodate small clamps, probably positioned near the bench.

It is important that the assembly area is well varnished and even waxed so that any excess adhesive that has set can be knocked off easily. The surface must be flat for testing the legs of chairs and tables. Fix a shelf above this space for adhesive and glue spreaders, and keep paper towels nearby for cleaning up any spills.

To get the most glue possible, turn tubes upside down when not in use.

An assembly table makes the gluing up projects enjoyable and accurate.

Sash clamps need to be readily available, and are best stored on a rack.

Keep smaller clamps, for holding jigs, near the bench.

Machines to fit your workshop

Arranging machines around the workshop is an art in itself. As much as anything, you have to consider the direction and length of timber that will be passed across the machine, and where you will stand. Try to use varying machine heights creatively, since you may be able to position some equipment below the table height of another. Here are some of the key considerations.

Band saws. These saws are often used to cut narrow lengths of timber rather than sheets, and so the important factor is the length of cut you can do without hitting the wall of the workshop. I've found that band saws sit well in doorways, since you need to have only half the machine protruding, so it shouldn't get in the way too much. The table on a band saw is often quite high in relation to other bench-mounted machines, and you might be able to position a router table nearby without too much interference. Long boards being cut on the band saw will pass over the router table.

Radial-arm saws. These saws suit long, thin workshops, while saw tables are better in square areas that have plenty of space in the centre. The radial-arm saw only needs length, but isn't as good for ripping boards as the saw table, which, since it needs both width and length, is space-hungry.

Surface planers, thicknessers and planer-thicknessers. If you are lucky, you can position a surface planer and thicknesser at right angles, with the boards travelling underneath the out-feed or in-feed table of the surface planer. This has certainly worked for me, but I have an L-shaped workshop. Where workshop space is limited, planer-thicknessers are popular because they make such efficient use of the direction of work.

Timber. Store timber in the roof space if you can, since this will utilize otherwise dead space; however, remember that timber is heavy and can be difficult to manhandle up and down. If possible, keep boards of the same species together so that you can find them more easily, especially if they are rough-sawn and hence tricky to identify.

Store boards flat, with plenty of support to ensure that they don't sag, and in a well-ventilated space away from dampness. Check your stock from time to time for mould and insects. You don't need to separate dry boards with sticks as you do when they are seasoning, but make sure you don't let oak and some other species touch iron or steel fittings, since this can lead to staining of the wood.

Small scraps are useful for padding when assembling projects, though I prefer permanent pads on my sash clamps.

Shelves for offcuts and short lengths of timber are valuable, especially if they can be compartmentalized by species.

As your woodworking progresses, you will amass a growing stock of offcuts. These are very valuable and need to be easy to access for quick jobs such as making jigs. However, offcuts can easily overwhelm a workshop, and it is important you have an area dedicated to them that doesn't overflow into the rest of the workshop. Once your offcut storage is full, you can probably start burning some of it.

That said, keep hold of even the smallest bits of valuable exotic species. I have some exquisite Cuban mahogany – which is now impossible to buy – recycled from an old wardrobe, and I refuse to throw out even the tiniest piece.

Sharpening. Dedicate an area to sharpening. Ideally, this should be close to the workbench but in an area where water and metal filings won't contaminate projects that you are working on. You need especially good light for sharpening and a worksurface a bit higher than the bench.

Dust. All machines and power tools need extraction, but while this can be achieved with small vacuum extractors for tools that only produce dust or fine chippings, the surface planer and thicknesser need proper extraction for shavings. The best solution is to site this outside the workshop by running ducting from the machines through the walls. There are many systems that can achieve this using flexible hose, soil pipe or metal tubing.

If you have more than one machine connected to the same extraction unit you will need to fit blast gates at each source, otherwise you will lose too much pressure. These can be relatively simple affairs or electronically controlled by a central command box. When laying out the ducting, try

to keep the bends to a minimum, since these will undermine the flow.

If you are particularly concerned about dust, you might also consider an ambient filter, which works on a similar principle to the kitchen extractor, except that it filters dust within the workshop without ejecting it outside. The advantage of this, especially over an extractor housed externally, is that there is no need for air to come in from outside, which can have an effect on your heating system.

Heat. Though you have to take care with the obvious fire risks, wood-burning stoves are probably the most effective and economical way of warming a workshop, especially if you live in the countryside. Gas isn't so good, since it produces water vapour, but electric heating works well. Obviously, in a garage connected to the home, you may be able to run central heating to the workshop, and potentially add a dedicated pump and circuit so that you are only warming that room during the day when everyone is out of the house.

A wood-burning stove gives fabulous heat in the workshop.

Finishing. It is easy to forget the importance of finishing in woodwork, and yet this is often what separates the really good woodworkers from the ordinary. Invariably, when I've been a judge of amateur woodworking competitions, it is the quality of the finish that is the deciding factor, especially for wood-turning and carving. You need an area clear of clutter and dust where you can apply finishes to your projects. It could even share space with your sharpening area, where you may not be producing too much dust.

Foam applicators are cheap and good for applying many finishes.

Tools. When it comes to storing tools, accessibility is the important thing, though rustproofing comes a close second. I have problems with dampness in my workshop, but I don't like to store my tools in sealed cupboards, preferring to have them close at hand. To be honest, I'm not that well organized, but I do like tools to be in a logical place, with sash clamps hanging beside the assembly table and chisels at hand behind the bench. Storing all the rarely used tools I've collected over the years had always been a big challenge until the day I put them all in a big cardboard box and shoved them to the back of a cupboard.

Lighting. Successful woodworking depends on good lighting. Daylight is obviously excellent, but many workshops won't have this luxury, so other solutions are necessary. Striplights are good for ambient light, but nothing beats a number of spotlights directed at the area where you work. Use a light with a strong, weighted base, which takes a high-voltage bulb, to illuminate your work.

A small portable and powerful lamp is excellent for checking finishes.

Materials

All about wood – dealing with defects

Knots can add character to any project, but they are difficult to deal with, since the grain changes direction around the defect and there is a risk that the knot will fall out. It's often a case of judging whether you think the knot will survive and if it will get in the way of joints or profiles. Positioning knots in the centre of the board, rather than near the ends or edges, is important. You may well need to use a scraper (see Using a cabinet scraper, page 117) to finish the knot, and you might consider filling any gaps with epoxy resin to hold it in place. Try adding colour to the resin for contrast.

ADVANCED ADHESIVES

You can't underestimate the value of good glue for woodworking, and for most tasks, white cabinet-maker's adhesive (PVA) is ideal. However, there are many others to choose from, which can be used for specific jobs.

Polyurethane adhesives

Polyurethane glues react with the moisture in wood (or any other material) and foam as they escape the joint. They come in a couple of types, notably distinguished by the speed of set, with some fixing in no more than five minutes. What you gain in speed you lose in glue line, and the fast-setting polyurethane adhesives tend to leave a white crystaline deposit. Slower-setting types are usually stronger, and the best have a darker glue line that can't be seen once you apply a finish.

Advantages

Excess glue can be knocked off the surface after assembly, especially if you've applied a finish first. The glue doesn't dull blades and cutters, and is easy to work. They are simple to apply.

Disadvantages

The glue can go off inside the bottle, with a thick film forming. Your fingers will end up black or brown with dried glue, though this can be removed with acetone.

Yellow glue

Once you get into woodworking more seriously, you will soon discover yellow glue, which is essentially an improved version of white glue. Many of the properties are the same, but it tends to set faster and is stronger. These aliphatic glues are more water-resistant than white glue but are very easy to use.

Advantages
Easy to spread and use.
Relatively inexpensive.
Strong.
Fast setting.

Disadvantages
It sets a yellow color, but not noticeably unless the glue line is obvious.
In hot weather it may give you only a few minutes to complete an assembly.

Two-part epoxy

Two-part resins are commonly used around the home for household repairs, but some woodworkers also use them for projects. Their selling point is that you can build them up to fill gaps, and there is the opportunity to add colour or fillers. They set quickly and are very hard. I use them for some repairs and occasionally for laminating because they are easy to apply with a brush and you can adjust the mix of catalyst and resin for a longer open time.

Advantages
Quick drying.
Can fill gaps and be mixed with colors or fillers.
Very strong.

Disadvantages
Expensive.
Can be brittle, and don't always adhere well in dusty conditions, so watch out when using for repairs.

Cyanoacrylates

Usually referred to as superglue, cyanoacrylates are designed to bond quickly but are not necessarily chosen for longevity. They tend to be fairly brittle and can survive pull stresses, but are often easily broken with sheer pressure. It is worth buying the more expensive brands, and you can find some that set more slowly and are also less brittle. This sort of adhesive is useful in the workshop when you need to make jigs or hold something temporarily. You can also use them alongside longer-term adhesives when clamps won't work. The cyanoacrylate holds the pieces together long enough for the other glue to set for a permanent bond.

Advantages
Sets fast.
Very strong, at least in the short to medium term.
Various types available.

Disadvantages
Too brittle for long-term use.
Can easily stick fingers to wood! Make sure you have a bottle of debonder.
Expensive.

Hot glues

Dispensed from a heated gun, hot glues set very quickly and are very useful for temporary fixtures. Some people use them all the time, but I've found that the glue sets so fast that you don't always have time to complete the job. Woodturners swear by them for holding wood on the lathe. These glues certainly have their uses, and it's worth buying an inexpensive gun, but don't expect to be using it every day.

Advantages
Quick-setting.
The glue has some flexibility.
Low wastage.

Disadvantages
Delay waiting for gun to heat up.
Glue can set too quickly.
Glue is only ever a temporary fixture.

Hide glue

Traditional hide glue used to be kept warm in a pot, emanating the most horrible stench. It was used by furniture-makers, and some antiques restorers and repairers still employ it for authenticity. However, these days you can buy a sanitized and improved version in a bottle. It takes a long time to set and is very strong, with the same honey consistency of traditional hide glue.

Advantages
Traditional.
Adheres well to almost anything.
Long open time for adjustments.

Disadvantages
Slow-drying.
Very vulnerable to damp.

Contact adhesive

Some woodworkers use contact adhesives for applying veneer. It is certainly strong but tends to be messy to use and takes time.

Many woodworkers favour contact adhesive for gluing down veneer.

Project Sideboard 1

For the hallway

This sideboard can be used in many rooms around the house, but the drawer is ideal for phone directories in the hallway. The pine here is reclaimed, and the project is a good opportunity to practice tenons and mortises. Next lesson we will make the drawer (see page 214).

510 mm (1 ft 8 in)

1110 mm (3ft 7¾ in)

19 mm (¾ in)

370 mm (1 ft 2½ in)

255 mm (10 in)

945 mm (3 ft 1¼ in)

430 mm (1 ft 5 in)

12 mm (½ in)

840 mm (2 ft 9 in)

220 mm (8¾ in)

70 mm (2¾ in)

921 mm (3 ft ¼ in)

340 mm (1ft 1⅜ in)

960 mm (3 ft ¾ in)

340 mm (1 ft 1⅜ in)

45 mm (1¾ in)

B A C E G J H F D C E F D C

Cutting list (table frame)

Part	Material	Quantity	Dimensions length, width, thickness	Part	Material	Quantity	Dimensions length, width, thickness
A Top	softwood	1	(1110 x 508 x 19 mm) (43¾ x 20 x ¾ in)	**F** Lower side rail	softwood	2	400 x 70 x 19 mm (15¾ x 2¾ x ¾ in)
B Top bearer (not shown)	softwood	3	430 x 38 x 19 mm (17 x 1½ x ¾ in)	**G** Drawer guide	softwood	2	340 x 45 x 19 mm (13⅜ x 1¾ x ¾ in)
C Leg	softwood	4	840 x 45 x 45 mm (33 x 1¾ x 1¾ in)	**H** Drawer runner	softwood	2	489 x 10 x 2 mm (19¼ x ⅜ x ³⁄₁₆ in)
D Front/ back rail	softwood	4	1006 x 45 x 25 mm (39⅝ x 1¾ x 1 in)	**I** Side panel	softwood	2	368 x 254 x 6 mm (14½ x 10 x ¼ in)
E Side rail	softwood	2	400 x 45 x 25 mm (15¾ x 1¾ x 1 in)	**J** Block support	softwood	2	50 x 21 x 21 mm (2 x ⅞ x ⅞ in)

1 Plane the components for the framework, including the legs, rails, drawer guides and drawer runners.

Cut the mortises in the legs (**C**) for all the rails, taking care not to break the grain where the mortises meet (see Marking and cutting the mitred tenon, page 194).

Cut the tenons on the rails, including the lower side rails (**F**), noting that each tenon is 27 mm (1³⁄₁₆ in) long. Make sure the distance between the shoulders is consistent. Test-fit all the joints; glue up the front and back frames, then the whole thing.

2 Pin and glue the drawer runners (**H**) to the lower side rails.

3 Clamp the drawer guides (**G**) to the lower side rails so that the guides are flush with the inside face of the legs. Mark the position and drill screw holes in the lower side rails. Then glue the drawer guides in place, screwing up from below.

4 Glue the blocks (**J**) in place so that they are flush with the outside of the legs.

5 Glue the side panels (**I**) to the rails.

6 The top (**A**) can be made from stripwood, bought ready-planked at a DIY store, or by gluing up narrower boards, then planing or belt-sanding the top smooth. Stop the top cupping by screwing three cleats (**B**) to the underside, ideally elongating the holes in the cleats so that the top can move a little (see Attaching tabletops, page 184).

Lessons learned

- Cutting accurate joints requires a flat bench top.

- You can't have enough clamps.

- Complex assemblies are best done in stages.

7 Rout a profile around the edges of the top, using a bearing-guided cutter or with the side fence attached to the router. Make sure you rout the end grain first (see Routing across the grain, page 137 and Routing around a board, page 181).

Lesson 3
Tails and pins

Getting started

I made my first dovetails as a boy at school, encouraged to build a toolbox from 25-mm (1-in) thick utile. It was too heavy to carry when empty, let alone when full of tools. The real error was that between myself and my teacher, we managed to position the dovetails the wrong way round, so that all the weight was held by the pins instead of the tails. Thanks to good glue, it didn't fall apart, but that was something of a miracle.

When to use a dovetail
The dovetail is the most decorative woodworking joint, as well as one of the strongest, relying very little upon the glue line. Perhaps only wedged or draw-bored mortise and tenon joints are inherently stronger without adhesive. The mortise and tenon is the joint of choice when connecting square-section or nearly square-section components like rails and legs, but the dovetail is useful for joining boards, restricting any tendency for the wood to cup and also providing good strength.

Dovetails are most commonly used in boxes, drawers and other high-quality cabinets. The visibility of the joint is something of a statement of ability, especially now that there are quicker alternatives like the biscuit joint (see Using a biscuit jointer, page 138 and Buying a biscuit jointer, page 140) and the mitre-lock joint (see The mitre-lock joint, page 149), which are just as good. Unlike the mortise and tenon, which hides the vital parts of the joints within itself, the dovetail is on view and any inaccuracy is highly conspicuous.

Lesson planner

Key techniques	Key tools and materials
• Variations on the dovetail • Marking up a through dovetail • How to make a box	• Quarter-sawing a log or board • Dovetail templates • Engineer's square • Japanese saws

Basic principles of the dovetail
There are many different types of dovetail jig that can cut the joint quickly and accurately, but there is a satisfaction in being able to produce a tight-fitting dovetail by hand. It isn't that hard, either; it just takes patience and care.

Throughout the lessons so far, we've been debating the benefits of cutting joints so accurately that you don't need to pair them off. Huge amounts of time can be saved by developing the skills that allow you to fit any tenon into any mortise when, for instance, constructing the under-frame of a table. With dovetails it's best to start afresh and assume that each joint is unique, at least until your experience and confidence grows. Without using a jig, it is very difficult to repeat a series of tails or pins, and one of its attractions is that each joint is slightly different.

Most woodworkers will cut the tails first. These are the fan-shaped parts that give the joint its name. On the other board you cut the pins, which fit between the tails. You use the tails on the first board to mark up the pins on the other. Usually you will have an equal number of tails and pins to the joint, though often you will start and finish with half pins, one at each end of the joint.

The way you lay out the tails and pins and vary the spacing are very much matters of style. Visually, it looks more interesting to have slightly wider tails than pins, and the finest work will usually have the thinnest pins, though the pins and tails can be roughly the same width. The angle of the tails, however, is important and depends on the strength of the timber you are using. For softer species you need a higher angle, while the hardest woods are strong enough to cope with a shallow angle. One common rule is that you use an angle of about 1:6 for softwoods and 1:8 for hardwoods.

Variations on the dovetail joint
There are fewer variations on the dovetail than for many other joints, but they are all useful for different kinds of joinery. Here are some examples you may use:
The through dovetail. The basic joint is for both the tails and pins to be visible, like interlocking fingers clasped together. This is used in box-making, cabinet-making, and for the joint between drawer sides and the drawer back.

The blind, mitred dovetail. Often referred to as the secret mitred dovetail, this is a joint too far for many woodworkers, combining two of the trickiest joints to cut and very difficult to achieve with jigs. This joint has to be cut

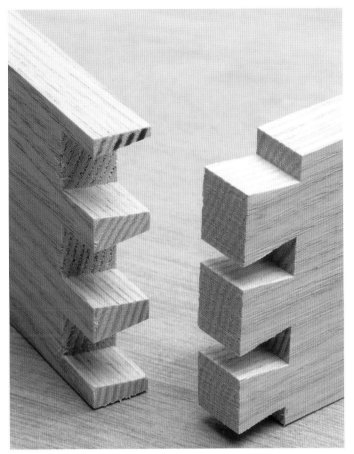

Making a clean, workable through dovetail takes a great deal of practice and skill, but it is essential for cabinet-making and items with drawers.

by hand, and it is no coincidence that it isn't used very much. Anyone who claims to have employed the blind mitred dovetail ought to be made to prove it because, of course, it is entirely hidden. What it achieves, however, is a mitred joint that is locked together, which almost no other technique can claim.

The tapered dovetail. Also known as the sliding dovetail, this joint is effectively a housing but has the advantage of being self-tightening, so it is ideal for the construction of items too large to manage with sash clamps. A dovetailed housing is cut in one component, tapering gradually to match a taper on a dovetailed tenon cut on the other piece. Only as the two pieces are slipped together do you discover the success of the joint, by which time it may be too late to get it apart again. It is not widely used these days but has its place.

Of course, you can also produce dovetailed housings that aren't tapered, which just slide together and rely on glue for the final bond. These won't pull the components together as tightly as the tapered dovetail, but are useful for inserting shelves into the sides of bookcases and similar. You can work a dovetail on one or two sides of the shelf.

The half-blind or lapped dovetail. Used particularly in drawer construction to hide the ends of the pins when looking at the front of a drawer, the half-blind dovetail shows the end of the pins and sides of the tails, but hides the ends of the tails. Surprisingly, it can be easier to cut because half the joint is hidden, though extracting the waste from the sockets between the pins can be awkward. Some commercial woodworkers get around this by cutting a normal through dovetail and then sticking a false front on the drawer, as we've done in this lesson's project, the Sideboard Drawer.

Marking up a through dovetail
Because you cut each joint individually unless you are using a special jig (**D**), the marking up is especially

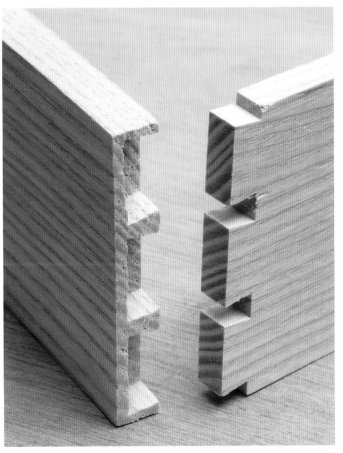

Unlike the through dovetail, half of this lapped dovetail is hidden. It is still a tricky operation, particularly extracting the waste from the sockets.

Having marked the depth line, use a dovetail template to mark the tails.

Put the board at an angle in the vice to cut down the tail vertically.

Shade the waste so that you cut to the waste side of the drawn lines.

Cut the half-pins at each end, taking care to cut vertically to the line.

important. It really is up to you how you divide up the tails and pins, and you have to experiment a few times to discover the effect you like. But always start by marking out the tails, using a dovetail template and small engineer's square to mark down the board and then across the end grain. A marking gauge sets the depth, though you can set this a fraction deep so that the tails are a little overlong and can be sanded back later.

Once you've cut the tails, which we'll explain later, you can use them to mark the positions of the pins. Initially it's a good idea to shade the waste areas you are removing!

Cutting a through dovetail

Whether you start with the tails or pins is a matter of personal habit. I tend to cut the tails first.

1 Cut down the tails, obviously cutting to the waste side of the drawn line. To get the angle consistent, it's a good idea to cut all the angles that slope one way, and then all the ones that slope the other. The same is true with the pins. This method enables you to build up a muscle memory, and you are more likely to keep the angle consistent. Stop just short of the depth mark.

2 Use a coping saw to remove the waste between the tails, taking care not to cut below the depth mark. Removing the waste relieves the pressure when it comes to cleaning up the line with a chisel. You will need a very sharp bevel-edged chisel for paring end grain. While the first cuts can be done with a mallet, the last ones are best solely with pressure from your arm, with your hand guiding the edge into the scored depth mark.

3 Clean up the tails. Then place the other part of the joint in a bench vice, with the end grain flush with the top of the bench. Lay the tails on top and mark across the positions. Mark the depth and then down the pins with the engineer's square.

4 Cut the pins and remove the waste as you did for the tails. Then you can start testing the fit, which always takes a bit of time. You want the fit to be firm without being too tight. The softer the timber, the tighter the fit, because the fibres will compress a little.

Assembling the through dovetail

When it comes to assembling the dovetail, the only important trick is that you cannot exert pressure on the

Let the little half-pin fall away and do the other one.

Use a coping saw to remove the waste from between the tails.

Chop down to remove the waste from between the tails.

Use the finished tail piece to mark off the pins on its neighbour.

The packing piece also supports the chisel to keep it vertical.

Cut down the pins and remove the waste with a coping saw. Then chop away the waste with a chisel.

To clamp up a dovetailed joint, cut fingers in an offcut allowing the pins to protrude. They can be sanded back later.

Use a brush to apply adhesive to the dovetails before assembly.

corners are neat. They are not particularly strong, and will probably need some reinforcement (see Reinforcing a mitre joint, page 76).

Generally, boxes are made from four sides, a base and a top, though you don't have to look far to find exceptions. The base is usually held in grooves that are routed into the sides. The same is often true of the top, depending on the design. It may also be glued into rebates or simply to the top of the sides. Or the top could be an independent frame and panel that is simply hinged to the back. The possibilities are endless, and boxes are a good opportunity to have a go at veneering and even marquetry.

To strengthen a long mitre joint, rout cavities for keys into the mitres.

corners, since the tails or pins might protrude. Instead, you need to position the clamps farther in, away from the joint, but as close as possible so that you don't bend the components.

How to make a box

Box-making has become very popular over the last fifteen years, with some remarkable designs produced. As a speciality it has the advantage of not taking up much space or timber, and everyone has a use for a box. However, it usually requires great accuracy, since boxes are inspected with microscopic degrees of curiosity.

Dovetails are often used for making a box because they hold the components in place. Another advantage is that with dovetails you can use thinner stock than for almost any other joint, since it is strong and you don't have to insert one piece into the other, as is the case for tenons, biscuits and dowels. Mitres are also popular for box-making, since they too don't require much thickness and the

The block stops the cavities from being routed too deeply.

Box-making tips

1 It's a good idea to make the box as a complete unit and then cut off the top after it is assembled. This can be done with a fine-bladed table saw (see Using a table saw, page 218), or with a narrow cutter in a router table. The trick is not to cut through the sides, but to stop just short. This way the top doesn't loosen, and you can make the final cut with a craft knife.

Put a thin cutter in the router table to separate the box from the lid.

Make light cuts, gradually working your way around the box.

Ensure that the lid isn't caught in the cutter when separated from the box.

2 You often don't need heavy clamps to assemble the box: use rubber bands and masking tape to hold the components while the glue sets.

If accurately cut, mitred boxes can be glued up with decorator's tape.

3 Lining the inside of the box offers the opportunity to introduce another type of timber – perhaps even using an aromatic species – and it also helps to align the top and sides of the box. The linings can be mitred inside the box, protruding just a little above the side to guide the top into position.

Use a mitred liner to achieve a better fit for the lid.

The lining needs to have a neat finish to match the rest of the jointing.

Tools

Dovetail template

You can make your own dovetail template easily enough, but they are usually inexpensive to buy and are very useful. There are various designs, often offering two ratios to cope with softwoods and hardwoods.

Engineer's square

A small metal engineer's square has many uses, not only for setting up machines but particularly when it comes to marking up dovetailed joints. The blade only needs to be about 76 mm (3 in) long. Check that it is square, both for the inside and outside edge of the blade.

Japanese saws

More and more woodworkers are using Japanese saws, sometimes to complement a tenon saw or to replace it entirely. Characterized by a long handle, fine blade, and teeth that usually cut on the pull stroke, the Japanese saw is ideal for cutting dovetails because it produces a particularly thin cut.

The long handle tucks neatly into the crook of your elbow for superb control, but I've found that some of the thinner blades have a tendency to wander and you have less control than with a fine dovetail or gent's saw. Japanese saws take a bit of getting used to when starting the cut into end grain, since the teeth have a tendency to bite into the fibres and don't ride over the timber quite as smoothly as a Western tenon saw.

Japanese saws have no kerf and are ideal for dovetailing.

There are many types of Japanese saw, and you won't regret buying one to experiment with. For dovetailing, you'll probably need a saw with about 24 tpi.

Materials

All about wood – aromatic timber

The bottom of a drawer is traditionally made from an aromatic timber, like cedar of Lebanon or incense cedar, to ward off insects and for a delicious smell as you pull the drawer open. These drawer bottoms are often left unfinished so as not to inhibit the aroma.

Quarter-sawing a log or a board

Drawer sides, which are sometimes known as drawer linings, are traditionally made from quarter-sawn timber.

1 By cutting up yew branches on a band saw, you'll soon learn how to quarter-saw a log.

2 Cut it into strips, perhaps 25 mm (1 in) wide.

The description derives from the technique of dividing a log into quarters along its length and then cutting boards with the growth rings at 90° to the face. Because wood shrinks more from the centre outwards (radially) than around the circumference (tangentially), this is the most stable cut. There is also less opportunity for the growth rings to 'straighten', which leads to the cupping of plain-sawn boards.

It can be difficult to find quarter-sawn boards, since most logs are plain-sawn. The most you will find is some quarter-sawn sections on a board, usually towards the edges. It is, however, very simple to convert a plain-sawn board into a quarter-sawn example.

3 You can see from the reassembled log how the grain on each board is at 90° to the surface. This is the most stable cut.

Project **Sideboard 2**

For your paperwork

A good, deep drawer is superb in the hallway
for storing phone books and all those items that
don't have a home in the office or the kitchen.
Making this drawer is an excellent exercise in
dovetailing.

1 ft 8 in (510 mm)

3 ft 7¾ in (1110 mm)

¾ in (19 mm)

1 ft 2½ in (370 mm)

10 in (255mm)

3 ft 1¼ in (945 mm)

1 ft 5 in (430 mm)

½ in (12 mm)

2 ft 9 in (840 mm)

8¾ in (220 mm)

2¾ in (70 mm)

3 ft ¼ in (921 mm)

1ft 1⅜ in (340 mm)

3 ft ¾ in (960 mm)

1 ft 1⅜ in (340 mm)

1¾ in (45 mm)

Cutting list

Part	Material	Quantity	Dimensions length, width, thickness
K Front	softwood	1	921 x 190 x 12 mm (36¼ x 7½ x ½ in)
L Back	softwood	1	921 x 181 x 12 mm (36¼ x 7⅛ x ½ in)
M Side	softwood	2	430 x 190 x 12 mm (17 x 7½ x ½ in)
N False front	softwood	1	921 x 222 x 10 mm (36¼ x 8¾ x ⅜ in)
O Base	ply/softwood	1	908 x 419 x 2 mm (35¾ x 16½ x ³⁄₁₆ in)

1 Plane all the parts to thickness, and cut and plane to width. There are a couple of points to note. Instead of cutting lapped dovetails, as an introduction to this most famous joint we are gluing a false front (**N**) to the drawer after assembly to give the impression of a lapped joint (see Types of lap joint, page 43). The fact that we've specified a plywood base influences the design of the drawer, although actually we've adapted the traditional approach used when a solid timber base is fitted to let it move (see Attaching tabletops, page 184), so the back (**L**) is narrower than the sides (**M**).

Rout the groove in the sides and front for the base, 6 mm (¼ in) from the bottom edge. It is easier to do this now than after you have cut the dovetails, when there's also a risk of taking chips out of the tails in particular.

Mark out the tails on the front or back at whichever corner you want, using a dovetail template to get the angle right (see Dovetail template, page 212). Cut the joint.

2 Use the tails to mark up the pins on the sides. Cut the pins and test the fit; do the same for the others.

Cut the plywood base (**O**) to size, and slot it into the sides and front; assemble the drawer without glue.

Glue up the drawers, using sash clamps with blocks to pull the joints together. Check the diagonals, then slide the base into the grooves and pin to the bottom edge of the back. You can support the base further with thin bearers glued to the sides and front beneath the groove.

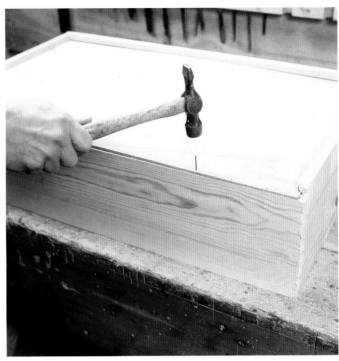

3 Use a block plane or belt sander to trim back the proud pins or tails (see Block planes, page 26 and Belt-sanding a board, page 118). Then glue the false front to the drawer. Once the glue has set, you can plane the edges and clean up the front.

4 Test the fit of the drawer in the sideboard. There should be a gap of no more than 1.6 mm ($\frac{1}{16}$ in) around the outside of the drawer and preferably a bit less. The important thing is that the gap is consistent.

Finish the outside of the drawer and screw the drawer pulls to the front.

Lessons learned

- Dovetails take a lot of practice!

- Don't worry if the pins protrude through the tails, as they can easily be sanded back afterwards.

- Experiment with the order of cutting dovetails. You may find you prefer to cut the pins before the tails.

- For the drawer to fit well, the case must be absolutely square.

Lesson 4
Crosscut to accuracy

Getting started

If you want to convert wide timber into manageable boards, buy a band saw. But if you want to achieve some really accurate results quickly and repeatedly, go out and get a table saw. When you buy one, though, make sure it's good, since, it will soon become your best friend and you'll discover uses for it you never imagined.

There's a bit of a cultural divide about the table saw. In the United States it has become a multi-purpose machine, used for many operations. In the United Kingdom the spindle moulder (shaper) and the dedicated tenoning machine are favoured, and the table saw tends to be used for fewer jobs. Some woodworkers prefer the radial-arm saw or its modern equivalent, the sliding chop saw or mitre saw. These are especially suitable for narrower workshops, because the work is laid on the table and the saw is moved. But they are not so useful for ripping timber and for cutting wide sheet materials.

Using a table saw

I don't believe that a table saw can compare with the band saw, surface planer, thicknesser or even the router table as a machine that will help an improving woodworker make a great leap forward, but it is certainly useful. It is also very versatile and has the potential for employment in many jointing jobs. It must, however, be set up very accurately.

Safety is an important consideration when using a table saw because it is a powerful machine. It is essential that you keep the riving knife fitted to the saw, since this keeps the cut open so that the board doesn't bind on the blade

Make sure the saw blade is square to the table.

With an angle setter you can set the blade at a specific tilt to cut joints for certain types of geometric angles.

and kick back at the operator. By keeping the guard in place, you ensure that any timber that flicks up from the saw can't go very far in the air and towards your face. Many top guards also have fittings for dust extraction. There are some operations on a table saw, such as tenoning, that can be done safely enough, but you should fit some form of home-made guard to house the blade and limit the consequences of kickback.

Table saws can be improved by fitting a home-made or store-bought insert where the blade projects from the table. When you are trimming small pieces off the end of a board, they have a tendency to fall down into the gap in the insert. If the gap is too wide, say more than 1.5 mm ($\frac{1}{16}$ in), there is

Lesson planner

Key techniques	Key tools and materials
• Using a table saw • Ripping with a table saw • Crosscutting with a table saw • Using a drawing	• The table saw • Alternatives to the table saw • Beading tools • Choosing a saw blade

There needs to be a good angle gauge on the saw to show the tilt of the blade.

It's good to have an off switch you can knock with your knee.

A guard over the switch seals it when you aren't in the workshop.

In an emergency, you can switch off the table saw with a push stick.

Some saws have a clip for a push stick on the rip fence, which keeps it close at hand.

a chance that trimmings will catch the blade and be thrown back towards you. Always wear ear defenders when using a table saw – or any machinery and power tool for that matter – and make sure the dust is extracted. I often wear a visor if I'm concerned that an operation might be hazardous.

It is very important that you have push sticks at hand for pushing the timber across the saw. You need two, one for each hand, but it's a good idea to have more around the workshop, since they always seem to get mislaid. Make sure you have them by every machine, particularly the table saw, band saw and router table. Get used to using a push stick even when you don't need it – it's a good habit to develop. However, remain aware of the risks you face, and don't assume that you are safe because you are wearing the gear and using a push stick. It is just as important to take note of the pressure you are having to

Make sure that the power is disconnected when you change the blade.

exert and to listen to the sound of the machine, since mistakes and accidents often happen when tools are under load and you are having to work too hard. I've noticed that you use more pressure with a push stick than you might with only your hands, and then when the cut finishes, your hand rushes towards the blade.

Ripping with a table saw

Personally, I cut boards to width along the grain (ripping) with a band saw as often as possible because you lose less wood in the cut. However, the band saw won't always cut beautifully straight, and a home woodworker's band saw is probably not as powerful or as fast-cutting as the home woodworker's table saw.

Usually you will rip with the board against the fence, which you should be able to adjust side to side and forward and back. By sliding the fence forwards a little, you gain more lead-in and counter any tendency for the wood to bind against the fence after the cut.

Use the rip fence for cutting along the grain.

When ripping long boards, it is useful to have a roller stand on which the timber can rest as it leaves the saw. These can be made from a piece of broom handle held in a frame, or you can buy various designs depending on your budget. I have only the most basic metal roller, and not the ball-bearing type, since most of my work is relatively short. But if you do a lot of work with long boards or whole sheets of plywood, it is worth buying a support that is accurate and smooth-running.

Crosscutting with a table saw

I use a table saw for accurate crosscutting operations more than anything else. For this you need a fine-toothed blade and an accurate mitre fence. These are the two essentials, but I would also add a flip stop, since it is so useful for repetitive cutting.

If you have a sliding carriage for the mitre fence, and I thoroughly recommend that you get one, it is worth

The sliding carriage on this saw locks the fence at 90° and 45°.

With the crosscut fence at 45°, you can cut accurate mitres.

A flip stop is essential for repetitive cutting to length.

Fix a false table to the crosscut fence to hold the workpiece solidly.

Use a fine adjuster, or your finger, to move the flip stop a fraction.

fitting a false 'table' that slides back and forth on the carriage. This way you can run the plywood 'table' right up against the blade for less breakout, and it also means that the join between the carriage and the proper table is bridged because it can be very difficult to level this join on cheaper table saws. The only disadvantage is that you lose a bit of available cutting height.

When it comes to cutting angles with a table saw, it's best to alter the fence, rather than tilting the blade. Resetting the fence afterwards is usually far easier than resetting the blade, though it does depend on the saw.

Common tasks for the table saw

There are a number of books that concentrate solely upon the table saw, for it is a versatile machine and can perform many operations.

1 **Tenoning.** The simplest technique is to cut tenon shoulders on the table saw, with the component against a stop on the mitre fence. You can then remove the cheeks on a band saw or with a tenon saw. However, you can also produce a carriage for the rail to be tenoned that uses the table saw for cutting the cheeks as well.

2 **Dovetails.** With the blade tilted to the appropriate angle, you can cut the tails. Then, with the blade upright and fence adjusted, cut the pins, at least to remove the bulk of the

Watch out that the saw does not bind if you run the tenon against the rip fence while using the crosscut fence.

Set the saw blade to the depth of the tenon.

Cut the shoulders of tenons on the table saw; cheeks on a band saw.

With a special jig against the rip fence, you can cut tenons easily.

The notch pushes the workpiece through the saw.

waste before you clean them up by hand (see Cutting a through dovetail, page 209).

3 Tapering. You can buy adjustable jigs that you fit to the rip fence on the table saw for cutting tapers. Or you can simply cut a piece of plywood 25 mm (1 in) thick, at the appropriate angle, and fit it to the rip fence.

4 Housings. Table saws are often used for cutting grooves, though you ought to replace the top guard with

With a home-made jig you can cut tapers with ease using a table saw.

a home-made alternative. Don't remove the riving knife. With multiple cuts you can use the table saw to cut housings wider than the kerf of a single blade, or you can buy kits for stacking blades. The use of wobble blades, which are canted over at an angle as they spin, is frowned upon in some countries.

5 Mitres. Though the radial-arm saw and the mitre or chop saw are often favoured by site carpenters for cutting mitres, the table saw is still an effective tool for the job.

Set the depth of cut with a depth gauge.

Using a drawing like an atlas

Working your way around a drawing is a bit like using a road map to search for identifying details, while using the cutting list for supporting evidence. A good drawing shows the construction clearly, with no doubts about the position and shape of components, and has as few annotations as possible.

Ideally, the cutting list should give the length of each component, though you may want to add a little to this when roughly cutting up all the parts. Those dimensions that are defined by the cutting list – such as the width and thickness of a part – don't need to be repeated in the drawing. There are, however, exceptions to this rule, specifically when parts are shaped or tapered, in which case you need to look for the angle and length of the taper and the final width or thickness. A good drawing should also show the distances between shoulders, such as on the rails of a table, which are not given by the cutting list.

When using a drawing, check that the dimensions tally with the cutting list before you start cutting timber. This not only reduces the number of wasteful mistakes, but also acquaints you with the construction. Check that the dimensions add up. Be particularly cautious when the measurements are given in both metric and imperial, since the conversions may not be correct. Try to establish which measurement was originally used by searching for the most frequent 'rounded' figures. If you are able to determine this, you can then make your own conversions and check their validity as you proceed.

Tools

Making a scratch stock

The scratch stock is a great little tool for beading, and there is something satisfying about making it yourself. Use an old piece of hacksaw blade for the cutter, inserted into a wooden stock and held in a groove by screws. Make very gradual, shallow cuts, slowly extending the blade from the stock. You can sharpen the blade as you might a cabinet scraper (see Using a cabinet scraper, page 117 and Sharpening a cabinet scraper, page 119).

Cut a short length of hacksaw blade for the cutter on the scratch stock.

Cut the stock of the scratch stock from a piece of hardwood.

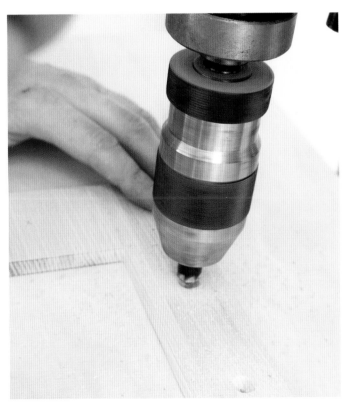

Drill and countersink each half of the stock. Insert the cutter between them and screw the stock together.

Using a file, work the shape of the cutter on the end of the hacksaw blade.

Tidy up the scratch stock on a disc sander.

Scratch stocks need to be held tightly, and gradually the bead is formed.

The table saw

When it comes to choosing a table saw, the first criterion is likely to be the size of blade, with the most common sizes being 203 mm (8 in) and 254 mm (10 in) for home woodworkers. Blade diameter often determines the power of the motor, the size and robustness of the machine, and the price. Generally, though, I'd favour buying an expensive small machine over a cheap, larger table saw.

The problem is that a 203-mm (8-in) table saw cannot cut boards 203 mm (8 in) thick. The amount of blade protruding through the table will be far less than this, and then you have to take into account the way the top guard fits on the riving knife, since this can further inhibit the cut depth. When using the blade on an angle, the depth of cut is restricted even more.

The best saws have cast tables, which are made from either aluminum or iron and ground flat. A good model will have a sliding carriage to make crosscutting easier and far more accurate. Some have extension tables to the sides and back, but a roller stand will do for the latter, and you don't need as much table space as you might imagine. The quality of the saw can also be judged by the type of motor used. The cheaper models are fitted with brush motors, which you can identify by their high-pitched screech. They also tend to start quickly, almost with a jolt. Induction motors are much quieter, which is a major consideration for home woodworkers, and many will have a soft start, thereby taming the beast a bit.

Alternatives to the table saw

The traditional approach to woodworking is to have a solid table saw that is used for ripping and crosscutting, but there are alternatives or additions you might consider, since they are better for some jobs.

Trade secret

Marking out a curve from two halves

When marking out a curve for cutting on a band saw, you need to draw only half the shape on a piece of card or paper. Transfer that curve twice on to a piece of thin plywood to create a template to use for marking all components. Don't be tempted to mark the first piece and then use this for the next and so on, since you are likely to alter the shape as you cut each piece.

1 **Radial-arm saw.** Favoured by anyone who rarely rips boards, and who often cuts to length. If you have a band saw for ripping boards, the radial-arm saw might be a good choice, especially if you have a long workshop with plenty of worksurface space, but perhaps not so much free space in the centre. Table saws, in comparison, are best in square workshops, where there is plenty of space in the centre of the room for both crosscutting and ripping. Radial-arm saws are not brilliant for cutting up sheet materials, since the length of cut is limited.

2 **Chop saw.** Also known as the mitre saw, and used extensively on site, the chop saw is very similar to the radial-arm saw, but usually has more sophisticated adjustments for cutting mitres. It also has a much shorter length of cut, so is more likely to complement a table saw than replace it. Like the radial-arm saw, you need plenty of wall space. It is excellent if you are cutting loads of mitres. Some chop saws now have a table over the top for ripping.

3 **Contractor's saw or saw site.** A lightweight version of the traditional table saw, the contractor's saw is usually relatively inexpensive for the cut it offers. It is certainly worth considering, and the flip-over version offers options for using the machine as a traditional table saw or as a chop saw.

Beading tools

Obviously you can use a router for beading, but sometimes for small jobs it's quicker and more satisfying to do it by hand. You can either make a scratch stock yourself (see Making a scratch stock, page 223), or buy a beading tool with ready-formed cutters.

Choosing a saw blade

Get used to changing the saw blade in the table saw, since the choice of blade has a significant impact on what you can achieve with the machine. It is certainly worth buying a good blade because the table saw lives and dies on the quality of the cut.

The number of teeth is probably the main consideration when buying a saw blade. Though there's

a temptation to select a general-purpose blade, say 32 teeth for an 203-mm (8-in) blade, this tends to fall short for both ripping and crosscutting. A finer blade, say 48 teeth for the same blade, will crosscut beautifully to a finish you can joint, while still being able to rip reasonably. I'd also buy a rip saw of 16 teeth for a much more aggressive cut to cope with the longer fibres when ripping. With fewer teeth, there are wider spaces for the dust to be ejected, but don't use this blade for crosscutting, since it will tear the wood.

You won't find a huge range of kerf widths when it comes to choosing a saw blade. Most are about 4 mm (⅛ in), but you can find finer. The majority of the teeth have relatively similar shapes, but some have what is known as negative rake for a finer cut and less chance of grabbing occurring in a mitre saw.

Cleaning and storing saw blades

If you have more than one saw blade, make sure they are stored safely so that their brittle tungsten teeth don't chip in the holder. Keep them well oiled to stop rusting.

It is an easy mistake to think that a saw blade is blunt when often it is just caked in resin. Ironically, cutting softwoods can do more damage to a saw blade than hardwoods. However, it is short-lived, since the build-up of dirt can be treated with a cleaning spray, which can also be employed for router cutters.

Materials

All about wood – abrasive timber

Some species are famously abrasive and dull blades faster than others. This isn't always because they are harder or heavier than others, since some timber contains abrasive particles that wear down an edge more quickly than others. Oak, for instance, can be abrasive, but it is the exotic species that are likely to be worst for this.

Project **Bookcase 1**

For the living room

Though it looks large, this bookcase is no more than
a cabinet, to the front of which is attached a frame
and doors. The cabinet can be joined together with
a biscuit jointer. Turn to page 240 to make the doors.

340 mm (1 ft 1⅜ in)
325 mm (1 ft ¾ in)
19 mm (¾ in)
1780 mm (5 ft 10 in)
655 mm (2 ft 1¾ in)
945 mm (3 ft 1¼ in)
445 mm (1 ft 5½2 in)
50 mm (2 in)
340 mm (1 ft 1⅜ in)
970 mm (3 ft 2¼ in)
100 mm (4 in)

Shopping list

Tools and materials

Brass shelf supports and lug supports: 16 of each
Beading cutter or beading tool

Cutting list (cabinet)

Part	Material	Quantity	Dimensions length, width, thickness	Part	Material	Quantity	Dimensions length, width, thickness
A Top/ bottom	cherry	2	933 x 343 x 19 mm (36¾ x 13½ x ¾ in)	**J** Cupboard back	plywood	1	676 x 952 x 6 mm (26⅝ x 37½ x ¼ in)
B Pot shelf	cherry	1	933 x 335 x 19 mm (36¾ x 13¼ x ¾ in)	**K** Plinth front	cherry	1	972 x 102 x 19 mm (38¼ x 4 x ¾ in)
C Side	cherry	2	1778 x 324 x 19 (70 x 12¾ x ¾ in)	**L** Plinth side	cherry	2	340 x 102 x 19 mm (13⅜ x 4 x ¾ in)
D Shelf	cherry	3	933 x 324 x 19 mm (36¾ x 12¾ x ¾ in)	**M** Plinth back	cherry	1	933 x 102 x 19 mm (36¾ x 4 x ¾ in)
E Cupboard shelf	cherry	1	933 x 286 x 19 mm (36¾ x 11¼ x ¾ in)	**N** Cornice front/back	cherry	2	972 x 67 x 19 mm (38¼ x 2⅝ x ¾ in)
F Front top rail	cherry	1	870 x 102 x 16 mm (34¼ x 4 x ⅝ in)	**O** Cornice side	cherry	2	340 x 67 x 19 mm (13⅜ x 2⅝ x ¾ in)
G Back top rail	cherry	1	933 x 51 x 19 mm (36¾ x 2 x ¾ in)	**P** Dustboard	plywood	1	865 x 254 x 6 mm (34 x 10 x ¼ in)
H Upright	cherry	2	1778 x 50 x 19 mm (70 x 2 x ¾ in)	**Q** Glue block	cherry	20	27 x 19 x 19 mm (1⁵⁄₁₆ x ¾ x ¾ in)
I Bookcase back	plywood	1	1083 x 952 x 6 mm (42⅝ x 37½ x ¼ in)				

1 Start by preparing the main components of the cabinet, namely the sides (**C**), the top and bottom (**A**), the pot shelf (**B**), and the back top rail (**G**). You can probably make do without the final part. Cut all the parts exactly to length and drill the sides for the shelf supports. Note that the pot shelf is 6 mm (¼ in) narrower than the top and bottom (**A**) to account for the thickness of the ply back (**I** and **J**), which is rebated into the sides, top and bottom.

2 Joint the horizontal parts (**A**, **B** and **G**) to the sides (**C**) with dowels or biscuits depending on your equipment and preference.

3 Rebate the back edges of the sides, top and bottom for the ply back. It's easier to do this with the router hand-held than by using a router table (see Lesson 5, page 136).

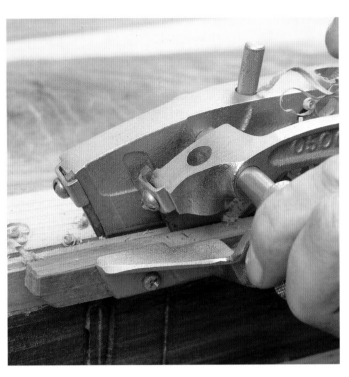

4 Cut the notches from the front of the top and bottom to accommodate the uprights (**H**).

Cut out the two pieces of ply for the back, making sure the cuts are accurate. Check the diagonals to test for squareness.

Glue up the cabinet using sash clamps to draw the sides to the horizontal parts. You'll need six sash clamps: two per shelf, front and back. Check the diagonals and screw the back in place to add support.

Prepare the timber for the uprights and front top rail (**F**). Note that the front top rail is slightly thinner than the uprights to make up for the beaded profile along the inside edge of the uprights.

5 Use a router, scratch stock, or a combination plane to shape the bead down the upright (see Lesson 6, page 146 and Making a scratch stock, page 223).

6 If you choose to join the rail to the uprights with a mortise and tenon, the rail will have to be a bit longer for the tenon.

7 Cut the curved recess from the top front rail with a jigsaw or band saw, having marked it up with a template.

8 You can glue up the rail and uprights now, then fix them in position with dowels (see Using the dowel joint, page 54), or wait until the doors are ready next lesson and cut the hinge recesses first.

9 Prepare the parts for the plinth (**K**, **L**, **M**). For strength, this is best constructed with reinforced butt joints (see Using the dowel joint, page 54 and Using a biscuit jointer, page 138), but it would be tidier mitred, in which case you might need to screw or glue right-angled corner blocks inside the corners. If you rout the profile along the top edge of the plinth after assembling it, the fact that the corners aren't mitred will hardly be noticeable.

10 Cut the shaped lower edge of the front plinth rail (**K**) using a template as a guide. Using a halved template is useful here (see Marking out a curve from two halves, page 224). Assemble the plinth. If you can do so, dry the bookcase on its back so that you can test the fit of the plinth against the cabinet. The bottom of the bookcase should fit neatly on blocks screwed and glued to the inside of the plinth.

11 Rout the profile on the cornice components (**N** and **O**) and also rout a rebate on the top inside edge to take the plywood dustboard (**P**).

Lessons learned

- Large assemblies are daunting, but actually not always as difficult as you might imagine.

- Mitres are one of the most difficult joints to get right, especially when they are as long as the ones on the cornice.

- Finishing shaped components is much more difficult than finishing straight parts.

12 Mitre the cornice parts and assemble with a band clamp, screwing the dustboard in place for support. You can screw or dowel the cornice to the top when you are ready. Prepare the timber for the other shelves (**D** and **E**) and insert on the support. Now you are ready to make the doors: see page 240.

Lesson 5
Frames and panels

Getting started

Medieval furniture was characterized by being made from solid boards in a simple style. An evolution of this approach has been to hold panels within a frame. This saves on wood and gives the piece greater strength and stability. However, making a frame and panel needs cutting and jointing skills and equipment.

I've always loved making panels. There is something very satisfactory about machining all the parts and then jointing the components to fit together. With so many options for ornamentation and decoration, you can stamp your individuality on a design and try out different effects. You will also need to experiment with more advanced techniques, and jointing accurately puts greater emphasis on the integrity of your work, so your tools have to be razor sharp and working well.

Panels can be made from plywood or MDF for economy, but the excitement comes from producing solid timber work. More care is needed to allow the wood to move, but you can experiment with various styles of cutter to produce different raised and fielded panelling.

The principles of frame and panel construction

One of the most important developments in furniture design was the evolution of frame and panel construction, which replaced the use of simple, solid boards for the doors and 'bodywork' of cabinets and chests. A panel within a frame makes better use of timber, is more stable, and provides more opportunities for decoration and individuality.

Today it means we can use man-made sheet materials in projects while retaining a sense of craftsmanship. This is economical, saves time, and makes the frame even easier to construct, though it may inhibit the potential for ornamentation.

The frame and panel offers the woodworker so many opportunities for individuality. You can alter the

When rails are moulded, you may need to meet profiles with a mitre.

The solid wood panel fits into a groove in the frame components.

Lesson planner

Key techniques	Key tools and materials
• Making a frame and panel • Variations on the mortise and tenon • Making a panel from thin strips	• Matched router cutters • Drilling jigs for shelves • Moisture meters • Horizontal drum sanders • All about wood – figure

dimensions of the rails and stiles in relation to the panel, with some of the Arts and Crafts designers doing this with spectacular results. The frame edges, particularly those facing inwards, can be profiled with any moulding, though it is the lack of any such decoration that distinguishes Shaker furniture. Study furniture of different periods to see how these small details help define the age.

In almost every case, the posts and rails are tenoned and mortised, with tenons worked on the horizontal rails and mortises cut in the posts. In this lesson we will look at some of the variations on the joint and discuss how they can be made by machine or power tool. There are any number of ways you can deal with the panel. Usually, it is inserted into grooves routed into the rails and posts, though you can also use a rebate and bead.

When gluing a solid wood panel into a frame, apply only a dab of glue so that the panel can move.

Trade secret

Judging the sizes of tenons
In deciding the depth of the mortise, you are trying to compromise the need for a long tenon to give the joint strength, without weakening the posts. I'd go for a mortise between half and two-thirds the width of the post. The same compromise applies when marking out the haunch. For a rail 50 mm (2 in) wide, the groove for the panel is likely to be up to 10 mm (⅜ in) deep. The haunch is about 12 mm (½ in) wide, and the tenon proper is 30 mm (1⅛ in) wide.

The panel itself can be flat, or raised and profiled, sometimes known as fielding.

Making the basic frame and panel
The simplest frame and panel has no moulding on the rails and posts, and the flat panel is fitted into a groove, which is the same width as the mortise. In these circumstances the panel will usually be plywood or veneered board, and it can be glued into the groove to help strengthen the assembly.

If, the panel is made from solid timber you must give it room to move, so the grooves in the posts (assuming the grain runs up and down) are cut deep enough to give the panel some extra space. In this instance you fix the panel in place by using glue in the groove down one post, or with a dab of adhesive at the centre of the groove on each rail. With the first technique, the panel can expand and contract across its whole width towards the unglued post, while with the latter technique the panel moves both sides away from the centre.

Making a simple frame and panel
1 **Leave a horn** of at least 25 mm (1 in) on the end of each post and cut the rails exactly to length. Extending the mortise to the end of the post would weaken the timber, so instead the tenon has a haunch to fit into the groove, which is routed the full length of the post. The haunch stops the rail from twisting.

2 **Chop out the mortises first.** Then rout the groove for the panel along the inside edge of both the posts and rails. It is easier to cut the mortise before the groove is worked, basically because you can see the marks more clearly, and the cutter isn't deflected. It doesn't matter that you cut the groove in the rails before cutting the tenons; in fact, it reduces the amount of work you need to do.

3 **Cut the tenon,** with the haunch fitting neatly in the groove. This has to be accurate for doors, since the top of the rail and post will be visible.
Alternative If you don't want the haunch to be visible on the top of the post but need the benefits a haunch provides (no weakness in the post and no twisting of the tenon), you can slope the haunch. Cut it just as you would any other tenon.

4 **Cut the panel to size.** If it is made from solid timber, rather than sheet materials, you need to leave at least 3 mm (⅛ in) for movement.

5 **Assemble the frame** and panel before you cut off the horns on the posts. You can apply a finish to the panel and the inside edges of the frame before assembly, but leave all the others unfinished, to be tidied up after the glue has set.

Check for squareness when clamping up a frame and check the diagonals.

Decorating the simple frame and panel

In Shaker furniture, the simple frame and panel was left entirely unadorned. However, you may want to add a profile on the inside edge of the rails and posts. There are a couple of ways to do this.

1 **The stopped chamfer.** The simplest solution, which gives a piece a country look and feel, is to chamfer the inside edges but stop short of the joints. If you use a router to do this, the end of the stopped chamfer will be slightly scalloped, which can be left like that, but is a telltale sign of this modern technique. For a more traditional look, pare back the ends of the chamfer.

2 **A bearing-guided router.** With the frame assembled dry, but without the panel in place, you can use a router with a bearing-guided cutter to shape a profile. The only problem is that the moulding narrows at the joints, though you can hide this with a little careful scribing by hand.

You may notice, on some budget furniture, that there is sometimes a V-section groove along the line of the joint. This is used to hide any inaccuracy in the joint and make finishing easier since you don't have to worry about cross-grain scratching.

Variations on the mortise and tenon

The way that the mortise and tenon is marked out and cut depends on two main factors. The first, as we've seen, is the way the panel is held in the frame, which is most tidily done with a groove. Fitting the panel into a rebate presents other challenges. Proper decoration of the frame can be done more effectively than the compromises we've explored so far.

1 **Rebated frame.** Some panels, particularly thick ones, are best held in a rebate, with pins or with a bead. This has consequences for the way the mortise and tenon are laid out. The solution is to have offset shoulders so that one tenon shoulder is longer than the other to fit into the rebate.

2 **Mitred mouldings.** The traditional, and most effective, way to join a post and rail that have a moulding along the inside edge is to mitre the profile at the mortise. This takes some care, but isn't as difficult as you'd imagine. The best solution is to make a jig to guide the chisel at 45°, to pare the mitre. Rout the moulding first, and the panel groove or mortise; then cut the mortise, just as you would normally. To mitre the mouldings, cut the edge of the post to the depth of the moulding and then mitre the end of the profile.

A horizontal panel-moulding cutter is large and must run slowly.

A vertical cutter is easier, although you have to hold the panel firmly.

Producing panels

There are many options for decorating the panel. The most traditional is with a long bevel, usually stepped at the top. This can be done with a plane, specifically a shoulder plane. Router catalogues are full of more complex shapes you can try, though the cutters are very expensive and need to be used in a router table. The least expensive and easiest to use are vertical panel cutters, as opposed to the much larger horizontal cutters.

Making a panel from strips

First, though, you have to make the panel. Normally you will have to do this by gluing up a number of boards with butt joints to produce a panel that is wide enough and stable enough. Very rarely will you find a single piece of timber that can be used as a panel over, say, 203 mm (8 in) wide without incurring some risk of the board cupping, though this does depend on the thickness of the panel. Very thin solid wood panels, of 6 mm (¼ in) or less, shouldn't have the strength to do any damage if they start to cup.

Assembling a panel from thin strips is also economical, since you don't have to rely upon wide boards. But it does mean you have to spend more time arranging the timber, joining the boards and cleaning up.

1 Start by planing and edging the boards, but at least 4 mm (⅛ in) thicker than the final thickness. Once you become better at judging the grain of wood, you will often find that you only have to edge the boards and can leave the faces rough-sawn from the band saw until they have been glued up as a panel. This way you don't end up surfacing sides twice, before and after gluing.

2 When it comes to arranging the strips, you must check from the end grain that the growth rings alternate, to diminish the consequences of the boards cupping. If they do start cupping because of a change in conditions, they should cup in opposite directions, resulting in a wavy line but not major damage.

3 Once you have this in mind, you also need to arrange the boards for visual effect. For a start, ideally you want an odd number of boards so that there isn't a conspicuous centre-line. Then it's a case of looking for boards that match and avoiding joints that certainly don't match. Watch out for knots or defects that have been cut in half, since these will show up clearly along a join line. When the grain on one board is curving or the rings are far apart, you don't want to put it next to another that has very straight grain with close marking. Remember you are trying to recreate the effect of a real board and doing your best to hide the lines.

With panel boards, find an arrangement that has an even grain pattern.

4 Glue up the board. I use polyurethane adhesive for this job because it is very strong, and much easier to pare off when set than most other glues (see Foaming adhesives, page 89 and Advanced adhesives, page 200). You shouldn't need to reinforce this sort of joint with biscuits or dowels, but if you do, plan them carefully so that they aren't revealed when it comes to fielding the panel.

5 Glue up the panel, using sash clamps above and below if necessary to stop it from bowing.

6 Once the glue has set, clean up the joints and plane. If the panel is very wide, you may need to surface it by hand, though horizontal drum sanders can take much wider panels than most thicknessers and surface planers (see Horizontal drum sanders, page 238). This is when it's good to have learned excellent hand-planing skills.

TIP: When assembling panels wider than your surface planer or thicknesser can cope with, consider producing the panel in halves. Surface both halves and then join them together, perhaps using biscuits or dowels to ensure that they are level. Then you'll have far less hand planing or belt sanding to do to clean up the panel.

Always rout across the end grain first with the vertical moulding cutter.

Conditioning panels

To be sure that panels won't bow, it is a good idea to leave them a day or so before surfacing and cleaning up. In large workshops, you will often find a stack of panels, glued up but rough. This gives the boards time to do any moving and also means that you have plenty of panels to plane to the same thickness at the same time.

Preparing for movement

There is a very good chance that any solid wood panel will shrink inside its frame once it is in a centrally heated home. This is why some woodworkers condition wood under the bed to get it well acclimatized. Given that the panel will contract, it is very important to apply finishes to the panel before inserting it in the frame, especially stains. Otherwise, when the panel contracts, a contrasting line will be exposed.

Tools

Matched router cutters

The modern solution to mass-producing doors is to use matched router cutters that mould and groove the rails and posts, and can then be used to cut an exact reflection of the moulding and groove on the end of the rails. This dispenses with the need to mitre the moulding, and also means you don't need to cut mortises and tenons, but the technique can only be used for smaller doors that don't take too much wear and tear. They are designed for use in a router table.

With matched router cutters, where accuracy is important, hold the work piece firmly.

When cutting across the end of a rail, support the rail with the mitre slide.

The joint works well for small doors, because the panel sits in the groove.

A shelf-drilling jig is set up very easily by holding the two runners on a purpose-made sash clamp.

By using a special lug, you can move the whole assembly for further drilling.

You can change guide bushes in the mechanism of the jig for different drill bits.

Make a drilling jig from plywood, using a collar on the drill bit for depth control.

Drilling dowel holes for shelves

The dowel joint may not be as popular now as it was twenty years ago, but dowel jigs are superb for laying out repeat holes for fitting shelves and the like. Alternatively, you can make your own by simply marking up a length of plywood and drilling holes in the appropriate places to create a template.

The home-made drilling jig has guides underneath for accurate positioning.

Moisture meters are ideal for testing the condition of boards.

Moisture meters

Once you start making panels for furniture, you will need to start considering the moisture content of the timber you are using. Because the boards can be wide, any movement caused by changes in temperature or humidity will be amplified and could damage the piece you are making. Moisture meters cost about £30 upwards, and you can choose one with spikes or one that measures the resistance through electromagnetic waves. It is important, though, that the scale goes down below 10 per cent moisture content, since timber used in projects in hot, dry homes will need to be down to 9 per cent.

Horizontal drum sanders

The horizontal drum sander is growing in popularity. This has a moving rubber conveyor that feeds a panel or board beneath a spinning drum covered in abrasive. Not only are they extremely accurate and can remove tiny quantities of waste at a time, but they are also open-ended, so that you can pass a panel through the sander two ways, doubling the available width. A typical small sander may be 406 mm (16 in) wide, so can thickness or plane a panel 813 mm (32 in) wide.

The sanding drum is raised or lowered within a frame, with the weight of the motor acting as a balance or cantilever so that the drum doesn't dip at the open end. That said, I have seen some woodworkers fit a secondary support at the open end to nullify the tendency for cheaper models to dip. Generally speaking, though, these machines are so accurate that you can use them to produce your own veneers and even to tidy up marquetry panels.

Materials

Veneer and veneering

For centuries, since the first exotics were imported from the tropics, woodworkers, particularly cabinet-makers, have been using thin veneers to produce panels. The savings in expensive timber are obvious, and there can even be a saving in time, since the veneer only needs light sanding after gluing to the core. Of course, veneered panels cannot be fielded or moulded, though I've seen some startling designs that reveal the layers of veneer and core, and make a feature of this.

Originally, cabinet-makers would apply veneer to a softwood core, but today we tend to use ply or MDF, which are both perfectly flat and need no preparation. You do, however, need to apply veneer to both sides of the core because the veneer is stronger than you imagine and will try to bow the core unless it is counterbalanced. The balancing veneer is often invisible within a project and doesn't have to be the same quality or species.

Traditionally, cabinet-makers used animal glue to stick down veneer. If you are doing a lot of gluing, you will probably use yellow glue, though you could use liquid hide adhesive. For small projects, contact adhesive is excellent. It is quick to use and the veneer is fixed immediately, with some limited opportunity for adjustment.

Veneers are cut in all sorts of ways to reproduce the effects of plain-sawn or quarter-sawn boards, with the bulk of veneers peeled from the log to produce the wide grain patterns of a plain-sawn board. Most veneers are sliced to between 0.6 and 1.0 mm thick, though you can also buy constructional veneers up to 2.0 mm, which are especially useful for laminating. Veneers come into their own when you start working, with the amazing burls and figure that are found in some timber.

All about wood – figure

You will sometimes hear woodworkers talking about the figure of a board. This has two meanings. Generally, the word refers to the grain patterning, a well-figured board having an interesting pattern created by the growth rings. More specifically, figure refers to unusual effects that are found in some boards, but are not created by the arrangement of the growth rings. The acer family of species, which includes maple, sycamore and plane, is famous for the subtle rippled, mottled and curly figure you find in some boards, as well as the extraordinary bird's-eye maple that resembles the explosion of a firework.

Apply contact adhesive to the ground, making sure it is only a thin layer.

Then apply a coat of contact adhesive to the veneer.

Test the tackiness with the back of a finger.

Glue down the veneer with a roller.

Project **Bookcase 2**

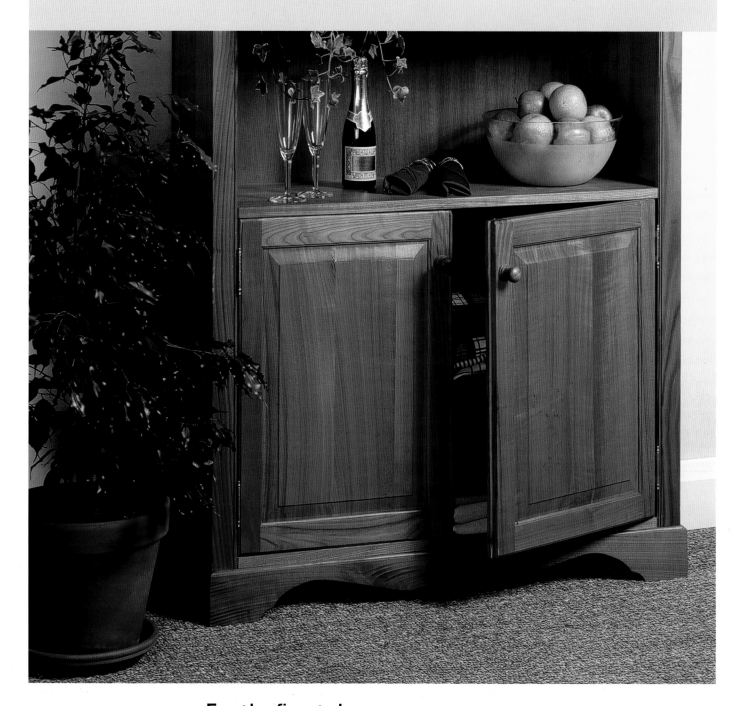

For the finest doors

In the last lesson we studied the construction of the cabinet for the bookcase, and now we are going to make the doors. Quantities given here are per single door: obviously, you will need to double this for two doors. Length given for the rails assumes a tenon 38 mm (1½ in) long. Length and width given for the panel assumes the panel is set 10 mm (⅜ in) into the grooves in the rails and stiles.

1 ft 1⅜ in (340 mm)

1 ft ¾ in (325 mm)

¾ in (19 mm)

5 ft 10 in
(1780 mm)

2 ft 1¾ in
(655 mm)

3 ft 1¼ in (945 mm)

1 ft 5½ in (445 mm)

2 in (50 mm)

1 ft 1⅜ in (340 mm)

3 ft 2¼ in (970 mm)

4 in (100 mm)

Cutting list (per door)

Part	Material	Quantity	Dimensions length, width, thickness
R Stile	cherry	2	654 x 51 x 19 mm (25¾ x 2 x ¾ in)
S Rail	cherry	2	419 x 51 x 19 mm (16½ x 2 x ¾ in)
T Panel	cherry	1	571 x 362 x 19 mm (22½ x 14¼ x ¾ in)
U Beading	cherry	1	1829 x 6 x 6 mm (72 x ¼ x ¼ in)

Shopping list

Tools and materials	Extra tools for the job
Brass butt hinges: 1 pair of 51 mm (2 in) per door **Turned doorknob** **Magnetic or ball catches**	**The doors** can be made by using matched router cutters, which are excellent for quickly producing doors that don't need the strength provided by a mortise and tenon. You will need to use them in a router table (see Using a router table, page 146).

1 Prepare the two stiles (**R**) and two rails (**S**) for each door. Start by cutting the mortises on the stiles. Notice that the tenons are haunched. Mark up the tenons on the rails.

Rout an ovolo profile along the front of the rails and stiles.

2 You can either rout a groove along the rails and stiles for the panel (**T**), or cut a rebate around the back and hold the panel in place with beading (**U**). We've chosen the latter option.

3 Cut the tenons on the rails.

4 Mitre back the moulding on the stiles and rails where they meet. Check the fit of the tenons in the mortises.

TIP: Make a jig for paring the mouldings at 45° by creating a sandwich with 45° ends that you hold over the rail or stile for mitring the moulding.

5 Test-fit the frame and check the diagonals for squareness. Once satisfied, you can glue it up.

Glue up boards for the panel (see Making panels, page 84) and then plane and sand smooth.

6 Use a raised panel-moulding cutter in a router table to shape the panel, working across the end grain first.

7 Fit the panel in the door frame, and pin the beading to the frame so that the panel can move as the ambient humidity changes. Drill a hole for the doorknob and fit.

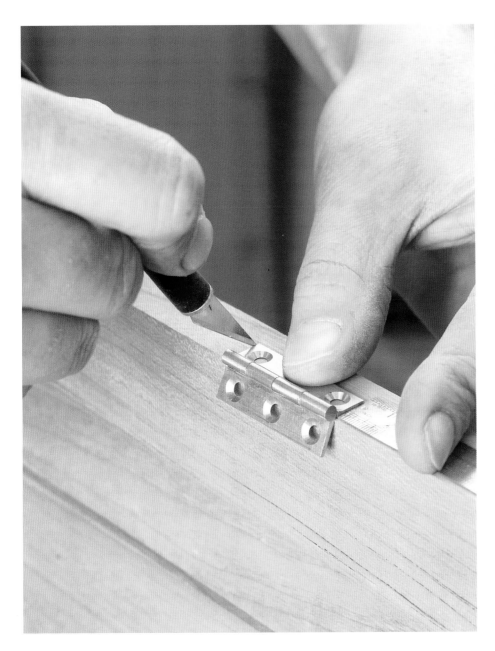

8 Cut the hinge recesses in the door and screw in place. Offer the door up to the bookcase upright and mark off the positions of the hinges. Cut the recesses and screw in place.

Clean up the completed door and finish. Fit the catches to the door and the underside of the pot shelf.

Lessons learned

- Even with a router table, it takes a lot of effort to work an even moulding around a panel. Often you will need to clean up with a shoulder plane.

- Make sure the doors are a snug fit inside the cabinet. Sloppiness here will be highlighted, and the gap must be consistent around the door.

- Fitting hinges takes much practice. Your first ones often look untidy, but gradually your technique will improve.

- Experiment with cutting mortises and tenons on components that are grooved, rebated or profiled, or a combination of them all. Understanding the layout is difficult and has to be done through trial and error.

Lesson 6
The craft of chair-making

Getting started

Chair-making
Of all the woodworking skills, chair-making is perhaps the most advanced, though it doesn't have to be so. The principle distinction from most other types of woodworking is the need to cut joints at various angles, and not just the 90° for which so much of our equipment is designed. This requires an ability to set up machines and marking devices accurately, and/or having a very good eye for angles and good coordination. The fact that chairs take more stress, especially from tilting, than most projects further complicates the issue.

Formal chairs that are largely produced from square- or rectangular-section rails, legs and stretchers, require very accurate jointing, usually with the mortise and tenon. These angled joints need careful planning and accurate marking up. More informal country chairs, like this lesson's project, the Kitchen Chair, have greater margin for error and usually employ the round mortise and tenon, the latter being lined up by eye or with a jig.

More often than not, country chairs have a solid seat, into which are drilled holes for the legs, back and arms. More formal chairs have framed seats, with the comfort provided by cane or upholstery. A compromise is the rushed or woven seat that has rails, but these are largely hidden and are usually drilled into the legs.

Angled mortise and tenon
Look at the seat of most chairs and you can't help but notice that it splays out from back to front. Look from the side and you'll see that the back support is laid back at an angle for comfort, and the seat is often tilted upwardsa little to force the sitter's lumbar region into the chair and to stop the sitter's bottom from sliding forwards. As a result, the mortise and tenon is often angled.

To cut an angled mortise and tenon you have to decide how you want to arrange the angles. To produce the splay of the seat, you would normally cut the shoulders of the rail at the appropriate angle. You'd also cut the tenon at the same angle. This way, the mortise on the legs would be cut 'square'.

The shoulders are quite easy to cut at an angle, but cutting the tenon at an angle can be tricky, as well as undermining the strength of the joint because the grain may be 'short' in the angled tenon. This is certainly the way you would always do it for the front leg. However, you will sometimes find chairs that have the rear legs twisted outwards at the same angle as the splay. Here, the joint between the side rail and the back leg is normal and square, but the joint between the back rail and back leg is at an angle.

Marking and cutting an angled mortise and tenon
In some cases, when the angle is very slight and the leg into which you are mortising is quite sturdy, there may be space to angle the mortise, keep the tenon straight, and for you to only have to angle the shoulders, but it's six of one and half a dozen of the other.

1 Set the adjustable square to the appropriate angle for the splay. Make sure the wing nut that fixes the square doesn't interfere, since you may well need to use both sides of the blade and stock.

2 Mark up and cut the mortise either in the leg or in an offcut to use as a test piece.

Keep an offcut
1 One of my rules of woodworking is to always keep an offcut of every component in a project: I either keep a complete extra piece, or just the waste that has been cut

Lesson planner

Key techniques	Key tools and materials
• Marking and cutting an angled mortise and tenon • Drilling angled holes • Basic turning • Bending wood	• Chair-making tools • Sharpening turning tools • Using grain direction • Finishing turned parts

off the end. I write on the offcut which piece it is, then use it for setting up marking gauges and machines, and for testing joints. By testing each joint first, you reduce the margin of error, and by actually cutting the first joint on a piece of scrap, you will hopefully made your mistakes (which are bound to happen) on an offcut and not on the real thing.

Cutting a preparatory joint prepares you for what will happen and how the tools or machines will react, and it builds up your muscle memory of the operation. The last joint of a batch that a woodworker cuts is always the best, and the first is usually the worst – so I've always wondered why we don't cut the last one first!

Keeping a few offcuts from parts of a project helps when it comes to setting up machines.

2 Use the adjustable square to mark up the shoulders on the rail.

3 Mark up the angle of the tenon itself along the grain (or at least at an angle to the grain). When it comes to selecting timber for the rails, this is a time when a piece with grain that curves at the end can be ideal, providing added strength to the tenon. Mark the position of the tenon on the shoulder line, and then use the adjustable square to mark up the angled tenon. It's certainly worth doing a trial joint first and potentially using this as a template.

4 Cut the tenon as you would normally.

Drilling angled holes

In the making of country chairs, holes have to be drilled at angles for the legs and other parts to splay. You can do this with one or two adjustable squares (or templates), with a cordless drill or brace and bit by eye, or you can set up an angled table on a drill press. This will certainly speed things up, especially for repetitive drilling, but according to some chair-makers, it isn't necessarily in the spirit of chair-making.

This sort of jig can be very simple, no more than a piece of plywood with a batten underneath to raise it to the appropriate angle. If you seriously get into chair-making, you could make an adjustable drilling jig, with a screw to raise and lower the table for variable angles.

Use a sliding bevel to guide the freehand drilling of angled holes.

A simple jig for a drill press makes angled drilling so simple.

Set up the tool rest roughly level with the centre of the workpiece.

Honing can be done on a slow grinder, in this case with a leather wheel and paste.

Basic turning

To produce basic country chairs, you will probably need to turn some components. This is known as spindle turning, with the workpiece held between a drive centre at the motor end and a pointed centre at the other. This is the most basic form of turning, but a very good place to start. You learn the foundations of using a roughing gouge to round the piece and a coving gouge to form the shapes.

Some slow grinders have a shaped wheel for honing the inside of gouges.

Turning depends on sharp tools. Make sure you have a good tool rest on your grinder for sharpening turning chisels.

The important thing, when turning, is to use sharp tools that are ground properly. I was fortunate to be taught in my teens how to sharpen turning tools by one of the finest turners in Great Britain. I've watched many novice turners flounder because they don't understand the importance and simplicity of this essential skill.

The key lesson when it comes to sharpening turning tools is that, unlike normal chisels and plane irons, there must only be one bevel on the turning tool. And the bevel should be concave so that it touches the wood at the end and then at the back of the bevel for support. If the bevel is flat or convex, it will only touch at the edge, and will then judder and catch, making the whole process impossible.

Sharpen turning tools on a grinder. Some people use water-cooled, slow-turning grinders for this, but I've always found it difficult to watch the edge with the water tumbling down the tool. Certainly there is less risk of burning the steel with such a machine, and I have found them to be very useful for fine carving tools, but for turning I advocate the use of a normal grinder. Make sure your grinder has a good tool rest (see Using a grinder, page 120) so that the turning tool is well supported, although I remember clearly being

On a roughing gouge like this, you are aiming for a continuously smooth, single bevel for the gouge to run well.

Skew chisels are difficult to sharpen as the point easily blues, and it is hard to achieve a straight edge and even bevels on both sides.

For roughing, hold the gouge like this for stability.

With a smaller gouge, you can hold the tool gently in your fingers.

Notice how the gouge is held at an angle to the spinning wood.

For a bead, use a small fingernail gouge, twisting the gouge in your fingers as it rolls over the bead.

Mark up any features with pencil.

shown how to develop a feel for the bevel by sharpening the turning tool without a rest and purely by feel. Don't do this yourself.

To sharpen, gently pivot the turning tool towards the spinning wheel and feel for the bevel. This is really important. Once the whole bevel is rubbing, any vibration will disappear. Check to see what you have ground on the bevel. Gradually raise your lower hand, which should be at the end of the handle, until the sparks are pouring over the edge. Then you know the tool is sharp.

This is pretty much the same action as you will use for turning: presenting the bevel until it rubs, and then raising the handle to engage the edge. Turning is really very simple, and is based on this principle, so get it right from the beginning and you will always be able to turn. It is entirely a question of touch.

Start with the roughing gouge, which looks like a big 'U', and present it to a spinning piece of wood until you hear and feel it rubbing against the timber, without the edge touching. Slowly raise the handle until the edge starts to cut the wood. The higher you raise the handle, the deeper you cut. Tilt the gouge to the left and start cutting towards the

left. Then go the other way. Soon you'll get the hang of it, and after a while you can try a coving gouge, which is sometimes referred to as a fingernail gouge. For a slicing action, like a plane, use a skew chisel, but only cut with the bottom third of the edge or the tool will jump and catch because the edge isn't supported. The tip of the skew can be used for cutting grooves and lines in the wood.

Advanced turning

Woodturning has become a hobby in itself, with more gadgets and tools produced for turners than any other woodworking speciality. It can be very satisfying, with shapes emerging from beautiful pieces of timber and heaps of shavings growing around your feet. Spindle-turning is fine for chair-making, but anyone who gets into turning will soon want to make bowls and other vessels, for which you will need to buy a chuck to hold the blank without support from the tail centre.

Bending wood
There are two techniques for bending wood, and both are great fun – in fact, this is possibly my favourite part of woodworking.

1 **Steam bending.** The most traditional technique is to use a steaming chest, in which you put the piece to be bent for a few hours. The combination of heat and moisture makes the fibres more pliable. Once it is 'cooked', remove the piece and quickly bend it around a former, holding it in place overnight for the fibres to find a new position. You'll need to bend it further than you think because there will be a tendency for the bent wood to spring back a bit.

You can make a steaming chest quite easily, perhaps even from a drainpipe if you don't have many pieces to cook at the same time. It needs to be sealed to raise the pressure as far as possible. Insert pegs for the timber to rest on, so that the steam can reach all the parts. Produce the steam by heating an old drum of water, with a rubber hose connected to the steaming chest.

The length of time the wood needs in the steamer depends on the species and the dimensions, but expect it to take at least two hours for a length of ash 25 mm (1 in) square – one of the easiest species to bend. Many species can be bent, with varying degrees of difficulty, but the important thing is to ensure the grain is straight, with no weakness or curved grain that is likely to break under pressure.

Laminating. The principle of laminating thin strips of **2** wood or ply has amazing potential, but is more complex than steam bending. With steaming you really need only one former, around which you pull the timber. For successful laminating, you need a male and a female former so that the glue line between the laminations is invisible, though this can be achieved with a strip of metal if you get into laminating in a big way. The beauty of it is that it's quick, and you don't need to make a steaming chest and wait for the wood to cook. I use the technique for making handles, and it is also used in chair-making.

Ergonomics of chair-making
When it comes to designing chairs, there are some principles concerning the human form that help us define the measurements. For a fuller explanation of chair design and ergonomics, invest in a book on furniture design – I recommend *Designing Furniture* by Seth Stem.

Dining chair

Height of seat: 451 mm (17¾ in)
Seat slope: max 25 mm (1 in) front to back
Seat width (front): 457 mm (18 in)

Seat width (back): 394 mm (15½ in)
Slope of back: 90–95°
Arm width: 489 mm (19¼ in)
Seat depth: 413 mm (16¼ in)
Back height: 813 mm (32 in)

Tools

Chair-making tools
Some tools used for chair-making are part of many standard toolkits, but other equipment may only be available from specialist suppliers, direct from manufacturers, or from second-hand dealers.

Rounders
Lathes are often not long enough for the turning of chair legs, stretchers, rails and backs. This is also a tricky operation, with time needed to prepare the timber for the lathe, and the long, thin spindles have a tendency to vibrate and the cutting edge to judder. Rounders are designed to convert square-section timber into round rods, working a little like a pencil sharpener.

Brace and bit
The brace and bit has largely been replaced by the cordless drill, but when it comes to drilling larger holes the cordless drill doesn't always have the torque for the job. That is when the brace and bit works so well, and is in many ways easier to control. There is also a beauty in the sound of the bit biting into wood and cutting the fibres.

The sticks in chair backs can be rounded with a spokeshave.

Spokeshave and drawknife
The spokeshave is useful for many woodworking jobs beyond chair-making, and is available with either a

curved sole or flat sole. The former is more versatile for shaped work, the flat spokeshave being used for shaving the edges off straight boards. The drawknife is simply a long blade held between two handles; it has very little to control the cut, so it tends to be used for more aggressive, freehand shaping.

Adze

An unusual sight in most woodworking workshops, the adze is like a small axe, except that the blade is at right angles to the handle and is curved to shape seats.

Choosing a lathe and tools

A lathe needs to be able to perform various tasks so that there is plenty of scope for experimenting with different types of turning. It needs to be long enough between centres to turn a chair leg, but with space to turn a bowl or platter up to 305 mm (12 in) in diameter. It doesn't need to be particularly expensive, or have more than four or five speeds.

Turning tools are often sold in sets, and this is usually a cost-effective approach. Look for a set with a roughing gouge, parting tool, skew chisel ideally 25 mm (1 in) wide, 13-mm (½-in) and 6-mm (¼-in) spindle gouges, and a 10-mm (⅜-in) bowl-turning gouge. The latter is machined from a thicker bar to give the edge more support when cutting into the end grain of a bowl.

Materials

All about wood – using grain direction

The builders of wooden boats and old vaulted roofs looked out for curved boards that could be used for the ribs. This was so that the fibres weren't disturbed and the strength of the wood was retained. The same is true for chair-making, especially when the back legs of a chair are long and curving. Timber for steam bending must be straight, with no weaknesses that might cause it to break under pressure.

Finishing turned objects

There are many sanding options for cleaning up turned projects, though a sheet of sandpaper will do to start. Just be careful not to burn your hand when holding the abrasive against the spinning wood, or to get your fingers trapped against the tool rest. Always wear a dust mask or respirator when sanding at the lathe, since huge quantities of dust are produced. Preferably, keep sanding to a minimum, and work on improving the finish straight from the tool edge. Not only is this

quicker in the long term, but the finish is cleaner with the fibres less bruised.

The simplest finish to apply to turned items is sanding sealer, either shellac or cellulose, which can be applied on a rag with the item spinning slowly. Do this a couple of times, cutting back with 320-grit abrasive between coats; then hold a stick of carnauba wax against the spinning wood. This hard wax can then be buffed to a high shine.

Wear gloves to avoid the risk of burning your fingers.

Apply sanding sealer with a cloth while the lathe is turning slowly.

Polish with carnauba wax, which is tough and finishes to a good shine.

Project **Kitchen chair**

For your kitchen

Chair-making is simultaneously the most difficult
and the simplest woodworking skill. The angles are
tricky to work out, but you need very few tools and
a wheel-back kitchen chair certainly requires less
accuracy than last lesson's bookcase.

1 ft 6¼ in4
(65 mm)

1 ft 6 in
(460 mm)

1 ft 7½ in
(495 mm)

1 ft 5³⁄₁₆ in
(438mm)

1 in (25 mm)

1 ft 3 in (380 mm)

457mm
(1ft 5⁷⁄₈ in)

93°

70°

85°

1 ft 2⁷⁄₈ in
(337 mm)

1 ft 4³⁄₈ in
(415 mm)

95°

Cutting list

Part	Material	Quantity	Dimensions length, width, thickness
A Seat	elm/cherry	1	437 x 381 x 40 mm (17³⁄₁₆ x 15 x 1⁵⁄₈ in)
B Leg	ash/beech	4	454 x 45 x 45 mm (17⁷⁄₈ x 1¾ x 1¾ in)
C Stretcher	ash/beech	2	378 x 30 x 30 mm (14⁷⁄₈ x 1⅛ x 1⅛ in)
D Centre rail	ash/beech	1	416 x 30 x 30 mm (16⅜ x 1⅛ x 1⅛ in)
E Splat	ash/beech	1	(464 x 105 x 10 mm) (18¼ x 4⅛ x ⅜ in)
F Back bow	ash/beech	1	1245 x 32 x 30 mm (49 x 1¼ x 1⅛ in)
G Stick	ash/beech	8	495 x 16 x 16 mm (19½ x ⅝ x ⅝ in)

Shopping list

Tools

Steaming chest
Spokeshave
Drawknife
Angle grinder

1 Plank up boards to make the seat (**A**), ideally using a very strong polyurethane glue, or whatever you trust most. Use biscuits to strengthen the joint. Preferably use an odd number of boards to make up the seat (see Making panels, page 84).

Cut the seat to shape and 'bottom' the top. You can do this traditionally, or by using an angle grinder with a woodcarving disc attached. It takes time to get the seat right, and each seat should be better than the previous one.

2 Drill holes 25 mm (1 in) in diameter for the legs, using an adjustable square to help you judge the splay. The splay is 95° back and front, and 85° to the sides. Make sure you don't drill through the seat, though the legs on many such chairs do protrude the whole way through and are wedged. Alternatively, drill the holes using a drill press, with a sloped jig setting the angle.

3 Turn the legs (**B**), stretchers (**C**), and centre rail (**D**) 90°.

4 Fit the legs into the seat and mark the position for the stretcher holes.

5 Drill and assemble the under-frame; then do the same for the centre rail.

6 Make a note of which part of the under-frame fits where and then glue up, adjusting the parts until the legs wobble as little as possible. You can always trim them later.

7 Drill the holes in the seat for the bow back (**F**), either using adjustable squares as sighting guides, or by using a jig in the drill press. Make them 25 mm (1 in) in diameter.

8 Make a former slightly tighter than the radius of the bow back. Put the piece in a steamer for at least two hours; then bend around the former and hold in place with G-clamps and sash clamps. Alternatively, laminate thin laths with glue around a former, but you will need a male and female former for this job.

9 Next day, clamp the bow in a vice and mark off the length of the tenons at the ends. Cut around the shoulders and cut off the corners. Then pare back the tenon to a circle, checking the fit with a suit hole drilled in an offcut (rather than offering up the whole seat).

10 Check the fit of the bow in the seat. Then drill the 10-mm (⅜-in) holes for the sticks (**G**), and chop out the mortise for the splat (**E**). Once again you can do this by eye with an adjustable square, or by using an angled jig.

11 Cut the sticks roughly to length and offer up to the bow to line up the holes. Then drill the 10-mm (⅜-in) holes in the bow. Use a couple of offcuts to measure the length of each stick. Before you round the full length of each stick, test the fit in the bow and seat: you don't want to waste time getting a stick perfectly round and then make a mistake cutting it to length!

13 Use a coping saw or fretsaw to shape the splat and check its fit in the seat. Then cut a corresponding pair of mortises in the bow. Attach the turned roundel to the splat.

12 Round the sticks with a specialist tool or a spokeshave (which I prefer). Sand smooth.

Lessons learned

- Chair-making is all about accurate drilling. Notice how any gaps will be seen, but the tapered components can often be pushed in tight.

- Turning identical components is very awkward and requires loads of practice. But remember that chair legs are further apart than you might imagine, and many people won't notice any differences.

- It's best to make chairs one at a time, as they are so difficult to replicate. There is a time saving in batching parts, but it's still a challenge to make the match.

14 With all the parts cleaned up, you can assemble the chair, though many chair-makers will recommend that you do all the finishing, right up to the wax, before assembly.

Lesson 7
Making tables

Getting started

Tables always impress people. Non-woodworkers don't realize that they are one of the easiest of constructions to produce. A wide expanse of gloriously finished wood looks fantastic and any deficiencies in the under-frame are usually hidden away, as long as it doesn't rock. Many tables are so heavy that they won't budge anyway.

The greatest challenge when making a table is usually, for the home woodworker, assembling the whole thing, and clamping up wide panels like the top. This isn't a worry for small side tables, but kitchen and dining tables are often quite large. One option is to use bolts to draw the end frames together, or you could look back to our technique of draw-boring tenons (see Draw-boring, page 128). Or you could make your own long sash clamps by acquiring some special clamp heads and fitting them to a wooden bar.

The thing is that by this stage, woodworkers should be thinking for themselves, and starting to devise their own solutions to the challenges they face. That is one of the measures of success and the sense of independence is one of the rewards of building up a stock of skills and tools.

Making a table

Compared to producing chairs, designing and making tables is intriguing and fortuitously simple. Though tables may be large, and the top can be challenging to finish, the construction is, at least in principle, relatively straightforward. It's a question of choosing the appropriate under-frame and then devising a shape and style for the top. And few projects offer the woodworker quite the same opportunity to display the beauty of wood.

Options for the under-frame

The most common design for a table is to position four legs at the corners and join them with four rails. This is a good design for dining tables because it gives you plenty of space to place the chairs and for diners to stretch their legs. The downside is that such under-frames have inherent weakness because their legs are not supported or reinforced with lower rails.

One way to get around this is to use deeper rails to lengthen the join line between the rails and the legs, and reduce the tendency for the legs to pivot. This, however, can interfere with the legs of anyone sitting at the table, and there is a tricky compromise between the height of the tabletop and the height above the knees of the rails. This problem can be nullified by shaping the rails so that they are narrower at the centre than at the joints. Another option is to use thicker material for the rails, thereby increasing the joint strength.

Many old tables have four low rails near the feet, but the result is heavy-looking and more restrictive. A compromise is to join the legs low down at the ends and then use a full-length rail (or stretcher) to join the end rails. For desks, which are only used from one side, you can offset this central rail so that it doesn't interfere; indeed, it becomes a perch for the sitter's feet.

To produce a slender, elegant design, table legs are often tapered on any of the four faces, with contrasting results depending on which side is tapered. The two outside faces are the most commonly tapered, but it doesn't have to be done like this. Legs can be round, square-section, hexagonal, octagonal or rectangular. They can curve or splay. The options are endless. You can even support the top on a single pedestal, which is great for small, round tables, especially if they are made to tilt. On larger dining tables, the pedestal is both hidden and potentially unstable.

Lesson planner

Key techniques	Key tools and materials
• Options for the under-frame • Options for the top • Ergonomics of a table • Five ways to taper table legs • How to cut a sliding dovetail	• Skew chisel • Trammel bars • Locks and fitting them • All about wood – the mighty oak

Options for the top

The proportions of the top depend largely upon the space it has to fill and the table's purpose. Round tables are welcoming but waste space because so much of the top is a dead zone in the centre. Rectangular tops are the most efficient; however I've always loved elliptical tables because the sitters can all see each other, there is very little wasted area, and the changing curves are intriguing. My father once produced a fabulous range of coffee tables, with a Christmas theme, only to discover that the downside of a holly-shaped top is laddered stockings and bruised shins.

Solid wood tabletops are often cleated at the ends, with a loose tongue joining the cleat to the end of the boards. This stops the boards from cupping, but allows them to move across their width. On one table, I made the mistake of joining the cleat to the tabletop with dowel rods, only for the top to split terribly when it couldn't move at the centre.

Ergonomics of a table

Based on the average dining chair being about 457 mm (18 in) high, the lower edge of the rail or apron needs to be about 622 mm (24½ in) above the ground, with the average tabletop 737 mm (29 in) high. Ideally, the tabletop should overhang the rails by about 229 mm (9 in).

The number of people who can sit at a table depends largely upon the arrangement. For instance, a table 1270 mm (50 in) in diameter can sit six people, while eight people can sit at a table 1219 mm (48 in) square. You need to give each person about 660 mm (26 in) space around the circumference of a round table, which can be converted into the diameter by multiplying the number of people by 26, and then dividing by 3.14. Sitters at square or rectangular tables need only 610 mm (24 in).

Use a jig to taper table legs on a table saw.

Five ways to taper table legs

With most of these techniques, you taper adjacent sides with some form of jig first, and then remove the jig to taper the opposite faces.

1 **The table saw.** You can buy a tapering jig, but it's just as simple to cut a piece of 25-mm (1-in) ply to the appropriate angle and clamp it to the rip fence. With a fine blade, this will only need a little finishing.

2 **The band saw.** Some band saws have fences that can be set at any angle to the blade. If yours does not, then simply clamp a wooden straightedge to the table and use it to cut the taper. The finish from a band saw isn't that great, but it is a good way of removing waste.

3 **The thicknesser.** Just as for the table saw, you need to insert a carriage into the thicknesser to taper boards. The jig can be designed for tapering along the length or across the width of a piece of wood. It gives a good finish, but takes more time to set up than on the table saw.

With a template, you can taper with a router table.

4 **The router table.** It doesn't help to angle the fence on a router table, since the cutter will still produce a straight edge. A simple solution is to make a plywood template of the tapered leg (which is a good idea anyway for marking up) and fix it to the board with double-sided tape or hot glue, and then use a bearing-guided trimming cutter to rout the taper. Work with the grain by starting at the wide part of the leg and rout towards the foot.

A slightly more complicated method, but quicker once it is set up, is to make a jig that slides in the groove for the mitre fence. By holding the workpiece at an angle to the groove with stops and toggle clamps, you can easily taper the leg.

Use a router table to cut a tail on a board for a sliding dovetail.

5 **By hand.** Of course, you could taper the leg by hand, in which case all you need to do is mark the top and bottom points and plane away the waste.

How to cut a sliding dovetail

The dovetailed housing is a useful joint for attaching rails, as with the centre rail in this lesson's project, the Dining Table. It is also commonly used for making compartments within drawers, since it is naturally strong and helps to reinforce the construction. A stopped version makes sure you can't see the joint. The basic joint has parallel sides, and is best produced by routing the 'tenon' on a router table, and the 'housing' with the router hand-held.

A more complicated version is the sliding dovetail, which is self-tightening. Both the socket and the tail are very slightly tapered along their length so that they only tighten right at the end. Tapering the socket with the router hand-held is simple because you only have to move the straightedge you are using as a fence fractionally. But to taper the tail you will need to make a carriage for the rail, sliding it in the router table's groove for the mitre fence. This sort of jig takes time to produce, but is worth it in the long run.

Tools

Skew chisel

When it comes to cutting lapped dovetails, one of the greatest challenges is cleaning up the corners inside the sockets. You can buy skew chisels specially designed for the job, or you can take an old bevel-edged chisel and grind it to a sharp angle. Unfortunately, you will need two because the operation is 'handed'.

Trammel bars

Trammel bars are used for cutting or routing circles with a router. A simple version can be made easily enough from a length of plywood screwed to the base of the router and then pinned or screwed to the centre of the workpiece. Often, you will need to use a trammel bar from underneath the tabletop, or whatever you are cutting, so that the fixing mark isn't seen. If fixing on the top face cannot be avoided, it's a good idea to temporarily glue a block to the workpiece, to which you can fix the trammel.

Keep aside any jelly jars because they make an excellent home for tiny screws and fittings in your workshop.

Adjustable trammel bars, which fit in the fence-bar sockets of the router's base, are available from various manufacturers. When using a trammel, watch out for changes in grain direction as you work around the circle. You need to work against the rotation of the router cutter, which means there will be times when you will be routing against the grain. Make very light cuts at those stages.

Use the best brass fittings: they will certainly improve your project.

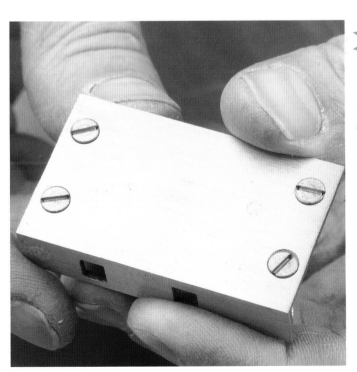

Screw heads that aren't lined up in a lock will look untidy.

Materials

Locks and fitting them

There's no great secret to fixing locks in place, but care is needed to make the job tidy. The keyhole can be very awkward to shape tidily, but an escutcheon hides any inaccuracies. For the best finish, use brass slot-headed screws, and try to get the slots all lined up in one direction, or leave them proud and then grind them back to look like rivets.

All about wood – the mighty oak

Oak is probably the finest of all hardwoods, with various species offering subtly different effects. White oak is superb: it incorporates an even grain and good patterning that make it easy to use, there is little wastage and it is a warm, medium-brown colour. Red oak is richer in colour and cheaper, but doesn't have quite as interesting a grain. European oak is wilder than them both, with amazing flame-like medullary rays and a richer honey-brown colour. Diseased oak turns brown, to varying degrees, and tends to be softer. Japanese oak is the palest of the species, while Tasmanian oak is the coarsest of all.

Trade secret

The beauty of screws

There are a couple of really unexpected uses for screws. Grind a notch out of the head of a flat-headed screw and you can make it into an improvised scratch stock, fixed into a small block. When you don't have wide enough sash clamps, you can use a screw to draw the joint together, though not as you might expect. The trick is to insert the screw into the edge of one board and then drill a corresponding hole in the edge of the adjacent board. From the hole, elongate a groove beneath the surface, with only a gap for the screw's shank. By adjusting the depth of the screw, you can loosen or tighten the joint as the screw slides in the slot.

Project **Dining table**

For the dining room

This table will seat four to six people and has a neat drawer at one end. The tapered legs lighten the design. In this case it is made from cherry, but you can use whatever you have.

840 mm (2 ft 9 in)

1530 mm (5 ft)

A

673 mm (2 ft 2½ in)

50 mm (2 in) square

140 mm (5½ in)

C

770 mm (2 ft 6⅜ in)

E

H   **D**

D

H

H

D

1371 mm (4 ft 6 in)

I

38 mm (1½ in) square

J

H

80 mm (3⅛ in)

F

65 mm (2½ in)

F

125 mm (5 in)

83 mm (3¼ in)

G

710 mm (2 ft 4 in)

90 mm (3½ in)

G

50 mm (2 in)

B

M

660 mm (2 ft 2 in)

I

L

L   **N**

90 mm (3½ in)

676 mm (2 ft 2⅝ in)

K

510 mm (1 ft 8 in)

521 mm (1 ft 8½ in)

Shopping list

Materials

Drawer knob
Dowels: 8 x 8 mm (⅝₆ in) in diameter
Right-angled expansion brackets to fit the top: 8

Cutting list

Part	Material	Quantity	Dimensions length, width, thickness	Part	Material	Quantity	Dimensions length, width, thickness
A Top	cherry	1	1525 x 840 x 22 mm (60 x 33 x ⅞ in)	**H** Runner/kicker	cherry	4	651 x 45 x 19 mm (25⅝ x 1¾ x ¾ in)
B Leg	cherry	4	711 x 50 x 50 mm (28 x 2 x 2 in)	**I** Drawer guide	cherry	2	651 x 19 x 19 mm (25⅝ x ¾ x ¾ in)
C End rail	cherry	1	737 x 125 x 19 mm (29 x 5 x ¾ in)	**J** Runner block	cherry	2	79 x 25 x 21 mm (3⅛ x 1 x ⅞ in)
D Side rails	cherry	2	1435 x 125 x 19 mm (56½ x 5 x ¾ in)	**K** Drawer front	cherry	1	508 x 90 x 16 mm (20 x 3½ x ⅝ in)
E Centre rail	cherry	1	797 x 125 x 19 mm (31⅜ x 5 x ¾ in)	**L** Drawer side	cherry	2	660 x 90 x 16 mm (26 x 3½ x ⅝ in)
F Drawer rail	cherry	2	724 x 50 x 19 mm (28½ x 2 x ¾ in)	**M** Drawer back	cherry	1	508 x 73 x 16 mm (20 x 2⅞ x ⅝ in)
G End fillet	cherry	2	89 x 83 x 19 mm (3½ x 3¼ x ¾ in)	**N** Drawer bottom	cherry	1	721 x 521 x 6 mm (28⅜ x 20½ x ¼ in)

2 Cut the top drawer rail (**F**) to length and mark out and cut the double blind dovetail.

1 The sub-frame of this table looks a bit daunting, but you should realize by now that the way ahead is by splitting it into two end frames, which you assemble first. Only when they are glued up and tidy do you attempt to join them with the side rails (**D**). The centre rail (**E**) slides into place later, when you also fit the kickers (**H**).

Prepare the legs, but don't taper them yet. Mark up and cut the mortises (see Marking out a mortise, page 99) for the side rails and the end rail, and also the mortise for the lower drawer rail. Notice that the mortises aren't centred on the legs, but offset towards the outside so that there is a 6-mm (¼-in) return on the legs.

3 Use the tails on the top drawer rail to mark out the sockets on the top of the legs (**B**). Drill the holes in the legs for the end fillets (**G**) that fill the space on either side of the drawer.

TIP: Apply glue to the dovetails with a small brush so that it gets into all the difficult to reach corners. When not in use, keep the brush in a solvent or water, depending on the type of adhesive you are using.

4 Taper the leg (see Common tasks for the table saw, page 222) on a table saw to 38 mm (1½ in) square at the bottom. Clean up with a bench plane. Prepare the materials for the rails. Cut the tenons and check the fit. You will probably need to pair off the joints (see Cutting in pairs, page 75) because they are all quite complex, and there isn't a huge amount of repetition.

5 Cut the housings in the side rails (**D**). These go the whole way across the rail and can be cut as sliding dovetails if you prefer, which will hold the side rails in position better.

Rout 6-mm (¼-in) grooves along the inside edge of the drawer rails (**F**). These take a loose ply tongue, 6 mm (¼ in) thick, which makes it easier to assemble the kickers (**H**) and centre rail (**E**). Work the bead along the bottom edge of the side rails, using either a hand-held router, a router table, or a scratch stock (see Making a scratch stock, page 223).

6 Assemble the two end frames. The dovetails at the drawer end should hold that frame together without the need for sash clamps, which helps if you don't yet own many.

Clean up the end frames once the glue has set. Then join them together with the side rails, which will probably be too long for any sash clamps that you own. This is when the technique of draw-boring (see Draw-boring, page 128) is an advantage, since you don't need clamps.

7 Prepare the centre rail and the components for the drawer runners, kickers and guides. Cut the 6-mm (¼-in) housings in the outer ends of the kickers and runners, then drill the dowel holes in the ends of the kickers. It's hardly worth setting up a jig for this, so you can use dowel-markers (see Using dowel-markers, page 57) to mark these positions on the centre rail.

8 Fit the centre rail and the kickers to the under-frame. Screw the drawer guides (**I**) to the runners and the blocks (**J**) to the centre rail.

Cut the end fillets to length and drill for the dowel holes. Glue in place. Then screw brackets to the under-frame to attach the top.

10 Clean up the top with a try plane or belt sander and cabinet scraper. Round the corners and run an ovolo cutter around the edges, guided by a bearing. Screw to the under-frame, making sure the brackets allow for movement in the tabletop (see Attaching tabletops, page 184).

9 Make the drawer by the usual technique (see All about wood – aromatic timber, page 212), cutting the tails first and then the pins. In the drawing, we've shown ply being used, with the grain running from front to back. If you use solid wood, position the grain running from side to side. Drill the drawer front (**L**) for the knob.

Glue up the boards for the tabletop (**A**). We've shown four boards on the drawing, but I'd favour three or five, since odd numbers look more interesting (see Making panels, page 85). To make the joints more accurate and to reduce the amount of cleaning up, use biscuits (see Using a biscuit jointer, page 138 and Buying a biscuit jointer, page 140).

Lessons learned

- The use of dovetails helps to hold the end frames together and reduces the need for long clamps.

- With a little ingenuity, you can taper table legs very easily and accurately.

- A drill press is superb for accurate drilling.

- Neatly fitted locks and hinges work better and look more professional than poorly fitted ones.

Lesson 8
Onwards and forwards

Getting started

So here we are: the final lesson. It's been an interesting ride and I hope you've enjoyed it all. I've tried to convey the many possibilities of woodworking and hope that this acts as a springboard for anyone wanting to take up woodwork. You'll find books that tell you more about the detail of joint-cutting and tool fettling, but I hope you will have picked up some of the fun that can be had by learning how to make your own furniture and by developing a workshop to be proud of.

A couple of lessons ago we explored turning, and that is just one of many paths you might take. I've come across all sorts of woodworkers in my time as an editor of woodworking magazines, and they're constantly changing direction, testing new techniques and challenging their skills. The arrival of a new jig might spark a new idea, and in this lesson we will be studying the most modern jigs you can buy.

Woodwork is not easy. You'll 'waste' plenty of timber because of misjudgments, but that's all part of the learning process, and if you're not making mistakes, you're not trying hard enough. Then again, woodwork doesn't have to be difficult, and usually the more challenging projects only seem daunting because of their size. Once you break them down into manageable bits, the fear diminishes. As many famous philosophers have said, a journey of a thousand miles starts with a single step. I hope your woodworking journey has been rewarding so far and continues to be so in the future.

Chest construction

This lesson's project, the Shaker Cabinet, is a superb example of how to make a chest of drawers. These days, with so much sheet material used, it is pleasing to see a cabinet built around a frame. It is also an example of how a construction gradually becomes stronger and stronger as more components are added.

The rails at the front are jointed into the sides, as are the top and bottom back rails. Along the sides are runners to support each drawer, also acting as kickers to stop the drawer from tipping forwards. The top edge of the drawer at the back is sometimes bevelled slightly so that it only tips forwards just before it is fully open. A stop fixed to the underside of the front rails stops the drawers from falling out, though by beveling the bottom back edge of the drawer a little you can lift up the drawer front enough to get the drawer in and out. The dustboard fits into a groove in the runners/kickers and rails. It is ever so simple and yet very effective.

Each part reinforces the construction further, from the rails to the dustboards and then the top and the back and the plinth. Screw holes must be elongated wherever appropriate to allow for expansion and contraction.

Specialist options

With our course almost over, it's time to look ahead and explore some of the avenues for future woodworking!

Carving tools with octagonal handles won't roll off the worksurface!

Lesson planner

Key techniques	Key tools and materials
• Chest construction • Woodcarving • Marquetry and scrollwork	• Dovetail jigs • Woodrat routing centre • Innovation for joints

Woodcarving

You need very few tools, but plenty of skill and hard work, to take up carving. A band saw is useful for cutting out blanks, and a solid bench and holding device are essential. Only a few tools are needed to get going, perhaps a shallow gouge and a firmer chisel, but you will very quickly discover what suits your projects. There are also various rotary burrs and sanding devices that can be fitted into miniature drills and grinding tools. Many people start with chip carving because it is the most regimented, a bit

Micro carving chisels are useful for getting into awkward corners.

To hold a small carving, glue a round disc to the bottom to be held in a vice.

There are many types of carving burr to fit a rotary tool.

Using a carving burr in a rotary tool.

Carving by hand is very rewarding work.

Hone carving chisels on the leather wheel of a slow-turning grinder.

like carving out a house name, but with greater potential for creativity. Chip-carving tools are pretty cheap, and you don't need many. Relief carving puts images into three dimensions, normally cut from a relatively thin board, whereas carving in the round is nearer to sculpture and is probably the most difficult.

Marquetry

It is easy to become intoxicated by veneers and the amazing woods that you can sample for low cost. Making them into images takes patience and a good eye but needs little more than glue and a craft knife, at least to start with. Suppliers offer plans and kits of veneer. Ambitious practitioners dye their own veneer and shade it with hot sand to give it a three-dimensional look. Pyrography is also popular for adding burned details to marquetry pictures, or for producing scenes.

A development from marquetry is practice of assembling a pattern of veneers into a block. By cutting the block in different ways, extraordinary effects can be produced. This is known as parquetry.

Scrollwork

Many books have been written for woodworkers looking for projects to make with a scroll saw. The scroll saw is certainly a versatile machine, and can be used for marquetry as well as intarsia, which combines marquetry and low-relief carving to produce three-dimensional scenes from contrasting pieces of wood.

Finding out more about woodwork

Magazines are superb sources of information for woodworkers, not least because many of them are full of advertisements. Poring over a catalogue is an excellent way to learn which tools do what and to pick up some of the jargon. The best magazines test tools and equipment and give honest assessments of their performance, but watch out for those publications that can never find anything wrong. The Internet has some woodworking sites and is valuable as a forum for woodworkers stuck alone in their workshops. It is very useful for finding out details about suppliers and for picking up techniques from other woodworkers.

Tools

Dovetail jigs

Dovetail jigs come in various designs, almost all of them employing a router to cut the pins and tails, though I have a very old Arcoy dovetailing jig that is powered by

The fingers on the Leigh dovetail jig guide the router cutter to cut.

To make the pins, a straight cutter is guided by the angled fingers.

The fingers can be adjusted to lay out the joint in whatever pattern you want.

an electric drill. The majority of dovetail jigs today have an arrangement of metal fingers that guide a bush attached to the router base. Most use a dovetail cutter for the tails and a straight cutter for the pins, and both can cut through lapped dovetail joints.

The cleverness of a dovetail jig is that you simply turn the comb of fingers over to cut the other half of the joint.

You can fine-adjust the jig to adjust the fit.

The best dovetail jigs have variable fingers that can be adjusted to produce whatever spacing you desire. Before you buy one, make sure that it can be used for cutting small dovetails if you are into box-making or drawer-making. And find out what else it can do. Some can be employed for many of the jobs you'd use a router table for, or even as a drilling jig for dowel joints or to space shelf supports. Others can cut sliding dovetails and housings.

Woodrat routing centre

If you are making a series of dovetail joints, as in the Shaker Cabinet this lesson, and want to explore small-scale batch production, a dovetail jig will soon earn its keep. Do plenty of research to discover the machine or jig that suits you best. There are some intriguing jigs these days that work on a router table. The Woodrat routing centre shown below has a variety of uses.

The Woodrat routing centre is used for dovetails and jointing techniques.

The Woodrat mechanizes the methods you would use cutting dovetails by hand, and employs a rack to use one half of the joint to cut the other.

Underneath, you can see how the dovetail cutter creates the tails.

Once cut, the tails are held at the left-hand end of the Woodrat.

Innovation for joints

Over the last five or ten years there have been various innovations in the cutting of joints, to make them stronger and easier to work. After years of the router dominating innovation in tools and equipment, there has been something of a return to the drilled joint, but in a completely new form.

The Woodrat is used for tenons, mouldings and other routing operations.

1 For years, woodworkers have used drills to remove the waste from mortises, but we've all experienced the drill bit sliding out of control when it hits the previous hole. With a jig, however, you can drill holes as close together as you like, and use a special loose tenon to fit perfectly into the wavy mortise. The 'tenons' are supplied as a strip of moulded hardwood, looking like a piece of child's modelling clay. Alternatively, you can make your own tenon with a special router cutter.

Miller dowel acts as a wooden screw, but is decorative and obviates the need for a wooden bung.

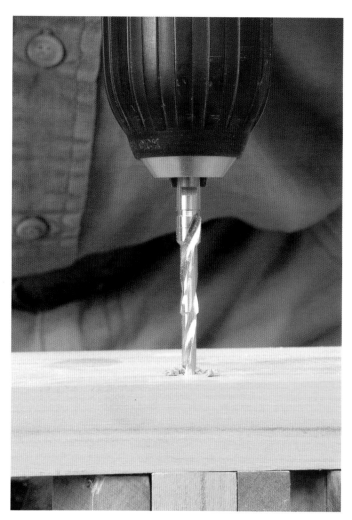

A special drill bit is used to make the holes for Miller dowel.

2 One of the challenges of woodworking is that there are few options for assembling a project without mechanical joints and adding the reinforcement later. Screws and nails are a compromise because you will invariably be fixing them into end grain, which isn't satisfactory, because the fibres are forced apart without binding. The screw or nail will usually pull free.

The modern solution is a ribbed and stepped dowel known as Miller dowel, which is inserted into a stepped hole that is drilled after assembly using a special bit. The dowel acts as a wooden nail, with the holding qualities of a screw, except that it can be glued into the end grain effectively. Depending on your view, the downside or upside is that the end of the dowel is visible, though some woodworkers make a feature of this by doming the head. As the dowels are available in various hardwoods, you can probably find one to match most common timbers.

When the Miller dowel is tapped home, it pulls up any gap.

The Kreg jig, and similar pocket-screw drilling devices, cuts an angled cavity in a board with a clearance hole for a hidden screw.

Various designs of pocket-screw drilling jig are available, with different combinations of hole. Notice the depth stop on the bit.

3 To overcome the problems of screwing into end grain, the pocket-screw jig also enables the woodworker to add fixings to a joint after assembly. The smaller portable jigs can be clamped to a rail using the stepped drill bit to make a cavity for the screw head and a pilot hole for the thread. It isn't one of the strongest joints, but is very useful around the workshop for making jigs and stands.

It's a good idea to make a rack for sash clamps so that they are stored safely but are ready for action.

Project **Shaker cabinet**

For the bedroom

A multiple-drawer cabinet, like this one in Shaker style, is ideal for storing clothes and oddments. If you can complete a project like this, you can do anything, and it is only complicated by the many frames you have to produce. Planning is essential.

440 mm (1 ft 5¾ in)

502 mm (1 ft 7¾ in)

360 mm (1 ft 2¼ in)

E

406 mm (1 ft 4 in)

111 mm (4⅜ in)

356 mm (1 ft 2 in)

325 mm (1 ft ¾ in)

420 mm (1 ft 4⅝ in)

420 mm (1 ft 4⅝ in)

380 mm (1 ft 3 in)

J

J

C

F

F

360 mm (1 ft 2¼ in)

J

F

B

330 mm (1 ft 1 in)

J

G

B

J

G

B

125 mm (5 in)

J

G

G

B

J

G

B

150 mm (6 in)

K

J

G

B

1134 mm (3ft 8⅝ in)

A

G

G

B

150 mm (6 in)

G

D

B

A

150 mm (6 in)

356 mm (1 ft 2 in)

G

G

H

340 mm (1 ft 1⅜ in)

B

162 mm (6⅜ in)

H

G

B

D

R

D

430 mm (1 ft 5 in)

M

162 mm (6⅜ in)

75 mm (3 in)

L

D

N

M

60 mm (2⅜ in)

I

O

502 mm (1 ft 7¾ in)

60 mm (2⅜ in)

M

L

L

N

O

335 mm (1 ft 1¼ in)

P

403 mm (1 ft 3⅜ in)

360 mm (1 ft 2¼ in)

390 mm (1 ft 3⅜ in)

P

S

Cutting list

Part	Material	Quantity	Dimensions length, width, thickness		Part	Material	Quantity	Dimensions length, width, thickness
A Side	cherry	2	1133 x 406 x 30 mm (44⅝ x 16 x 1⅛ in)		**K** Plywood back	plywood	1	1133 x 422 x 6 mm (44⅝ x 16⅝ x ¼ in)
B Top front rail	cherry	7	422 x 30 x 16 mm (16⅝ x 1⅛ x ⅝ in)		**L** Plinth front/ back mitred rail	cherry	2	514 x 70 x 16 mm (20¼ x 2¾ x ⅝ in)
C Top back rail	cherry	1	422 x 30 x 16 mm (16⅝ x 1⅛ x ⅝ in)		**M** Plinth side mitred rail	cherry	2	444 x 70 x 16 mm (17½ x 2¾ x ⅝ in)
D Bottom front/back rail	cherry	2	422 x 30 x 27 mm (16⅝ x 1⅛ x 1¹⁄₁₆ in)		**N** Plinth front/ back rail	cherry	2	454 x 30 x 16 mm (17⅞ x 1⅛ x ⅝ in)
E Top	cherry	1	502 x 440 x 30 mm (19¾ x 17⁵⁄₁₆ x 1⅛ in)		**O** Plinth side rail	cherry	2	387 x 30 x 16 mm (15¼ x 1⅛ x ⅝ in)
F Top runner/kicker	cherry	2	362 x 25 x 16 mm (14¼ x 1 x ⅝ in)		**S** Plinth leg	cherry	4	60 x 60 x 60 mm (2⅜ x 2⅜ x 2⅜ in)
G Middle runner/kicker	cherry	12	330 x 25 x 16 mm (13 x 1 x ⅝ in)		**Q** Front plinth moulding	cherry	1	502 x 19 x 16 mm (19¾ x ¾ x ⅝ in)
H Bottom runner/kicker	cherry	2	362 x 281 x 25 mm (14¼ x 11¹⁄₁₆ x 1 in)		**R** Side plinth moulding	cherry	2	430 x 19 x 16 mm (17 x ¾ x ⅝ in)
I Plywood bottom	plywood	1	356 x 340 x 6 mm (14 x 13⅜ x ¼ in)		**P** Plinth supports	cherry	6	19 x 19 x 16 mm (¾ x ¾ x ⅝ in)
J Plywood dustboard	plywood	7	356 x 324 x 6 mm (14 x 12¾ x ¼ in)					

The drawers are designed to cascade, with the top drawer 125 mm (5 in) deep, the next three 152 mm (6 in) deep, and the bottom two 162 mm (6⅜ in) deep. The sides and backs are the same respective depths, so for brevity's sake, we've only listed the lengths and thicknesses of the parts. Notice that each drawer back is narrower than its drawer front by the distance from the bottom edge of the drawer front to the top of the groove for the drawer bottom. This should be about 12 mm (½ in).

Cutting list

Part	Material	Quantity	Dimensions length, width, thickness
T Drawer front	cherry	7	391 x 19 mm (15⅜ x ¾ in)
U Drawer side	cherry	14	356 x 10 mm (14 x ⅜ in)
W Drawer back	cherry	7	391 x 10 mm (15⅜ x ⅜ in)
X Drawer bottom	cherry	7	349 x 381 x 6 mm (13¾ x 15 x ¼ in)

Shopping list

Tools and materials	Extra tools for the job
Drawer pulls: 14	**Sash clamps:** lots **Dovetail jig** **Skew chisels** for cleaning out lapped dovetails

1 Prepare the sides (**A**). There's no harm in leaving them 51 mm (2 in) overlong at this stage, to make cutting the bottom and top mortises easier, with less risk of breakout. Mark out the mortises to correspond with the cascading depth of the drawers. It's a really good idea to do a trial mortise and tenon on scrap to test the technique and the fit.

2 Cut the mortises by hand or with a mortiser, making sure they are identical.

3 Plane and thickness all the rails (**B**, **C**, **D**) and runners/kickers (**F**, **G**, **H**). Cut the fingered tenons at the end of each rail (see Identifying tenons, page 195) and check that they fit in the mortises, testing that any tenon fits in any mortise. By now, you should be able to repeat cuts like this without having to pair up each joint.

4 Groove the rails and runners/kickers for the plywood dustboard (**J**). The middle runners/kickers have a stub tenon 6 mm (¼ in) thick, which fits into that groove at the front. The bottom and top runner/kicker (**F** and **H**) are joined to the front and back rails with either a vertical tenon or with a dovetail.

5 Assemble the seven frames one at a time, checking the diagonals and that each frame is identical.

With all the frames assembled, test-fit the sides to the frames. This is probably best done with the cabinet on its back, using a sash clamp level with each front rail. If you have enough sash clamps, raise the assembly off the ground and insert sash clamps underneath as well.

7 Prepare the parts for the drawers (**T**, **U**, **W**, **X**), making them in batches – start with the single top drawer, then the next three down, and finally the bottom two, though you can groove all the parts at the same time for the drawer bottom. You can do this on a router table, or a table saw (see Using a table saw, page 218).

Cut the tails on the sides, marking them out so that they are a fraction (no more than 0.8 mm/1⁄32 in) overlong (see Cutting a through dovetail, page 208). Cut out the tails, then use these to mark up the tails on the front and back. This is when a dovetail jig is so useful (see Dovetail jigs, page 270).

Cut the drawer bottom to size and test the fit. If you make the drawer bottom from solid timber you will need to have the grain running across the drawer so that the bottom can expand and contract underneath the drawer back. Drill the drawer fronts for the pulls, and fit and finish.

6 Screw the plywood back (**K**) into place to add rigidity to the cabinet, though with quite so many frames it shouldn't be that important.

Glue up the boards for the top (**E**). Smooth and cut to size. Then rout the edges with a decorative moulding, working the end grain first.

Now start working on the plinth, first by cutting the short legs (**P**) to length. Mark up and cut the mortises and then cut corresponding tenons on the rails.

Cut the mitred rails (**L** and **M**) to length, and drill the screw holes to attach them to the plinth rails.

Assemble the plinth rails and legs, and screw the mitred rails in place to hold it all together. Afterwards you can add the little supports (**S**), which are in fact short lengths of the moulding.

Lessons learned throughout this book

By now you have the skills and equipment to do almost anything as a woodworker. Here, though, are some of the key lessons I've learned and would recommend you follow:

- When cutting joints, always prepare too much wood so that you have spare components in case of mistakes. Also, make sure you have offcuts that can be used for testing cuts and marking up.

- Buy some disposable medical gloves for gluing and finishing. It keeps your hands clean and makes the whole process a joy.

- Don't panic that your workbench isn't exactly flat or that your vice doesn't work perfectly. It will never be good enough, and you will be able to improve your kit and tools as the improvement in your skills demands. I have a rule that if you have a choice between doing something that needs to be done today and another that will help tomorrow, do the one for tomorrow first: you can always work late into the night to finish the job, and you will gain more and more by investing ahead.

- Always do a dry run of any assembly, and prepare all your clamps ready. Always check the diagonals on frames and carcasses. The moment that glue is introduced, everything will become twice as complicated.

- Check the grain direction carefully before any planing, especially if it is a final cut. Never plane a finished piece without checking the depth of cut on your plane.

- Connect dust extraction to all your machines.

- Level your workbench to ensure that there is no rock.

- Enjoy your woodwork and be flexible with your deadlines!

Conversion Charts

In this book we've included both metric and imperial (also referred to as 'standard') systems for most measurements and weights. But old habits die hard. There are products, materials and practices so steeped in the old 'non-metric' terminology that in many cases, only the 'imperial' terminology and measurements are used.

Case in point: A 2x4, which actually measures 1-½ x 3-½ in., is still called a 2x4 in both countries. Very few people refer to it as a '38 x 89.' Pipe, drill bits, plywood, nails, tile, insulation, doors and many other building materials and products, at the time this book was printed, continue to be referred to (and sold) by their 'imperial' names.

When in doubt about converting from metric to standard and vice versa, consult the information on these charts.

English system to metric system

To Change:	Into:	Multiply by:
Inches	Millimeters	25.4
Inches	Centimeters	2.54
Feet	Meters	0.305
Yards	Meters	0.914
Miles	Kilometers	1.609
Square inches	Square centimeters	6.45
Square feet	Square meters	0.093
Square yards	Square meters	0.836
Cubic inches	Cubic centimeters	16.4
Cubic feet	Cubic meters	0.0283
Cubic yards	Cubic meters	0.765
Pints	Liters	0.473
Quarts	Liters	0.946
Gallons	Liters	3.78
Ounces	Grams	28.4
Pounds	Kilograms	0.454
Tons	Metric tons	0.907

Metric system to English system

To Change:	Into:	Multiply by:
Millimeters	Inches	0.039
Centimeters	Inches	0.394
Meters	Feet	3.28
Meters	Yards	1.09
Kilometers	Miles	0.621
Square centimeters	Square inches	0.155
Square meters	Square feet	10.8
Square meters	Square yards	1.2
Cubic centimeters	Cubic inches	0.061
Cubic meters	Cubic feet	35.3
Cubic meters	Cubic yards	1.31
Liters	Pints	2.11
Liters	Quarts	1.06
Liters	Gallons	0.264
Grams	Ounces	0.035
Kilograms	Pounds	2.2
Metric tons	Tons	1.1

Fractions and Metric Equivalents

Inches (in.)	1/64	1/32	1/25	1/16	1/8	1/4	3/8	2/5	1/2	5/8	3/4	7/8	1
Feet (ft.)													
Yards (yd.)													
Millimeters (mm)*	0.40	0.79	1.0	1.59	3.18	6.35	9.53	10	12.7	15.9	19.1	22.2	25.4
Centimeters (cm)*							0.95	1	1.27	1.59	1.91	2.22	2.54
Meters (m)*													

Inches (in.)	2	3	4	5	6	7	8	9	10	11	12	36	39.4
Feet (ft.)											1	3	3-1/4†
Yards (yd.)												1	1-1/12†
Millimeters (mm)*	50.8	76.2	101.6	127	152	178	203	229	254	279	305	914	1,000
Centimeters (cm)*	5.08	7.62	10.16	12.7	15.2	17.8	20.3	22.9	25.4	27.9	30.5	91.4	100
Meters (m)*											.30	.91	1.00

*Metric values are rounded off. † Approximate fractions.

(actual size)

Temperature

Celsius (C)   Fahrenheit (F)

- Water boils — 100° / 212°
- 90° / 194°
- 80° / 176°
- 70° / 158°
- 60° / 140°
- Average body temperature — 50° / 122°
- 40° / 104°
- 30° / 86°
- Average room temperature — 20° / 68°
- 10° / 50°
- Water freezes — 0° / 32°

The two systems for measuring temperature are Fahrenheit and Celsius (or centigrade). To change from degrees Fahrenheit, to degrees Celsius, subtract 32, then multiply by 5/9. For example: $68°F - 32 = 36$; $36 \times 5/9 = 20°C$. To convert degrees Celsius to degrees Fahrenheit, multiply the degrees by 9/5, then add 32 to that figure. For example: $20°C \times 9/5 = 36$; $36 + 32 = 68°F$.

Nails

Nail lengths are identified by numbers from 4 to 60 followed by the letter "d" which stands for "penny." The imperial and metric equivalents are listed here.

4d	1-1/2"	38mm
5d	1-3/4"	44mm
6d	2"	51mm
8d	2-1/2"	64mm
10d	3"	76mm
16d	3-1/2"	89mm
20d	4"	102mm

Index

Acknowledgements

The Ultimate Woodworking Course was written over a period of months in 2004 and 2005. The book could not have been produced without the nudging and care of Miranda Sessions at Collins & Brown, the photographic and woodworking skills of Michael Wicks and doubtless other designers and creatives I haven't met, or have forgotten to mention.

I'd also like to thank Martin Godfrey for supplying a Woodrat (www.woodrat.com), Keith at BriMarc (www.brimarc.com) for the Leigh dovetail jig and other bits of kit, and Stanley Tools for sending us a box of tools (www.stanleytools.com). Axminster Power Tool Centre also supplied us with photographs.

Obviously the book would never have been produced without the tolerance and support of my family, Tina, Lara and Sasha, who all had to cope with the disruption of late nights and photoshoots. And finally a big thanks to Jude Adam and Jane Gazzo from BBC 6 Music for their entertaining radio show.